"Such a wonderful fu adventure." ~ **Lieutei**
former
(Albert Wallace's wartime
and still-existing RCAF squadron)

"Once I started, I couldn't stop. It was an incredible read that I couldn't put down. As a member of the RCAF, a pilot, an overseas veteran, and a history student I was engaged at every level. It's hard to express all the feelings that this story digs up. [...] A truly incredible read I will not forget."
        ~ **Greg Zweng,** military historian

"This book has detailed not only the life of Trendos' father, but the lives of all airmen, the sacrifices and the hardships not only of being a POW but of flying a tour of 30 bombing missions with the chances of survival being less than 10% . I was unable to put the book down and have since read it again. The author has written a history that should be read by all."
        ~ **Stuart Hunt,** roommate of Albert Wallace
            at Stalag Luft III and current friend

As familiar as military authors can be with their subjects, they can always gain knowledge and inspiration from fellow writers. What Barbara Trendos accomplishes in *Survival* – besides revealing her father's eagle eye for detail, wisdom of the moment and devilish sense of humour – is to give casual readers and experts the deeper view of the Commonwealth airman's war, between 1941 and 1945. Her careful assembly of Albert Wallace's flight log notes, and more important his wartime log entries, draws a vivid picture of his youthful innocence in training, his dedication to service on operations, and his resilience during imprisonment at Stalag Luft III. No wonder he stood a better chance of survival. A blessing he bestowed the gift of his memories to his daughter.
        ~ **Ted Barris,** author of
            The Great Escape: A Canadian Story

Albert B Wallace
419 Sqdn RCAF

SURVIVAL

My Father's War as
an Air Force Gunner and POW

BARBARA TRENDOS

*I hope you enjoy
Dad's story.
Lest We Forget*

Trendos

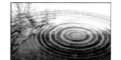

**STONE'S THROW
PUBLICATIONS**

Copyright © 2015   Barbara Trendos

Cover Photos: Photo Albert Wallace; Postkarte; RAF Identity Card; Albert Wallace Collection.

Map showing layout of Stalag Luft III North Compound: *Forced March to Freedom,* Robert Buckham, Canada's Wings, Inc., 1984, pg. 11. Reproduced with permission of Nancy Buckham

Book Layout and Cover Design: Sue Reynolds

ISBN 978-1-987813-01-2

Published by Stone's Throw Publications

Port Perry, Ontario, Canada

www.stonesthrowps.ca

Printed in Canada

1 2 3 4 5 6 7 8 9 10

"There are no words with which I can do justice to the aircrew who fought under my command. There is no parallel in warfare to such courage and determination in the face of danger over so prolonged a period, of danger which at times was so great that scarcely one man in three could expect to survive his tour of thirty operations...it was, moreover a clear and highly conscious courage, by which the risk was taken with calm forethought...it was, furthermore, the courage of the small hours, of men virtually alone, for at his battle station the airman is virtually alone. It was the courage of men with long-drawn apprehensions of daily 'going over the top'. Such devotion must never be forgotten."[1]

Sir Arthur Harris, Air Marshall of the Royal Air Force

Contents

suggest you read the

reface first. It sets

he stage for how I

rote the book.

njoy and thank you.

rbara

Preface

E LOG

It was June 1943, shortly after my dad, Albert (Wally) Wallace, arrived at Stalag Luft III, a *Luftwaffe* (German Air Force) run prisoner of war camp for captured Commonwealth and American Air Force officers, located 100 miles southeast of Berlin, near the town of Sagan in Silesia, Germany (now Żagań, Poland). The Canadian Y.M.C.A. made its first distribution of *A Wartime Log* books to Canadian prisoners of war. The book, not to be confused with an aircrew Flying Log Book used to record flight details,

k slate for the men to use as they saw fit to record ʒtches, poems and stories of prison camp life: a way to fill time, to cope, to capture the day-to-day routine of an utterly un-routine life experience.

Like many of the POWs, Dad began keeping a logbook to help break up the monotony of camp life. However, when the men were forced to evacuate Stalag Luft III on foot in the bitter cold of January 1945 to stay ahead of the advancing Russian army, they were able to take with them only what they could carry. For the prisoners who had heavily invested themselves in their logbook, there was no question of leaving such a legacy behind. For Dad, however, it was simple: the logbook, or chocolate and smokes. There was no contest.

So this book is not Dad's actual wartime log. Rather, it's his story, written by me, one of his daughters. That I chose to write it in the style of a wartime log in his voice was purely a matter of creative license. The transcribed text from the *kriegsgefangenenpost* and *postkartes* he wrote home from the prison camp, the official war correspondence, telegrams and prison camp photos, all so lovingly saved by my grandma, Kathleen Belle Wallace, are, however, "the real McCoy", as Dad would say.

The occasional blacked-out areas in the letters represent censorship at work, although whether the product of a German or Canadian censor isn't known, since prisoner mail was censored at both ends. I found the family pictures in an old beat-up photo album. Few were dated, so I confess I fit them into the timeline and story at my convenience. Together with official documents from Dad's Royal Canadian Air Force service file, it all provided a framework I felt compelled to fill in. And to portray a more complete account of his war experience, I expanded the log idea using Dad's 1941 enlistment date and his 1945 liberation date as bookends.

Memories, anecdotes, and photos helped to fill in the gaps as did World War II history that lives in the public domain. I spent time on the BBC News web site, On This Day: World War II, perusing the timeline of key events and headlines, and listening to actual audio news clips. Through secret prison camp radios, the BBC had been the POWs' pipeline to accurate war reporting, so I made it my pipeline too.

I also mined talks and interviews I heard Dad give through The Memory Project, an insightful educational initiative of Historica Canada that offers veterans and Canadian Forces staff an opportunity to share their service experiences with students and communities. Last, I relied on accounts written by, or told to me by, other Stalag Luft III ex-POWs, especially during the time period of the two horrendous forced marches across Germany in the final months of the war when the letters abruptly stopped. So this book is a mosaic of Dad's memories, research, and my imagination.

And, as Dad himself would hasten to point out, no POW would ever have written some of the things I took the liberty of writing in his voice. After all, Stalag Luft III was the prison camp of The Great Escape, in which 76 POWs pulled off an ingenious escape March 24/25, 1944 that Hollywood made popular in a 1963 movie starring Steve McQueen. The camp held many closely-guarded secrets, known to only a select few. A POW would, at best, only whisper about tunnels or escaping, and certainly never commit them to writing (other than in code), even in a logbook that was carefully hidden from prying enemy eyes.

I laughed and cried as I wrote this book. I am blessed to have been able to take this journey with my dad, and to get a glimpse of the young man who became the man he is.

I dedicate this book to Dad and to the spirit and memory of his crewmates, especially the two who died in the early hours of May 13, 1943, when their Halifax bomber was shot down over Germany:

SERGEANT WALTER HERBERT DAVID (DAVE) ALISON
Wireless Operator, RAF
Age 28

WARRANT OFFICER FIRST CLASS GLEN ALLAN (MAC) MCMILLAN
Pilot, RCAF
Age 22

Hotton Cemetery, Belgium

Rheinberg War Cemetery, Germany

I also dedicate this story to Dad's ex-POW friends past and present, and to all those who bravely served in Bomber Command both in the air and on the ground. Where would we be without their selfless commitment to our freedom? In the spirit of "Lest We Forget", stories like Dad's must be told while there's still time to capture them, and then retold, over and over.

Barbara Trendos,
2015

Prologue

They took me out into an office to be interrogated by an officer and he knew more about the war than I did. He knew more about our bombing squadron. I didn't have to tell him anything. He could tell me everything that they needed to know about our bombing. He told me who our commanding officer was and how many aircraft we could put up on a maximum effort and oh, he knew far more about the air base than I did.

So anyway, I was only there a few days and then I was taken out, put into a compound with other prisoners and then a few days later, we went on a train trip and I ended up at Stalag Luft III [a Luftwaffe POW camp near Żagań, Poland], where the Great Escape took place. It was just a great barbed wire enclosure. The camp was at least 15 acres in size. It was a brand new camp. It had only opened in April of 1943 and I was arriving in May of 1943. So I was there only six weeks after it had opened. And it had about 700 or 800 men in it when I arrived, but it would eventually have about 1800 or 1900.

It was a big camp, double barbed wire fences around it, about ten feet apart. And then in between the two fences, there were great coils of barbed wire to make it very difficult, literally impossible to get through. There were guard towers at different points all around the camp and the guards in the towers had machine guns. The towers had searchlights that were on all night in the camp.

I made arrangements with the guy that was in charge of the block that I was in to move to another room. So I moved to another room in block 104, and block 104 was the barrack block where the big tunnel was. And the room I moved to into was the room where the tunnel started. I didn't know it at the time, of course, because I was quite a newcomer. And everything about escaping was very secretive in the camp and really wasn't talked about a great deal. I mean, even some of the chaps in the room had nothing to do with the tunnel.

There was one chap in the room named Pat Langford and he was called the 'tunnel fuhrer'. He was the one who opened and closed the tunnel when they were going to send men down or bring men out or take sand out. And it wasn't, in my view, a very good room to live in, because when the tunnel was open, there were blankets all over the floor to catch any sand and the room was in effect off limits. You couldn't go back and forth into it. So I was in that room for I think only two to three months and then I made arrangements to move out of there.

I did do a little bit of work on the tunnel on sand disposal. I was a 'penguin' a few times where I had the bags of sand down my pant legs and dispersed it out in our garden or around the circuit where we walked, around the perimeter of the camp. But that was the only thing I did on the tunnel.

Everybody in the camp knew what was going to happen that particular night they were going to break out. Throughout the day, everybody in hut 104 moved out except for the men who were going out, and all of the men that had been selected to go out moved into that hut through the day with whatever they were taking with them on the escape. That night, when they opened the tunnel to the surface, they had a few hangups through the night. They had a hard time breaking through the ground to the surface and then when they finally broke through, they found out that they were short of the pine trees around the camp where they thought they'd be. They were about 20 feet short. But fortunately, they were about 30 feet behind one of the guardhouses. And the guardhouse was up there with a guard in it, of course, with a searchlight, but he was shining it into the camp. So he really wasn't a problem.

But the Germans also had guards on foot outside the main wire around the camp. And they walked back and forth with their guns. So the men used a rope they had in the camp. A man at the tunnel face held one end of the rope while another took the other end, and when the guards turned and walked away, crawled out the tunnel and into the woods. He would pull the rope to signal the coast was clear and one or two men in the tunnel would jump out and crawl to the woods. Well that way, they were able to get 76 out.

But through the night, there was an air raid on Berlin. And whenever there was an air raid, all the lights went out. So the lights in the tunnel went out and things of course were stopped for an hour or maybe an hour and a half during this air raid, during which time they didn't get anybody out of the tunnel. And then they had a couple of cave-ins in the tunnel when men going through knocked out some of the supporting boards. So they had to be repaired before the escaping could continue. So these different little hang-ups slowed things down.

Well, I remember that night. I was lying in my bunk and I don't think I slept much because I knew the tunnel break was taking place and I just wondered when things were going to happen. Well, sure enough, I think around 5:00 in the morning, I heard a rifle shot, one single shot. And I said, oh, that's probably it. Well, that was it. One of the guards on duty around the camp veered off towards the tunnel. He was going to have a leak, you see. And he nearly fell in the hole, he was so close to it. And just at that moment, the boys got their signals mixed up. One had pulled the cord in the woods and the one inside thought that was the clearance to pop out and he jumped out of the tunnel right in front of this guard and the guard - I guess he must have been quite shocked - whipped his rifle up and fired a shot. He missed the man, but the tunnel was over.

50 of the 76 were shot and they were just murdered. I mean, they were taken out in small groups and just shot in the back of the head. That was how they went. The Germans didn't admit that, they just said that they were shot while trying to escape. And of course, our commanding officer, when he was told this said, "Well, how many were wounded?" "Well," the Germans said, "well, none, they were all killed." That told them right away that they had been murdered. The camp all knew immediately that they had all been murdered and we all wore black bands for several weeks afterwards to signify to the Germans that we knew what had happened.

So it was a tough time around the camp because so many people had lost friends in those 50 guys who went out. A lot of them had been prisoners for three or four years and here they were, all of sudden, their lives blotted out, boom, like that. It was a tough time in the camp.[1]

Early Years
1941-1942

Dad was born September 9, 1920 at home on Brock Avenue in Toronto, Ontario and grew up in the city with his parents, Robert and Kathleen Wallace (née Campbell), older sister Eleanor Jean and younger sister Kathleen Elizabeth (Betty). The family later lived on Bristol Avenue, then Gladstone Avenue and St. Clarens Avenue. Grandpa was a good man, a hardworking and hard living Northern Irishman from Belfast, who, after imbibing a few whiskeys in the childhood days I recall, had a penchant for painting things green in an ode to the old country. His antics always had my sisters, my cousins and me laughing, and Grandma scolding. Grandma, known as Kate or Katie, was a country gal, born and raised on a farm near the village of Brechin, Ontario, the second eldest of 15 brothers and sisters. Grandma and Grandpa both worked in the needle trade in Toronto, he as a cutter, she as a seamstress.

Dad attended Dovercourt Public School and in 1935 entered the Industrial Course at Central Technical School, still an operating high school today, whose cornerstone was laid in 1913 by the then Prime Minister, Sir Robert Borden. Dad's name is listed on the CTS War memorial. While at school he worked part time as a delivery boy for Herbert Nimmo Carload Grocery and Peggy O'Neil Box Lunch. But he had no taste for school, preferring to read books. Dad stuck it out for a year, one not-so-fond memory being of the shop teacher inspecting his steel working project, wordlessly removing it from the vice and throwing it on the shop floor. With that, Dad left school and took a job at Beare's Limited Stationers for $7.00/week to help out the family. He worked at Beare's until 1939 when he joined Loblaws Groceterias for a better opportunity.

It was a time when the church often played a role in the social lives of young people, even if they didn't actually go to church. I suspect their mothers had something to do with it. Hence the references in Dad's letters and logbook to the Presbyterian church bible class and the Anglican camp.

In 1938, and in keeping with his fondness for guns, Dad became a cadet with the Queen's York Rangers Militia, 1st American regiment of the Canadian Militia at Fort York. In 1939, after Canada joined Great Britain in the war on Germany, Private Wallace was called up to do guard duty on the Welland Canal. It was during this time that the "Adventure in the Skies!" trumpeted on the cover of the Royal Canadian Air Force recruiting brochure caught Dad's attention. So, with youthful optimism that bad things happen to other people, a need to find his way in the world and a desire to do his part in the war, Dad obtained his discharge from the army and enlisted with the R.C.A.F.

In his 1940 R.C.A.F. application, Dad recorded baseball and bicycle riding as his favourite pastimes, and under question 24 called "Special Qualifications, Hobbies, etc., useful to the R.C.A.F.", he answered "Collector of Rifles". This last would figure prominently in his life. Always fascinated by guns, over the years he had taken any opportunity to pick off tin cans at his Uncle John and Carl's farm, shorten the life of a few nuisance groundhogs at the farm with "lead poisoning", hone his accuracy at skeet shooting, and, with his best friend Roly, shoot out the odd downtown Toronto streetlight on the fly from his CCM Road Racer. He would have been considered a juvenile delinquent by today's standards.

Once called up by the Air Force, all recruits began their career at one of the five Manning Depots, located in Toronto, Brandon, Edmonton, Quebec City and Lachine. In Dad's case, it was Toronto. Training lasted for a few weeks and focused on transitioning the recruits from civil life to military life.

Jan. 13, 1941

It's official – I'm air force. Finally called up today & report tomorrow to #1 Manning Depot based at the C.N.E. here in Toronto. I'm not old enough to legally drink a beer but 20 is good enough for the RCAF. Albert Randall Wallace, service number R-88911, at your service. My best pal Roly already enlisted & is out in Newfoundland working ground crew as an airframe mechanic. But I want to be up in the air. It was a full moon tonight - they call it a bomber's moon. An omen?

Mug Shot

Jan. 14, 1941

I'm here for 2 to 4 weeks. I have a rank so I feel kind of important already even though mine is Aircraftman Class II or AC.2 which happens to be the bottom rung on the RCAF ladder. But I was already used to that being a Private in the Militia. $1.30 a day. Have to start somewhere since I didn't even come close to finishing high school. So it's ground crew for now in Standard General Duties until I prove myself enough to apply for aircrew. It's gunnery training I want. Hopefully by then they'll have relaxed the 2 years of high school education requirement. It could be months before I'm selected for aircrew, maybe years, maybe not at all. Basically means I'll do anything in the meantime! First order of business – military haircuts for the lot of us.

Jan. 15, 1941

I'm billeted in the Coliseum building. Ottawa has taken it over as barracks for all new recruits. There must be thousands of us here. It's like a big holding tank. Very crowded. We get only 15 min in the morning for ablutions & that's a challenge with so many of us. We sleep on the upper level in iron, double-deck bunks. There are more boys living next door in the Horse Palace too. They get to sleep in old horse stalls! I think I got the better of the deal.

Introduction to military life began with rules, regulations, drills, orders, exercises, a seemingly never ending series of inoculations (sometimes in both arms at the same time), a visit to the dentist, and issue of a kit: leather boots, shoes, jacket, trousers, shirts, ties, socks, underwear, wedge cap, braces, greatcoat, jacket, mitts, overshoes, badges, cutlery, overshoes, brushes for polishing buttons, boots and teeth, a "housewife" sewing kit for do-it-yourself mending. No mother here to do anything for you. Recruits learned how to march, and when and how to salute. Precision and unity were key, so there wasn't much room for individuality. Food was generally considered poor, certainly not like the cooking the boys were used to at home.

Jan. 17, 1941

Our first inoculation parade this morning. We'd been warned about it. Rolled up both sleeves & walked between swabbers, doctors & extras to catch the fainters. Record number of shots in record time. Quite a few of the lads keeled over & I'm happy to say I wasn't one of them. Learned how to wear my wedge cap. Right side of the head, centred from front to back, 1 inch above the right eyebrow if you please. I like to give it as much of a rakish slant as I can get away with!

It helped that the young recruits shared the same goals – to fight for Canada and fly. Camaraderie made the road more tolerable.

Jan. 20, 1941

After lights out last night some guy called out *ANYBODY HERE FROM THE WEST?* Some smart aleck yelled back *FUCK THE WEST!* We laughed our asses off. Then some other guy joined in & yelled *ANYBODY HERE FROM THE EAST?* We all yelled back *FUCK THE EAST!* Sure hope it gets easier to sleep.

Feb. 8, 1941

Today it was pecker inspection. We all had to drop our pants right on the parade ground while the doc walked up down checking us out. What a sight! Row on row of all these bare asses. The guys who are already being treated for the clap or something have got blue balls from whatever medicine they're taking. No secrets or privacy here.

Feb. 11, 1941

That's it for me. I'm moving on for gunnery training. Posted to the No. 1 Bombing & Gunnery School near Jarvis, Ontario, out near Hamilton. It's the first bombing & gunnery school & part

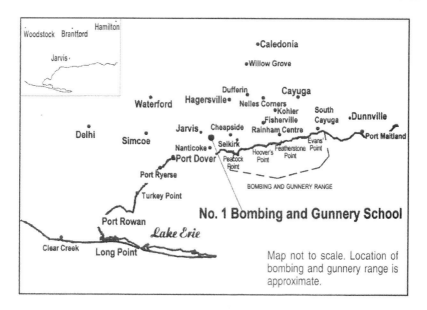

Woodstock Brantford Hamilton
Jarvis
•Caledonia
•Willow Grove
Dufferin Cayuga
Waterford Hagersville• Nelles Corners
•Kohler South
•Fisherville Cayuga •Dunnville
Jarvis. Cheapside Rainham Centre
Delhi
Simcoe Evans
Nanticoke • Selkirk Featherstone Point
Hoover's Point
•Port Dover Peacock Point
Point
Port Ryerse
BOMBING AND GUNNERY RANGE
Turkey Point
No. 1 Bombing and Gunnery School
Port Rowan *Lake Erie*
Clear Creek Long Point
Map not to scale. Location of bombing and gunnery range is approximate.
Port Maitland

of the British Commonwealth Air Training Plan. Commanding Officer is G/C George Wait. For now I'm going to be ground crew working on the B&G ranges. Sure glad I said I collect rifles & like to shoot skeet when they asked me about my hobbies.

The British Commonwealth Air Training Plan (BCATP), an agreement signed on December 17, 1939 by Canada, the United Kingdom, Australia and New Zealand, outlined a program to train Commonwealth pilots and aircrew. Canada was the perfect location for such a program: distant enough from the fighting in Europe, convenient for transporting men and equipment to England, and full of space for training facilities and practice operations. 107 schools were eventually set up across Canada. By March 1945 when the plan came to an end, 131,553 aircrew had graduated: pilots, navigators, bomb aimers, wireless operators, air gunners and flight engineers.[1]

Feb. 14, 1941

This is sure some place. I hear it was originally built in the 1930s by American Airlines to use in case of emergency landings but they stopped using it. Guardhouse, individual barracks & mess for officers, NCOs & airmen, civilian quarters & mess, control tower, fire hall, recreation building, hospital, drill hall, library, ground instruction school, sports field, parade square, 6 huge hangars, 4 landing strips, a dentist & the best part for me

– a 25 yard machine gun range & 4 indoor machine gun turret ranges. Hangar D is the gunnery hangar. Everyone calls the parade square Utopia Square.

Utopia Square

Feb. 17, 1941

The first European Allies (Norwegians) arrived today to train as Observers & Air Gunners under the BCATP. There's a lot of interest in this place. Seems there are always newspaper reporters & photographers around. Anything to attract more recruits I guess.

Feb. 20, 1941

I live in one of the 6 airmen's barracks. There are 75 or 100 of us. We're all in double deck bunks that line both sides of the hall with a washroom & toilets at one end. The married guys & their wives are billeted with local families.

Feb. 21, 1941

The streets here have great names – Raid Avenue, Pee Street, Rotten Row, Rookie Row & Sleepy Hollow.

Feb. 28, 1941

Couple of us took the bus into Port Dover. Closest place to hang out off the station. Lot of the boys aren't used to our Canadian winter especially the lads from Australia & New Zealand. Nothing that a couple of good snowballs up the side of the head won't fix.

Mar. 6, 1941

This place needs some girls to liven things up. One of these days they'll let women join up. Lots of jobs available without going to the front.

March 12, 1941

Lot of news reporters visiting the station these days, Canadians & Americans. Since we're the first B&G school, everyone wants to know what we're doing & how we're doing it. Even LIFE magazine has been here. A big Hollywood movie producer from Warner Brothers studio is going to make a movie here starring James Cagney! It's about northern Ontario bush pilots who enlist in the RCAF. Supposed to promote enlistment.

The BCATP in Canada was attracting the attention of young men all over the world: Norway, Great Britain, New Zealand, Australia, United States, Poland, Newfoundland, Belgium and free France. (The British colony of Newfoundland would not join Canada until 1949; the United States would not enter the war until December 1941, following the attack on Pearl Harbour.) Americans could enlist without swearing allegiance to the King so that they were able to remain US citizens. British men were coming to Canada to train because Canada had more capacity and airspace to offer. The side benefit was that they didn't have to worry about being bombed themselves in Canada, although there was always the worry about friends and family back home. Britain had taken a pounding, especially in places such as Coventry that the Germans had practically destroyed in November 1940. A BCATP station was good for the local economy, some of which was still recovering from the depression of the 1930s.

Apr. 13, 1941

Promoted to Aircraftman Class I or AC1. Not sure if I did anything to deserve it or if I got it just because I'm still here & breathing. Anyway I'm not on the bottom rung anymore! I've been practicing on the 25 yard range. It's just a bit east of Hangar F. My aim is pretty good. Must be all the practice Roly & me got shooting at the church roof from the backyard at the old house

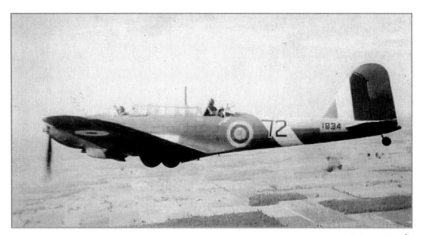

Fairey Battle

on Gladstone. Nothing quite like the ping of bullets off slate. Lucky we weren't arrested.

Apr. 30, 1941

All the air training here so far has been in Fairey Battle light bombers the RAF isn't using on the front line any more. Obsolete. No wonder – they're so large for a single engine aircraft. 1030 hp Rolls Royce Merlin. Open cockpit, no turret & slow as molasses. A lot of guys have got the chop in them. Stink of oil & glycol fumes all the time & some guys can't take it & end up washed out of their training. Most of them are painted yellow & some still have old RAF squadron markings. The Battles used for gunnery flights have a white band painted around the fuselage to identify them in the air. The ones used for bombing flights have a red band. Ones that tow practice targets have a black stripe.

May 11, 1941

5 hours straight bombing on London last night we heard. The worst yet. They don't even know yet how many were killed. Parliament, Big Ben, Westminster Abbey, thousands of homes all hit.

The Blitz (short for blitzkrieg, which means lightning war) was a period of extreme German Luftwaffe bombing of cities in England. It had begun on September 7, 1940, and culminated on Saturday, May 10, 1941 with a major raid on London.[2]

May 27, 1941

Big news today - the Royal Navy sunk the German battleship Bismarck in the north Atlantic. That would've been something to see.

June 7, 1941

Big wings parade today back at #1 Manning Depot in Toronto for 37 of our Jarvis air observer grads. Heard they had their wings pinned on by none other than Billy Bishop, the top Canadian World War I flying ace – VC, DSO, MC, DFC you name it. Can't get much more decorated than him. I'm getting a chance to work on the range crew. I'm game to try anything. One of these days I'll make it to aircrew.

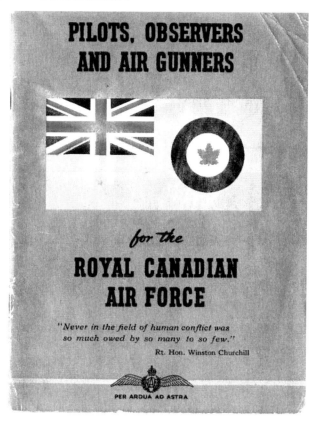

RCAF Recruitment Pamphlet

June 15, 1941

Got bounced around in the back of a panel truck today on the way to No. 1 target at Peacock Point on the shore of Lake Erie to be part of a range crew. I'm sure the driver is trying to kill us.

He must have his foot to the floor & every time he corners I'd swear the wheels come off the ground. At this rate we'll never make it overseas. There are 2 quadrant huts for the range crews & he dropped 2 of us off at the first one & then drove on to the second one about a mile away to drop the other guys off. The air observer students drop 11½ lb practice bombs on a target anchored out in the lake. Pretty shallow out there. Target looks like a pyramid, 30 ft or so across & floats on oil drums. Painted red. A big wooden arrow on the ground outside the huts points out to the target. The bombs release white smoke when they hit. We use telescopes from both quadrant huts to sight the smoke & phone the coordinates & the exact time back to the base where they plot them to rate the students. We keep a bomb sheet for each plane. By the time the students land their accuracy is all plotted out for them. Some of those guys sure are good.

Our quadrant hut

Floating bombing target

June 16, 1941

We got some flak from one of the guys whose bombs we sighted yesterday. He insisted he did better than what we reported. We were goofing off when 1 of his bombs hit & by the time I had the telescope ready to pinpoint it the wind had drifted the smoke a bit. Not that I was going to admit that to him. A direct hit would have cost him a round of beer in the mess anyway. He should thank me.

In an invasion known as Operation Barbarossa, Hitler amassed men, guns, tanks and aircraft to invade the Soviet Union, catching Soviet leader Joseph Stalin unprepared. It would last six months. The Germans were just a few kilometers from the centre of Moscow. Germany occupied what is now Belarus and most of Ukraine, and surrounded Leningrad (now St Petersburg). British Prime Minister, Winston Churchill called Hitler a monster and a "bloodthirsty guttersnipe" and said it was a turning point in the war.[3]

June 25, 1941

Back out on the range crew today. The practice bombs are neat little affairs. The head is made of lead & the tail end is full of some chemical that turns into smoke. When they hit, the pin goes in to explode the bomb & blows the tail end off that sends up the smoke. I "borrowed" one to take home with me. They say with all the bombing practice the water level in the lake has gone up quite a bit.

June 30, 1941

Over 100 trainees have reported to the school this month – Aussies, Canadians & even 1 American. His country's not even at war yet & he wants to help. It's official – we heard the Canadian Women's Auxiliary Air Force has just been formed. They're starting to recruit & train so it'll be a few months before any of the gals land here.

July 6, 1941

A Fairey Battle crashed & burned today in a training exercise. 2 Australian students killed even though their pilot safely bailed. The first training deaths here. We all know there's a good chance we might die in the war but no one expects to die in training. Never even occurred to me. Didn't know the boys myself.

Range crew lads loafing around off duty

"Training accidents would become an unavoidable fact of life at BCATP stations, although dying in training was certainly not the end that most students expected. With inexperience, take-offs, landings, aging aircraft and air manoeuvres, accidents were bound to happen, many of them fatal. Between October 1942 and September 1943, BCATP schools recorded over 6,000 accidents, over 300 of them fatal, 40 of them at Jarvis. 856 students were killed while training in Canada, more than half of them RCAF."[4]

July 7, 1941

Funeral today in Jarvis for the poor buggers killed yesterday. Pretty gloomy around here. No one can figure out why they didn't bail out when their pilot did. They buried them with full military honours at the Knox Presbyterian Church cemetery. They couldn't even send their bodies home to their families on account of the war.

July 13, 1941

Promoted to Leading Aircraftman or LAC for short. $2 a day now. Got my Propeller Badges & sewed them on my sleeves tonight.

July 17, 1941

      Out at the range hut today we saw these 2 civilians pull up in a truck hauling a boat on a trailer. We see them every week. They put on skin-diving gear & launch their boat. When bombing practice is over they ride out to the target drop area & go diving. At first we weren't sure what they were doing but today we figured out they're diving for the lead heads on the bombs. Lake Erie is pretty shallow. Must be selling the lead somewhere. There's gotta be 8 lb or more of it in every head – worth a lot. I guess there's a market for just about anything these days if you know where to sell it. Churchill wants everyone to use the V for Victory hand sign.

July 23, 1941

      The inquiry from the training accident a couple of weeks ago showed that 1 of the students deployed his parachute while he was still in the plane. What a tangled mess of silk that must have been not to mention a useless parachute. They figure the other guy went down trying to help him. No other explanation. Poor guys. Can't even imagine what that must have felt like. No one expects to be the one who gets it least of all in training. I've got 2 weeks annual leave coming up. Heading home & up to the country to see the family. Everyone wants to see me in uniform & the aunts all want to feed me. I can't wait.

Training accidents were rated with an A, B, C or D based on the damage to the aircraft. "D" meant it was minor & "A" meant the aircraft was written off.[5] There didn't appear to be a rating that indicated human casualties.

July 29, 1941

      Went to the AYPA camp up at Lake Couchiching with all my friends on my leave.

Aug. 9, 1941

      Leave was nice while it lasted but good to be back too. Sure miss the girls though. No. 16 Service Flying Training School just opened at Hagersville a few kilometers from here. They're training bomber pilots to fly twin engine Avro Ansons & fighter pilots to fly single engine Harvard trainers. That makes 5 airfields in the county in the BCATP – us, Hagersville, No. 6 SFTS at Dun-

AYPA Camp

nville, Kohler & Dufferin. Fighter pilot trainees at Dunnville are flying Harvards & Yales.

Aug. 15, 1941

Lot of the local types like to watch bombing practice over the lake from the shore. Some even bring the whole family for a picnic. Cheap entertainment these days. Boats can't go within 1000 yds of the practice bombing targets at B.1 Peacock Point & B.3 Evans Point.

Aug. 20, 1941

King George VI's youngest brother the Duke of Kent will be inspecting the school next week. Everyone is in a good mood & busy with spit & polish to make sure the station passes muster.

Aug. 24, 1941

Finished my Armourer course & scored 70%. Stripping & assembling, care & cleaning, troubleshooting, handling drills, sighting, ammo, maintenance & repair. Should've done better but good enough to get me a full time job in the Ground Instruction School, building #2.

Aug. 27, 1941

The Duke of Kent flew in to the station today. The CO & some senior officers gave him & his entourage an inspection tour of the base. I didn't get to meet him. Everyone was on their best behaviour. No brawls today! All the officers got to meet him at dinner tonight in the officers' mess. Sure would be nice to get a commission.

Sept. 9, 1941

My birthday today – 21. I can officially drink a beer although I could care less. There are close to 1500 of us working here at the station now.

Sept. 17, 1941

Bad news - Sgt. Jackson from the Ground Instruction School was killed in a car accident today while he was on his way back from leave.

Sept. 22, 1941

Got fingerprinted today. Just like in the movies.

Sept. 25, 1941

A YWCA Hostess House opened at the station where we can go in our off hours. Just inside the gate. There are darts, books, a piano, places to sit & shoot the breeze. The station even has its own orchestra. We even have our own newspaper – The Fly Paper.

Sept. 29, 1941

I'm pretty fast now stripping & assembling, especially the Vickers & Brownings. Blindfolded too. Armament is definitely one of my strengths.

Oct. 1, 1941

Promoted to Acting Corporal, my first NCO rank. Too bad

The Boly

no pay raise to go with it. Issued my 2 bar chevron shirt & jacket. Spud Hiscox is my best friend here. His real name is Earl & he's a corporal too. Most of the guys have nicknames – Spud is just one of the better ones. I go by Wally. Just add that to the other names I already have – Ab, Abe, Abby, Albie (only to Ma though).

Oct. 15, 1941

I'm now in charge of the GIS equipment room. I issue all the machine guns & other equipment for the air gunner class training. OK for now but I want to be IN that class some day soon.

Oct. 18, 1941

Some Bristol Bolingbroke IVs have arrived for training. We call it the Boly. It's built in Nova Scotia & compares to the RAF's Blenheim medium bomber. It's got a revolving mid upper turret – great for practice with the machine gun. Takes 3 students.

Oct. 30, 1941

An American Airlines passenger DC-3 crashed not far from here tonight. Near St. Thomas. They fly over us all the time.

Nov. 3, 1941

That American Airlines DC-3 that crashed was on its way to Chicago from New York City. No word on why it crashed but we were all grounded at the time on account of the lousy weather so at least we know it wasn't our fault. All 17 passengers & the 3 crew are dead. They're calling it Canada's worst aviation disaster.

Nov. 10, 1941

They asked those of us who won't be on leave at Christmas if we want to spend Christmas Day with a local family. Very nice offer but I'm more of a lone dog. I'll manage fine.

Nov. 19, 1941

Went to a big dance last night in the airmen's mess for something to do. Spud & me went (even though he's engaged to Flo) & there were loads of girls & chaperones brought in from the area although still way more of us than them. Had to be 10 to 1 so the competition for a dance was fierce. Those gals just about danced their feet off to music played by the station orchestra. I'll never amount to much in the dancing department.

Nov. 25, 1941

Medical exam today. Weigh 144 lb. Healthy as a horse & don't even smoke. Only thing I can remember having when I was a kid is measles. Had to explain the scar on my forehead so I told the doc about the Murphy bed falling on me when I was 3 & maybe giving me a concussion!

Nov 27, 1941

Hallelujah! I've been recommended for remustering to aircrew so I didn't waste a minute before applying. It's what I wanted from the start. I'm OK for vision, height & weight. Just waiting

Some of the lads in their flying gear

Scales of Pay for R.C.A.F. Aircrew

The following are the scales of pay for R.C.A.F. aircrew at various stages in their training:

AC2. (upon enlistment) ....$1.30 per day.

LAC. Airman Pilot, Air Observer or Wireless Operator (Air Gunner) (Received soon after training is commenced) ....$1.50 per day.

If you are selected for training as pilot or air observer, after completing training at an Initial Training School, you will be entitled to a special allowance of 75 cents per day, in addition to pay and allowances to which you are entitled at the time selected. This special allowance is paid continuously for the whole period during which you are undergoing flying training.

Over and above the daily rates of pay you receive, in addition, your meals and living quarters. You are also clothed, completely at the government's expense.

When you are mustered as sergeants at the conclusion of your training under the British Commonwealth Air Training Plan, your daily rates of pay, including flying pay, are as follows:

Airman Pilots	$3.70
Air Observers	$3.70
Wireless Operators (Air Gunners)	$3.20
Air Gunners	$2.95

In addition to the above rates you are also still provided with meals, quarters and complete clothing.

Upon embarking for overseas with, or in conjunction with the Royal Air Force, your pay will be in accordance with the scale of pay and allowances of the Royal Air Force. The deficiency, if any, in this rate from that of the Royal Canadian Air Force will be issued to you by the government of Canada as deferred pay, either on termination of service or otherwise in special circumstances.

For those selected as officers, the daily rates of pay, including flying pay are as follows:

Pilot Officer	$6.25
Flying Officer	$7.00
Flight Lieutenant	$8.50
Squadron Leader	$9.75

Officers are allowed $150.00 towards the purchase of their uniforms and receive, in addition free quarters and meals.

for them to relax the education requirement. Finally, a chance to get ahead doing something I like & think I'll be good at. I'll get a raise too!

Nov. 30, 1941

Since most bombing operations overseas are happening at night, night bombing practice has started for the air observer students taking their course at the GIS. They use the same lake targets used for daylight exercises only they're lit up. Can be seen up to 10,000 ft. They had to lay a submarine cable for power. The students use special bombs that flash for about a second when they hit the water so they can be plotted. They also take a gunnery course so I issue their equipment

27

& learn what I can from their course – sighting a machine gun, using tracer ammo, estimating ranges, learning gunnery techniques & turret types, recognizing the different A/C.

Dec. 3, 1941

Big sis Eleanor turned 23 today. Happy birthday El!

The face of the war changed dramatically on December 7, 1941 when Japan launched a surprise attack in two waves on the American naval base at Pearl Harbor, Hawaii, and declared war on Britain and the United States. By day's end, thousands, military and civilian, were dead or wounded. Japan also bombed the Hawaiian capital, Honolulu, the island of Guam, and the Philippines capital, Manila. On December 8th, Japan invaded Hong Kong, including attacks against the Canadian defenders, and US President Roosevelt declared war on Japan. Some of the 100 or so American staff pilots & students at the school resigned from the RCAF to join up with the US army air corps.

Dec. 9, 1941

Two of our Fairey Battles clipped wings mid air today near Fisherville. 1 of them actually made it back to the station. 3 are dead – the American RCAF pilot & 2 students, 1 of them RAF. 1 of them crashed with the A/C & the other 2 were found in a field.

Dec. 10, 1941

I was asked to be on the gun squad at the funeral parade of one of the guys killed yesterday. Poor sod. I didn't know him. 6 of us went to the funeral & cemetery. We fired off the rifle volley as they put him away. R.I.P. Every time someone gets killed in a training accident it feels like this place has a dark cloud over it. Something very unjust about being killed in a training accident when you're training to go to war.

The war was heating up. On December 11, Italy & Germany declared war on the United States. President Roosevelt immediately declared war on them.

GIS staff

Dec. 25, 1941

My first Christmas away from home. Some of the boys are away on leave & some are spending the day at private homes in the area. We had our own Christmas dinner right here in the airmen's mess served up by G/C Wait & some of the senior officers. There were around 600 of us. Britain surrendered Hong Kong to the Japanese. Merry Christmas to you too.

Dec. 31, 1941

G/C Wait recommended me for promotion to Temporary Corporal with pay. Complimented me on my work in the GIS. Nice way to finish the year. Should help me get into aircrew. Goal – my Air Gunner's wing badge.

Jan. 7, 1942

Didn't sleep well last night. The night bombing training planes were so loud, all night, most nights these days.

Jan. 20, 1942

I keep checking the DROs for an aircrew posting that I'm qualified for.

Jan. 26, 1942

Admitted to the hospital today with the worst sore throat I've ever had & fever.

Jan. 30, 1942

Sprung from the hospital this aft. Feel a lot better.

Feb. 1, 1942

Promoted to Temporary Corporal with pay. Scored 81% on my Drill & Ceremonial Qualification Report.

Feb. 15, 1942

CBS Radio was here at the station today to broadcast a wings presentation to the graduating air observers on its "Spirit of 1942" program. It played in New York & on CFRB in Toronto.

The RCAF band from my old stomping grounds at #1 Manning Depot in Toronto provided the music. G/C Wait emphasized in his remarks how critical bomber A/C are to the outcome of this war & why BCATP is investing so much to train bomber crews. There's hope for me yet. Singapore unconditionally surrendered to the Japanese today. Winston Churchill called it "the worst disaster and largest capitulation in British history".[6] The Japs say they've taken 60,000 prisoners!

Feb. 20, 1942

There are so many graduating classes of air gunners it's hard to keep up. Course 26 graduated its 1000th AG today. Maybe with the numbers they're putting through there'll be an opportunity for me soon.

On February 22, 1942, Air Marshall Sir Arthur Harris was appointed to lead Bomber Command. He set out to dismantle Germany's industry with new bombing tactics and aids. During his leadership, which would continue for the balance of the war, Harris became known as "Bomber Harris", a nickname that would follow him the rest of his career.

Me in the trainer

Feb. 27, 1942

Happy birthday Betty. Sweet sixteen! Ma'll be wishing I was around to fend off the boys.

March 14, 1942

Stood up for Spud & Florence Hiscox at their wedding. Real nice of Spud & Flo to ask me.

March 20, 1942

G/C Wait has been posted to No. 1 Training Command in Toronto. We'll sure miss him here. Never too big to stop & talk to even the most junior fellow. I admire that about him.

Group Captain Wait would become a role model for Dad. Much later in his own career, Dad would be well liked by all levels of employees for the very same reason.

March 22, 1942

A snowstorm caught everyone off guard today. Visibility was so bad that a few guys in the air got turned around. A few ended up landing elsewhere, some in New York. Heard 1 unlucky fellow from Hagersville flew right into the ground.

March 31, 1942

50 or so new aircraft for training – Avro Ansons & Westland Lysanders. Over 100 aircraft at the station now. The Anson is another combat reject like the FB but at least it has a built in bomb bay. It'll be used for bombing practice. The Lysander has these big black & yellow stripes so we call it the Bumble Bee. You can see it from a mile away. It'll mainly be used for towing drogues for air to air firing practice.

April 3, 1942

Some of the staff pilots aren't too pleased to be posted here. Bored to tears. Like the rest of us they just want to see some action overseas.

April 15, 1942

Our new station CO is W/C William Hanna from Winnipeg. FINALLY. Today's DROs had a posting looking for volunteers for the Air Gunner 35B course. For once it didn't state any educational requirements so I applied quick before they could change their mind. Have to wait & see now.

April 27, 1942

Finally we have WOMEN working at the station. 70 of them arrived today. That's swell news as far as I'm concerned! They call themselves the Royal Canadian Air Force Women's Division or WD's for short. They're doing administrative jobs for now. We'll have to get used to having them around & in the meantime mind our P's & Q's or we'll hear about it I'm sure. 7 days leave coming up on Thursday so I'm going home.

May 3, 1942

I came across the smoke bomb I brought home last year. Figured I better do something with it since it was armed. Ma wouldn't take kindly to knowing I had it in my room. I unscrewed the lead head & took the rest of it out back in the lane. I unscrewed the screw where they put the fluid into it & dumped it out in the laneway. There was so much smoke I thought for sure someone was going to call the fire department or the police. Good thing it was dark.

Cpl Wallace at ease

May 7, 1942

Back from leave. It was nice while it lasted. All the aunts & uncles came visiting. Betty & El invited all their girlfriends over to see me in uniform. Went to see some movies with Dorothy, a friend of El's. Walked around downtown.

Me & Dot

May 12, 1942

Met one of the WDs – Joan. Nice gal. She's a weather observer. Nice having girls at the station.

May 15, 1942

Went into Port Dover last night with Joan for something to do. Wandered around town & down to the beach. One of the boys missed the bus back to the station & had a LONG walk home.

May 22, 1942

Joan says she'd like to become aircrew but the RCAF won't allow it on account of the danger. Besides, I wouldn't be too pleased if she made aircrew before me.

It was around this time that Air Marshall Sir Arthur Harris, commander of Bomber Command, decided to execute his bold idea of amassing 1,000 bombers and sending them out in a single enormous raid on one German city (and do it more than once if possible as long as weather conditions cooperated). As the full moon approached, Harris selected Hamburg, Germany's second largest city, as his target; however, as weather conditions changed, Harris changed his target to Cologne, the third largest city in Germany. There would be two more 1,000-bomber raids, but neither would be as successful as Cologne due to the weather. The 1,000 bomber raids were pivotal for Bomber Command.[7]

May 31, 1942

We were stunned to hear about the massive 1000 Allied bomber raid on Cologne, Germany last night. A new tactic for sure. A success even though Bomber Command lost 41 aircraft.

June 3, 1942

A second 1000 bomber raid, this time on Essen. Not as successful as Cologne.

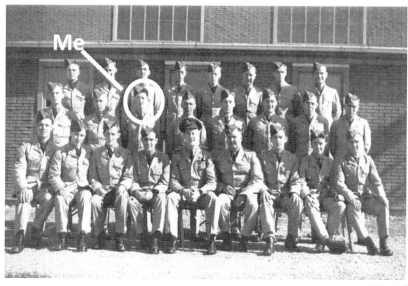

GIS staff

Keith & me in Toronto on Yonge St.

June 15, 1942

Had to go for another medical exam today as part of my air gunner application. 141 lb. Perfect vision & just under the maximum height of 6 ft. Pronounced fit!

June 17, 1942

Interviewed today about my application for AG & I think they gave me the all clear. Starting my 7 days annual leave tomorrow. So is Keith Fleming so we're heading to Toronto together with another lad.

June 26, 1942

Back from leave & heard that 1 of our staff pilots buzzed Hamilton for a laugh the other night. Too bad some upset citizens reported him. It's happened over Port Dover too. That's what boredom can do to you I guess. Another 1000 bomber raid on Bremen last night.

June 29, 1942

I made it to Aircrew! I've been recommended for air gunner training here at Jarvis. Finally I'll get a chance to go overseas & really do my part for the war. I start Course 35B on July 6 – for 12 weeks. Now I get to be a student at the GIS instead of a workie. George & me went to the Summer Garden dance pavilion in Port Dover tonight. Just for girling. The 2 of us aren't much for dancing. Nice spot – round and open air but with a roof over top. Heard the lad who buzzed Hamilton got a demotion & a 60 day detention. Hope it was worth it.

July 6, 1942

Started Stage 1 of AG training today. 25 of us in the class. All of us are re-mustered ground crew from different schools. Maybe we're an experiment. There's only a couple of us from here at Jarvis. We'll be evaluated on armament oral & written, anti-gas, aircraft recognition, navigation, math, signals & drill. I've started smoking now but who hasn't.

July 7, 1942

Using the Boly now too for training flights. At least it's got a gun turret – the Bristol B1 Mid Upper Gun Turret with twin .303 calibre Brownings.

July 10, 1942

I'm already good friends with Don Kelly in my class. He's from Richmond, Quebec. He really wanted to be a pilot but ended up here on account of his medical. AG training is swell so far. Totally different than high school but I'm at home around guns so it's right up my alley. At least I like to read.

July 14, 1942

Got to practice today at the 200 yard machine gun range at Hoover's Point not too far away. It's way bigger than the 25 yard range & has better technology. I fired at targets out in the lake using a Boulton Paul hydraulic gun turret – 4 Browning .303s. It's a real tail turret that can fire 4,800 rounds a minute. Not bad. Won't be the same as real aerial fire but the Fairey Battle doesn't have a turret so this might be as good as it gets until I'm in a bomber. My main job as AG is to be the lookout for fighters & protect the bomber. Know in a split second what to shoot at & then pour it on. But never fire unless necessary because it gives our position away. Instruct the pilot to take evasive action.

July 15, 1942

Spending a lot of time in the Aircraft Recognition room so I'm already getting pretty sharp at it. Over 80 types of planes too. The walls are plastered with the A/C shapes. Models of Wellingtons, Dorniers & Hurricanes on brackets have lights in their wings to look like guns. Our instructor is F/S Steiss – a Canadian fellow who was with RAF 76 squadron. Flew in Whitleys.

July 17, 1942

Another good guy in my class is Doug Storey. From Vancouver. A bit older than the rest of us. Introduced to map reading today. Practiced again at the 200 yard machine gun range only this time with a Frazer Nash turret. The locals must wear earplugs all the time or just get used to the never ending firing.

July 23, 1942

Three more guys bit it today in a Boly Mk IV training accident out near Target No. 1 at Peacock Point – 1 American RCAF,

Some of our class
Back row: *Cliff Hildreth, Gavin Nichols, Geo Lindley, Norman Notley, me, John Hucker, Ed Webb.*
Front row: *Don Kelly is 3rd in, then John Richmond, Keith Fleming, Doug Storey*

1 RAF, 1 RAAF. Pretty depressing. I sure hope I don't end up as a bag of personal stuff shipped home to Ma with a Silver Cross.

The Silver Cross, or these days referred to as the Memorial Cross, is an award created in 1919 by the Government of Canada for the mothers and widows of Canadian sailors, airmen and soldiers who died for their country. The son or husband's name, rank and service number were engraved on the back of the cross. Today, Canadian forces members can designate up to three Memorial Cross recipients.[8]

July 25, 1942

Me & John Hucker from my class have become great pals. Everyone calls him Huck. He's from Toronto too. I told him about the time Roly, Mousie & me were fooling around in the cellar with our guns & Roly took a shot in his leg. The bullet's still

Hucker

in there & he's got the lump to prove it! Good thing Ma was at work or there would've been hell to pay. His mother still doesn't know. He must have had to come clean about it in his enlistment medical.

July 26, 1942

The school is growing again. Course 58 is for a new aircrew position – Air Bomber – that along with the navigator replaces the air observer. Longer training. They're building new barrack blocks & adding a new runway too. I'm friends with another boy in my class too – Cliff Hildreth from Stoney Creek. CO Hanna is moving on & as of today our new station CO is G/C Alan Bell-Irving. Highly decorated with not one but two Military Crosses. He served in World War I & shot down SEVEN enemy planes. Was shot down himself FOUR times! I think I'd have quit while I was ahead. He was pressing his luck.

Aug. 1, 1942

Stage 2 of our air & ground training is starting. We'll finally be airborne. Got my goggles, helmet, ear pads & Flying Logbook.

Aug. 4, 1942

Skeet practice today with a shotgun. Practiced getting kitted up for my first flight tomorrow. Between long johns, extra clothes, flying suit & parachute harness I understand why they tell us to pee first. Never wear the parachute in the aircraft – too bulky. Parachute clips on to 2 metal loops on the front of the harness. Clips don't look too sturdy to me. D ring to deploy it is on the right side – not good for a lefty like me. Hope I never have to use it.

Aug. 5, 1942

Flew today for my first time – 3 of us. It was swell to finally be airborne. First entry in my logbook! It was a Fairey Battle I & the thing is a flying tank just like I heard. I wondered if we were ever going to get off the ground. I feel sorry for the fellows who flew operations in them. They didn't stand a chance against the Luftwaffe ME 109 fighters. Have to be careful handling the parachute. If you accidentally open it in the A/C there'll be silk from hell to breakfast & then good luck if you have to bail out. I remember when it happened to a fellow here last summer & he never got out.

Aug. 8, 1942

In the past 2 months 10 of our aircraft have been in accidents. They found the body of another fellow who went down in that Boly crash in the lake last month. A fisherman found him in the water. Canadian RCAF. The Hamilton Spectator ran a write-up about us yesterday & some of the boys from class got mentioned - Don Kelly, Gavin Nichols. Practiced with the Frazer Nash Mid Upper Gun Turret at the 200 yard range.

Aug. 12, 1942

More skeet practice today & I'm pretty good at it. Shooting all those nuisance groundhogs at Uncle John & Carl's farm is paying off for a second time. First time was for 5¢ a groundhog!

Aug. 15, 1942

Spending a lot of time in the Aircraft Recognition room popping slides into the magic lantern & naming the A/C that flashes up on the screen. A few seconds is all you get. 80 A/C from just about every angle. We've had about 30 hours of this.

Aug. 18, 1942

Another bad training accident today. An Anson on a bombing practice & an FB on a gunnery exercise collided over B.3 target at Evans Point. The Anson crashed in some local's yard & the FB ploughed into the lake. Both pilots killed along with 4 students – 1 RNZAF pilot & the rest RCAF. Who ever thought they'd get killed training & never even make it to the front? It's been a bad summer for crashes.

Aug. 19, 1942

The Germans attacked Stalingrad today in southern Russia. The FB that crashed yesterday was the same one that survived the mid air wing clipping accident last December. I guess it's only a matter of time for these old kites.

Aug. 20, 1942

Huge Allied raid yesterday on Dieppe on the coast of France. Largest op yet. Big Canadian losses. 2 of the Canadian boys killed here on Tues. were in the first Air Bombers Course 58. They would have graduated next week. Sounds like some changes may be made to the bombing range to prevent any more accidents like it.

More of our class

The August 19, 1942 attack on the French coast at Dieppe would become one of Canada's worst military disasters. Of the 5,000 Canadians, who made up the majority of the attacking force, 907 were killed, 586 wounded and almost 2,000 were taken prisoner.[9]

Aug. 21, 1942

Practiced with a cine-camera gun that was loaded with 16mm film instead of bullets. Another aircraft simulated an attack on us & I fired on it. Using film saves a lot of ammo (200 to 300 rounds per student) & eliminates anything raining down on people below so we can practice anywhere. The film will show how accurate I was (or wasn't!).

Aug. 25, 1942

The air training is making this all more real to me but it's what I signed on for. I'm starting to get nervous about what's ahead. Quite a few flying accidents here in the last couple of months, Battles, Bolys, Lysanders, an Anson. Crashes on take-off, crashes on landing & more. Lot of guys dead. Hope it's not a bad omen. We heard tonight on the news that the Duke of Kent who visited here last year was killed in a plane crash today. No one's immune.

Aug. 26, 1942

Introduction to aerial practice today over the lake. Fired tracer bullets at the water to get a feel for the curvature & the drift. In a couple of days we graduate to aerial practice firing at buoys anchored in the lake parallel to the shoreline.

Sept. 2, 1942

More air to ground practice today. Next comes drogue firing. A Lysander tows the drogue a few hundred feet behind it on a cable. It's made of white nylon & looks like a giant windsock so it flits around pretty good in the air. Only about 3 ft wide & 12 ft long so it's going to be tough to hit especially from 200 yds. They say that if you score 8% you're doing okay. When an exercise is over the drogue operator releases the old target & sends a new one down the cable to set up for the next exercise. Local kids are stealing some of the shot up drogues after they've been released. Maybe some of the lousy shots are paying them off! Pretty harmless compared to Roly & me shooting out streetlights from our bikes. But we were smarter. Never got caught.

Sept. 3, 1942

Air to air firing exercise today shooting at the drogue. The pilot took Huck & me together in an FB & we positioned ourselves in the rear cockpit. My bullet tips were dipped in red paint to identify them & Huck's were blue. They count the colour rimmed holes in the drogue to rate our accuracy. I was afraid I'd hit the darn tow plane but they said it's never happened. I'll get a report about how I made out but I think I did okay.

Sept. 4, 1942

More drogue firing from different angles & speeds. That's about as close as my training will get to what real air combat will feel like.

Sept. 5, 1942

Flew today in a Bolingbroke IVT. At least it's got a Boulton Paul turret with 2 Browning .303s. Pretty tight in the turret. Good thing I'm skinny. The Brownings make quite a racket when they go off. It'll be a miracle if I'm not deaf after this.

Some of the lads in their flying gear

Sept. 9, 1942

Happy Birthday to me. 22 today. Another training crash this afternoon, a Boly this time, pilot & 2 students dead, all RCAF. It's been a bad few months.

Sept. 14, 1942

No one can figure out what happened to the Boly that crashed last week. It was supposed to be a routine air firing practice out over the lake but halfway into it the Boly headed inland & dove into the ground. The A/C is beyond written off so nothing likely to be learned from it.

Sept. 18, 1942

The WDs are getting promoted to bigger jobs on the base. There are gals in the control tower, doing bomb plotting & A/C maintenance. Means more of the ground crew are free to apply for aircrew.

Sept. 23, 1942

An editorial in the Globe & Mail today says that ALL aircrew should be commissioned. We all support that idea!

Sept. 25, 1942

Training's over. Can hardly believe it. I logged 15 hrs 40 min of flying time & 7 hrs 20 min of turret manipulation. That's as good as it gets for now. Graduation is tomorrow afternoon & then we ship out Sunday by train to No. 1 Y Depot in Halifax. Start of 2 weeks embarkation leave. Joan's shipping overseas soon too to work at RCAF headquarters in London. They're just starting to send WDs overseas.

Sept. 26, 1942

Graduation Day! We had our wings parade this aft & got presented with our AG wing badge. Ma, Dad & Aunt Rae came. G/C Bell-Irving pointed out that we're the very first course of re-mustered ground crew – all 25 of us - to receive our aircrew wings at Jarvis. I guess that means there's hope for us General Duties types after all. Some of us got special mention too. He singled out Doug Storey because he had over 772 hours under his belt operating the drogue here at Jarvis over the past 2 years. Called him up for personal congratulations even! He mentioned me too for having been a general duty clerk for 18 months before training. Maybe that's some kind of record for perseverance. Or maybe just for dumbness. Cpl William Clow came first in the class & received his commission to Pilot Officer. The only com-

Me and Aunt Rae

Sgt. Wallace looking very dapper

45

ROYAL CANADIAN AIR FORCE

TRAINING REPORT

AIR GUNNER

No. 1 B. & G. School

JM982

			Christian	
1.	Surname	Wallace	Names	Albert Randall
2.	Number	R88911	Rank	Cpl.	Course No.	35-B
3.	Posted from		Posted to	No. 1 "Y" Depot	Duration Prom	6-7-42
					of Course	To	25-9-42
4.	Aircrew Category	Straight Air Gunner	Height		Girth	

5.

	EQUIPMENT USED			
Type Aircraft	Type Guns		Type Turrets	
	In Air	Ground	In Air	Ground
Battle	V.G.O.	V.G.O.	Bristol IV	Boulton Paul Fraser Nash
Bolingbroke	Browning	Browning		Bristol
	Rifle Revolver			

mission in the class. And then he got married in the afternoon! A good day for him all round. I guess whoever comes first in the class automatically gets his commission. I got 87.5% & came 2nd & I couldn't be more proud of me. I've never scored 87.5% in anything in my life so I'm pretty happy. At least I got promoted to Temporary Sergeant with pay. The rest of us will have to wait & see if Ottawa awards any more commissions. I'm keeping my fingers crossed. First thing I did was run back to barracks and sew my wing badge on my jacket.

Sept. 27, 1942

The whole class of 25 of us shipped out today to Halifax. We're finally on our way. Officially on leave until Oct. 10. Stopped in Montreal overnight.

Sept. 28, 1942

Kelly knows Montreal real well so he showed us around & took Huck & me to a cathouse last night. That was a new one on me. We had a great time!! Picked up more fellows at the train station. Arrived in Halifax today & reported to No. 1 Y Depot. It'll be our last posting before we head overseas. Sent Ma a telegram to let her know I arrived. She'll be worrying already.

We made the news!

REMUSTERED GROUND CREW GIVEN WINGS

Drogue Operator With 772 Hours in Air Is Included in Graduates

Jarvis, Sept. 27 (Special).—"There is special interest on this occasion because this is the first complete course of remustered members of ground crew to get wings of aircrew here," Group Captain A. D. Bell-Irving, officer commanding No. 1 Bombing and Gunnery School, Jarvis, told a class of graduating straight air gunners Saturday afternoon. Some of the men with stripes of corporals, the graduates had previously been clerks, general duty men, service police and security guards, and one, D. S. Storey of Dryden, had, as a drogue operator, 772 hours and 20 minutes of flying time behind him.

Sergt. D. S. Storey.

"We fully appreciate the value of your service in the Royal Canadian Air Force and the spirit that makes you want to go into the air and take a combatant part," Group Captain Bell-Irving said. "We congratulate you and wish you the best of luck."

Leading the class was 21-year-old W. R. Clow of Belleville, who had corporal's stripes as clerk in the R.C.A.F. recruiting centre at Hamilton for two years. The day was outstanding for Clow. He got his half-wing, was presented with a gift from the school and classmates as honor student, received a commission as

PO. W. R. Clow.

pilot officer and was married to Miss Edith Hastie, daughter of Mr. and Mrs. Andrew Hastie, Hamilton. Sergeant Pilot Storey had congratulations heaped upon him by officers who had witnessed his work in his 772 air hours as drogue operator at Jarvis over a period of more than two years. He had done a fine job,

they said. Storey, the son of Mrs. G. E. Storey, was called out of ranks on parade and brought before Group Captain Bell-Irving to receive his commanding officer's personal congratulations. The honor was unexpected by Storey and he was a bit taken aback. Spectators applauded him. His job with the drogue, a long canvas sleeve towed behind a plane, was to release it for firing practice by air gunners.

Another member of the Jarvis staff to be winged was Corporal A. R. Wallace, 22, son of Mr. and Mrs. Robert Wallace, 270 St. Clarens Avenue, Toronto. For eighteen months he had been a general duty clerk on the station.

About a third of the remustered men were from Toronto. Practically all of them had two or three years in the service. R. E. Dillon, South Porcupine, who was a goaltender with the R.C.A.F. team that won the Allan Cup last season, was winged. He and Corporal Milt Schmidt, former pro hockey player and now physical instructor at Jarvis, were the two representatives of the R.C.A.F. team on the station.

The Globe and Mail. September 28, 1942

Sept. 29, 1942

Nothing to do until we receive our orders other than report in twice a day for roll call & occasionally parade.

Sept. 30, 1942

Last night I met a real nice girl who lives here. Her name is Aileen. I'm going to see her again tonight.

Oct. 2, 1942

Another date with Aileen. Went to the pictures.

Oct. 5, 1942

Aileen invited me for dinner with her folks. Very nice people but unfair of me to get involved with a girl at this point.

Oct. 7, 1942

Saw Aileen again. I think I'm in love. Bad timing.

Oct. 11, 1942

Still don't know when we sail but it must be getting close. I'm enjoying time with Aileen in the meantime. Had to fill out all sorts of documents today. Who to be notified in case of casualty. Next of kin. Do I have a will. Have I completed documentation for dependent's allowance. I added Aileen to my Next of kin. Lots of reminders that I may not be coming back.

Oct. 17, 1942

Received a telegram today telling me I've been awarded the King's Commission to Pilot Officer effective AG graduation day - Sept. 25/42. I'm an officer!!! Haven't heard of anyone else getting one so it looks like Clow & me might be the only 2 in our class. My old teachers at Central Tech will fall over faint when they hear – especially Mr. Lewis. I'm sure they never expected me to

10,

Suitability for further training as a Gunnery Instructor	Not at all Suitable	Moderately suitable	Definitely suitable	Extremely suitable
			X	

Mark "X" in the appropriate column.

11. Remarks : Good student; excellent application; very fine youngster with sufficient independence and initiative to take the lead; sociable and absolutely dependable.

Date: 25-9-42

(G.O. Godson) Squadron Lead
Chief Instructor

Date: 25-9-42

(A.D. Bell-Irving) Group Capt
Officer Commanding
No. 1 B. & G.S.

amount to much. What a swell day! All the boys are kidding me & saluting me & calling me Sir. I was worried they'd resent me. Ma'll be on the phone all night telling the world. And I'll get a pay raise too! My new officer's service number is J-14982.

Oct. 18, 1942

Reported to Pay Accounts this morning to collect $100 to help me pay for my officer's uniforms. More to it than I realized - trousers, shirt, tie, tunic, hat, trench coat, greatcoat, gloves. The $100 didn't even begin to cover it so it's a good thing I don't have to repay it. Had to ask Ma to wire me some money to make up the difference. Pretty swish. I feel like a million bucks wearing it although I'm self-conscious around the lads from my class. Wait'll Aileen sees me.

Oct. 21, 1942

Had to be sworn in & take an oath of allegiance to the King that I'm willing to serve on active service anywhere in Canada, beyond Canada & overseas for the duration of the present war & the following demobilization should "His Majesty require my services". The war we're already in is enough for me to think about. Had my official picture taken. Wasn't too hard getting that smile out of me. Celebrated in town.

Oct. 22, 1942

The harbour is full of anchored ships. I don't know which one is ours or if ours is even here yet. Some of them are pretty beat up. When we embark is still a secret. They don't tell us anything until they have to.

Cheshire cat

Oct. 23, 1942

We watched the Queen Elizabeth sail into port & dock this afternoon. She's a beauty even painted gray. And huge. Some-one said she's easily over 80,000 tons. She attracted quite a lot of attention – police, R.C.M.P., military guard - all guarding her. With luck maybe she'll be our ride out of here. I'm thinking she's got to be one of the safer ships to cross on.

Oct. 26, 1942

Bought Aileen a ring today so I guess that means we're en-gaged. Must be crazy. Hard not to be when it's so crazy around here.

Oct. 27, 1942

Was officially transferred today from No. 1 Y Depot to the RAF training pool. They told us we're confined to camp tonight so I think this is it. Finally it was confirmed that we set sail tomorrow on the Queen Elizabeth. Walked down to the harbour to see her this aft & fellows were already boarding. She hasn't been hit by a U-boat yet so let's hope her luck (& ours) continues. And I know luck. I'll never forget the close call I had trying to stop my CCM road racer by jamming my foot against the front tire. I ended up flying ass over teakettle over the handlebars & onto the streetcar tracks. Packed up my kit bag & made it an early night.

Oct. 28, 1942

Marched down to the boat yard this morning. Crazy down there. Everybody saying goodbye to everybody & hugging & crying. Just made me want to get away from it all. Finally it was time to board & I headed up the gangplank. No turning back. Just come back to me is all she said. I just wanted to get the show on the road.

There must be thousands of us on board – Air Force, Army and Navy & they're still coming. As I boarded an officer handed me a card with my cabin number on it. I'm sharing a stateroom on an upper deck with a few other officers. Trouble is, the Brits are in charge now & they don't think much of officers fraternizing with OTHER ranks. Kelly, Hucker, Cliff, Keith & the rest of the guys are sergeants so they're stuck down below. I heard they have to sleep in hammocks hanging from the ceiling & they're packed in pretty good. We at least get bunks – mine's the lower.

I'm going to bed & we're still sitting in port. I don't know when we're supposed to sail. I wonder if Aileen misses me yet.

Oct. 29, 1942

Still in port this morning when I woke up. Guys are still boarding. Not much to do. We don't have meetings or parades or anything. Mostly I just explore the ship. There are anti-aircraft gun stations mounted on the upper deck. Already lost some of my money playing blackjack.

Oct. 30, 1942

Still in port. Must be some hang-up. I get to eat 1st class in the officers' dining room. Heavy china & silverware, thick linen serviettes. Posh. Served by a waiter dressed in white. Ma would

51

say it's for the fancy people. Breakfast was fruit, oats, bacon & eggs, warm rolls, marmalade, coffee, you name it. La-di-da. I could get used to this. Best enjoy it while I can. Another day of doing nothing.

Oct. 31, 1942

Finally at 09:00 hours we sailed. Went up to the top deck & said my own little good-bye to Canada. A war ship escorted us to start but once we left the harbour we were on our own. I thought we'd have a convoy escorting us all the way across but I guess they expect the QE is big enough to hold her own. I sure hope so. Wasn't long before it was just water as far as I could see. So far my stomach's good & I've got a pretty solid constitution so I'm not too worried about getting seasick. There's some motion but it's pretty gentle if you ask me. But some guys are sick. The Navy guys are laughing & saying it would be a lot worse if we were on a freighter.

The ship travels in a giant zigzag pattern supposedly so the U-boats can't track us. Hope they're right. It's nerve wracking all the same looking out over the water & wondering what might be under it. I'm trying not to think about the number of ships we've lost already in the Atlantic. I'll feel a lot better once we dock & I don't even know exactly when or where that'll be. Thought I'd never be able to sleep with the noise of the engines but I think I dropped off pretty fast. My first time abroad.

Nov. 1, 1942

Vibration of the engines never stops. A constant dull rumble. Few of lads still don't have their sea legs. Sure wouldn't want to be sticking my head out from one of the lower decks while the puke is coming down from overhead! I went exploring below deck today to find my pals. I lost count of how many flights of stairs I went down. Elevator is off limits except for the ladies & senior officers & there aren't too many of them. Kind of a waste. The farther I went down, the more I felt the vibration from the drive shaft & props. It got louder & louder. It was scary & all I could think was holy smokes, if this thing gets torpedoed I'm going to the bottom for sure. Pretty silly considering I'd likely be going to the bottom no matter where I was on the ship. So I changed my mind & hightailed it back to the upper deck. I'll see those boys in England. The dining room had a few empty seats in it tonight. The waiters think it's pretty funny.

Nov. 2, 1942

Found a high spot at the back of the ship where I can sit & just watch the giant wake zigzag out behind us. Looks like it stretches out for miles. Takes a long time for the water to calm down. Kind of hypnotizing to watch it. I tried sitting up front but when the bow dug into the water the spray came up & over & soaked me. And the North Atlantic is pretty darn cold for that. Went back out tonight to look at the stars.

Nov. 3, 1942

Foggy today. We played cards. Lost the last of my money. I'll have to cable Ma to send me more in England.

Overseas
1942-1943

Although nothing could dampen the thrill of having been awarded his commission, Dad was fast learning that ambition came at a price. New realities went along with being an officer in the military hierarchy, especially the RAF it seemed. There were desirable privileges to be sure: better quarters and meals, higher pay, respect, batmen/batwomen, the prestige of the uniform. On the other hand, for someone who came from the ranks, was comfortable in the ranks and had no airs, the separation of ranks was isolating. It had begun on the crossing and continued overseas. Dad wouldn't see any of his training friends from Jarvis again. Few would survive the war to see Canada again.

Nov. 5, 1942

  Arrived in the UK today in the port of Greenock in Scotland not far from Glasgow. I was happy to step on solid ground. Big port, lot of ships. Wet & cold. Hordes of us disembarked holding our papers while they sorted us out for our various destinations. Told me I was heading to the No. 3 RCAF Personnel Recruitment Centre in Bournemouth on the south coast. Marched straight to the station to board the train. An officer told us that all the Canadian & Australian aircrews meet in Bournemouth for orientation before we get assigned to our various training units & squadrons. Still didn't see any of the lads from my class. Maybe I'll see them in Bournemouth. The train was like the Queen Elizabeth – compartments stripped of any luxury & comfort that was there before the war in order to stuff more of us in. Damp & cold, no heat. Thank God for my greatcoat. Sat & looked out the window at the English countryside & tried not to think about how cold I was & what a target we must be from the air.

Nov. 6, 1942

Bournemouth is beautiful. Right on the English Channel. Overflowing with aircrew. I'm billeted at the Royal Bath Hotel with other officers. Seems the British government has taken it & all of the better hotels over. I don't know where the other fellows from class are. They may be billeted in private homes. Sent Ma & Dad a telegram to let them know I arrived safe & sound.

The role of the Personnel Recruitment Centre, or P.R.C., was to orientate airmen as they arrived overseas, have them checked out medically, and offer them refresher courses and lectures delivered by experienced aircrew. The P.R.C. also worked with the air ministry to facilitate aircrew postings. Life in Bournemouth introduced Dad firsthand to the day-to-day realities of war: the blackouts, blackout curtains on the windows, gas masks, the threat of air raids and bombings, air raid shelters, rest centres for those who couldn't return to their homes, anti-aircraft guns stationed around town. Although not a main Luftwaffe bombing target, over the course of the war over 2,000 bombs would be dropped on Bournemouth, killing 219 people and injuring 726. 250 buildings would be destroyed and over 13,000 damaged but repairable.[1] On May 23, 1943, 26 Focke Wulf 190 fighters would attack Bournemouth killing around 128 – no one really seems to know exactly - 51 of whom were servicemen, some RCAF.[2]

Nov. 7, 1942

I'm sharing a big room at the Royal Bath with some other officers. Very nice. Blackout curtains on the windows like they are all over England to make the city invisible to the Luftwaffe A/C at night. I've got a lot to learn about living in a war zone. This is the closest to the war I've got so far aside from the bombing damage I saw from the train. The bathroom has 2 toilets only one of them is more like a cross between a toilet & a sink??? None of us has seen anything like it before & we can't figure it out.

Nov. 8, 1942

Afternoon tea every day. That's one thing about the Brits. Put on a big dance for us. Lots of girls. At least they aren't stuffy like some of the British men.

Nov. 9, 1942

We have batman service at the hotel. He makes our bed, shines our shoes, brings us our morning tea. I guess it's the British way for officers. I could get used to it. Issued some emergency clothing coupons.

Nov. 10, 1942

Not a lot to do here. Just loafing until we get posted & no one knows when that'll be. They'll tell us when they tell us. There are some classes & lectures we can go to. Mainly we walk around the city, visit the parks, cycle, go drinking & girling at the pubs, play cards. It's like a pretend vacation. Issued a respirator in a bag that we're supposed to carry around with us in case of a gas attack. At night, the blackout makes it pretty dark – street lights off, car headlights covered, windows covered. Most traffic lights switched off. Have to carry a flashlight or a torch as the Brits call it.

Poster in Bournemouth

Nov. 11, 1942

We'll all have to upgrade our training to 4-engine heavy long range bombers. The RAF has been flying Short Stirlings & Handley Page Halifaxes since last year. Avro Lancasters more recently. What we're trained on will just depend on where we get posted.

Nov. 12, 1942

I wander around the city every day although lots of places are off limits. We're just across the Channel from German occupied France. Bournemouth is obviously a Luftwaffe target although not important enough to be a main target. Not allowed to go near the ocean or the beach. All barricaded off with barbed wire. There are anti-aircraft gunnery stations with 4 guns ready & aimed at the sky just waiting for the German fighters to come in low. Lot of bomb damage where the city's already been hit. Hope there isn't a raid while I'm here. Maybe I'll get back here some day & see it again in better times.

Nov. 14, 1942

Turns out the second toilet is called a bee-day & it's for washing your privates. Ha! Trust the Brits!

Another Poster in Bournemouth

Nov. 16, 1942

Walked around a lot today exploring.

Nov. 19, 1942

3 Soviet armies launched a massive counter-attack on Stalingrad today from outside the city.

The Soviets had been fighting intensely from inside the city of Stalingrad since the Germans attacked it in August. Victory for Germany would mean access to important oilfields, necessary to fuel the war machine. The fact that Stalingrad was named for Russian leader Joseph Stalin would make a German victory even tastier. A turning point in the war was about to take place.

Nov. 20, 1942

2 more Soviet armies attacked Stalingrad today. The German 6th Army is trapped inside the city.

Me outside the Royal Bath

Nov. 24, 1942

Went to a refresher lecture today about what to do if I have
to bail out & use my parachute.

- Wait 5 seconds to pull the D ring to be clear of the A/C &
  also to avoid deploying it while still in the A/C. Lots of
  awful stories about that. And a special reminder for all us
  lefties – the D ring is on the RIGHT side, so don't waste
  time grabbing around for it with your left hand when seconds might count.
- Keep legs together, bend knees, land & roll over to take the
  force of the landing upward.
- Be extra careful if you get hung up in a tree especially at
  night. Don't release your harness until you can see how
  high off the ground you are. He told us a story about some
  poor bugger whose chute was caught up in a tree who released his harness in the dark & ended up dying from his
  fall. Rotten luck that is.

No such thing as a practice jump. Terrifying to think that if I ever
have to use the chute for real it'll be my first time.

Nov. 25, 1942

Terrible sleep last night. Seemed like I dreamed all night
about bailing out. I think I'll study my notes from the lecture
every day, maybe sleep with them under my pillow.

Nov. 27, 1942

Raining today so I explored the hotel. It's pretty old –
opened on Queen Victoria's coronation day in June 1838. Lots of
royalty have stayed here. The rooms they stayed in all have signs
over the doors with their names.

Nov. 30, 1942

I'm so sick of brussels sprouts. I never liked them in the first
place & now we get them at every meal it seems. Even breakfast.
Just not a vegetable guy.

Dec. 1, 1942

All the aircrew are gradually moving out to different squadrons. Never did catch up with my Jarvis pals.

Dec. 3, 1942

Happy 24th birthday Eleanor. Sent her a telegram to let her

know I'm thinking of her.

Dec. 15, 1942

I got a surprise long distance call today from Bill Howell from Yorkshire. Bill & me went to bible school together at the Presbyterian church back in Toronto. Seems like a lifetime ago. Bill is the flight engineer with a Halifax crew & they're short a mid upper gunner. They'll be moving to 1659 Heavy Conversion Unit at the RAF base in Leeming to do some heavy bomber training in the 4 engine Halifax. They already know they're posted to 419 squadron flying Halifaxes in the new Bomber Command No. 6 (all Canadian) Group. 419 squadron is based in Middleton St. George in County Durham, northeast England. Anyway, I told him I'm your man. Leeming is about 400km from here. We're each going to talk to our COs to get all the transfer paperwork started. I forgot to ask Bill how he knew to find me here although I already know the grapevine works pretty good.

419 squadron was formed on December 15, 1941 at Mildenhall, Suffolk as part of No. 3 Group RAF Bomber Command. It was the third RCAF overseas bombing squadron. The Halifax squadron joined No. 6 (Canadian) Group Bomber Command, which became operational on January 1, 1943. 6 Group, made up of nine squadrons, was based in North Yorkshire and Durham. It moved from Mildenhall, to Leeming, Topcliffe and Croft for brief periods before it finally settled at Middleton St. George in November 1942 where it remained until the end of the war in Europe. It initially flew Vickers Wellington medium bombers, later converting to Handley Page Halifax heavy bombers and finally to Avro Lancasters in early 1944.[3]

Dec. 20, 1942

Lot of red tape to go through before I can crew up. Looks like I'll be here for Christmas. Received a parcel from home. Ma only has to address it with my name, rank, service number & RCAF OVERSEAS & it finds me…eventually. Surprisingly efficient.

Dec. 25, 1942

Another Christmas away from home. Hope Mom, Dad, El & Betty are having a good one. Bah. Humbug. Christmas dinner for us in the officers' mess. They treated us well.

Dec. 29, 1942

I'm officially now the mid upper gunner with Bill's crew. I've heard good things about 419 squadron. Lot of Canadians there. CO is Wing Commander Mervyn Fleming – decorated Canadian RAF. Just waiting to find out when I head out to Leeming to join up with them for heavy bomber training. I hear it's pretty cold & windy up there.

Jan. 5, 1943

Took the train today to RAF Leeming. Shared a compartment with 5 others from various places & we chatted along the way. Leeming is a permanent RAF aerodrome so the buildings are modern, brick. Good dinner in the officers' mess. Afternoon tea every day in the mess too.

Middleton St. George station

Jan. 6, 1943

Great to see Bill again & meet the rest of the crew after parade this morning. We are 7, 5 of us Canadian:

WOI Glen McMillan – Pilot. He's from Saskatchewan. RCAF. Nice guy with a great sense of humour. Back home he says he goes by Allan – his middle name but to us he's Mac. Been training for almost a year. He was in Nigeria, West Africa.

Sgt. Bill Klein – Navigator. Bill's RCAF too from Stratford, Ontario.

Sgt. Dave Alison – Wireless Op. He's RAF, a Brit from Middlesex. Dave's older than the rest of us & the only one who's married. Wife's name is Mary.

P/O Harry Enever – Bomb Aimer. Harry's RAF too, from Nottingham, England. Nice guy. Me & Harry are the only officers in the crew but after that first salute of the day we forget about rank.

Sgt. Hank Bees – Rear Gunner. Hank's RCAF from Winnipeg.

Sgt. Bill Howell – Flight Engineer. RCAF

And then there's me, P/O Albert Wallace. Mid Upper Gunner in the BP dorsal turret manning 2 Browning machine guns.

Jan. 7, 1943

Sometimes hard to understand the Durham accents.

Jan. 10, 1943

Two weeks ground school before we start flying. Lots to learn – new aircraft, new technology. Weather is stormy anyway. I don't mind this kind of school. We fly in any weather & here it seems it's mostly bad. Fog is normal.

Jan. 11, 1943

This base is in the middle of nowhere. Nothing to do, no-

Water towers

where to go at night. Lot of parties in the mess I understand, some of them like tonight's pretty energetic to put it mildly. Amazing how some of these stuffy Brits do a Jekyll & Hyde transformation at mess parties. Lot of the singing is hilarious & unrepeatable (& I'm no prude). As usual, only Mac, Harry & me can eat together – sergeants are in their own mess.

Entrance to the bomb shelter

Jan. 12, 1943

Learned what's in an escape kit today in case I have to survive & evade capture in enemy territory. Pretty compact – not much larger than a couple of decks of cards side by side. Holds all sorts of stuff like a cloth map of Europe, some money (Dutch, Belgium & French), a small compass, a chocolate bar, a jack knife, can opener, Horlicks tablets, some hard candy & tablets for purifying water. Hope I never need it.

Jan. 13, 1943

Hally tour today. First time for me & what a beautiful kite she is. Handley Page Halifax Mark II with 4 Rolls Royce Merlin engines. Much bigger & heavier than the Boly – over 35,000 lb before crew, ammo, fuel & bombs. Loaded at 60,000 lb we'll be a flying bomb ourselves. Max speed 270 mph. 21,000 ft service ceiling. Pilot sits on the left side of the cockpit. To his right there's an opening down to where the wireless op sits directly below. Bomb aimer & navigator sit in the nose. FE sits behind the pilot & has his own set of instruments. I'm farther back midship. For take off, Bill Klein & me will sit on the floor in the fuselage in the rest position between the main spars. That's where I'll hang up my parachute too until I need it (hopefully never) – no room to spare in my turret. Two escape positions plus the RG's. Mine'll be the rear hatch. At least it's big. There's a dinghy in case we ever have to ditch but I sure hope we never have to. It would be a nightmare trying to get out of a sinking A/C into freezing water at night. Pretty cramped in there with all the equipment sticking out. 3 BP electric turrets – front, dorsal (mine) & rear. Mine sticks out about 2 ft on top of the aircraft – midship just behind the wings. Looks like a barrel. All plastic so I can see out. Very tight & compact. I have 2 Browning .303 machine guns & a gun sight. I can turn the turret around full circle. Luckily the interrupter gear won't let me shoot the tail plane. My seat in the turret is very small & folds up so I have to push it down to sit. My head & shoulders are in the dome. It's going to be cold up there. Hank is the rear gunner so his turret is at the back of the aircraft. He's got 4 .303's. There's a catwalk going back to his turret. He's way more exposed if we get hit, but if that happens we're all likely goners. Mind you, I heard of an A/C coming back from an op intact other than the whole rear turret being gone. I didn't tell Hank.

Much to the chagrin and morale loss of Halifax crews, the Halifax bomber received short shrift in the war in favour of the Lancaster. Sir Arthur Harris had taken a dislike to the Halifax due to early design problems. Compared to the Lancaster, it had a lower service and cruise ceiling, lower bomb load capacity, took longer to reach altitude, had a shorter operational range, had lower maximum cruising speeds, and was prone to rudder problems. The Halifax, however, was a more versatile work horse and was easier for crews to escape from, attested to by crew survival rates.[4] 419 squadron would fly the Halifax II until April 1944.

Jan. 17, 1943

Our flying suits are heated. Sure didn't get that luxury at Jarvis. It plugs in inside the turret. Bomber Command isn't doing too well this month by all reports.

Jan. 18, 1943

Learned about the bombing process today. The pre op briefing, stream, Aldis lamp green signal to take off, waves, armament, Pathfinders. The Pathfinder Force helps with navigation. They drop marker flares at turning points & over the target to guide the bombers. The flares are colour coded for each operation – red, green or yellow. My job is to help Mac get us to the target & back to base safely. I watch for night fighters & don't fire unless we're fired on first.

Jan. 19, 1943

Our load can vary depending on the target but is made up of 1,000 lb high explosive bombs, containers of 8 x 30 lb incendiary bombs plus containers of 90 x 4 lb lighter explosives & we drop them in that order. A typical load might be 2 x 1,000, 48 x 30, 630 x 4. If we ever have a problem on take-off we'll be goners. Heavy bombs first do the major damage like blasting roofs off & exposing wood building frames. Incendiary bombs light the wood on fire & the lighter explosives keep it going & slow down firefighting. Can't even think about the people on the ground. 1,000 rounds per gun in my turret.

Jan. 20, 1943

Target practice today with the drogue. Just like we did at Jarvis. Dinghy training & drill in case we ever have to ditch. We'll carry homing pigeons for sending a message about our position in case the WO isn't able to report it before ditching. Can't even imagine floating round in a dinghy surviving on a tin of Horlicks praying to be rescued & relying on some stupid pigeon. Lots of guys who ditch aren't found for days if they're found at all. Can't think about that stuff.

Jan. 21, 1943

Covered barrage balloons today. They're huge balloons attached to steel cables anchored on the ground. They float at 2-3,000 ft over key targets like cities, factories, ports & the like.

They force low flying German bombers to higher altitude. Reduces the number of surprise attacks & also bombing accuracy. Also forces the Germans into the range of our antiaircraft guns. They give off signals to warn pilots who are flying too close. You sure as heck wouldn't want to fly into one of the cables. It would force an emergency landing at best & a crash at worst.

Jan. 22, 1943

Learned about mining or "gardening" ops today. Target is shipping traffic in ports & *Kriegsmarine* naval routes. We drop aerial mines by parachute from a very low altitude – as low as 600 ft. & they sink to the ocean floor. But dropping them makes us a great target for cannon flak from German mine sweeping ships. The mines have 2 safeties so they don't accidentally arm in transit. We'll get precise strategic coordinates from Royal Navy officers in our pre-op briefing. If we drop a mine in the wrong place the Germans can recover it when the tide goes out, defuse it to study our fusing technology & develop counter measures. So if we're not absolutely certain of our coordinates we have to bring the mines back with us. Referred to as gardening because we "plant" our mines & each area where we plant has a different code name – fruits & vegetables! Mines are about 9 ft long & 1500 lbs apiece. A small parachute on the end helps guide the mine so it enters the water nose first.

Jan. 23, 1943

Parcels arrived from home today. Aunt Jean sent me a sweater she knit & Ma sent me the suede jacket I asked her to buy for me. One from El too. I got that bad sore throat back again. Good news out of North Africa – Tripoli captured.

Jan. 24, 1943

Saw my flight training plan today & it looks like I'm not getting much training. Only 8 flights on it. I heard some guys are getting months of training. My throat was still so sore tonight I went to the infirmary to get it checked out & they admitted me. Maybe it's nerves.

Jan. 27, 1943

The US 8th Air Force hit Germany for the first time – Wilhelmshaven & Emden.

Jan. 28, 1943

Discharged from the hospital today & back to duty. Miss the nurses.

Jan. 29, 1943

First training trip today for the crew together. Went to the flight room to get our parachute, harness, helmet & Mae West life jacket. The sherabang driven by a gal took us out to the hardstand where our A/C was waiting. With all my layers of clothes, battle dress, flight suit, Mae West & harness I felt very bulky. My chest looked a little like Mae's. I wondered how tight it would be in my turret. Our A/C was V for Vic. Climbed up a little ladder into my turret once we were airborne & reported in to the skipper to let him know I was in position. Drafty as all heck.

Harry sat up with Mac & held the throttle on take-off so Mac could concentrate on keeping us straight. Harry can fly the A/C himself if he has to. Good to know that someone else in the crew can fly it because I sure couldn't. It was easy local flying around the base with air to sea firing practice. All I could hear was the roar of the engines. We'll all end up hard of hearing if we survive this war. Leather helmet & the headphones help to muffle it a bit. Crew voices crackled in my earphones. We keep the intercom open for Mac & don't talk unless we have something to report. Hank & me are supposed to fire a check burst over water to test our guns at the start of every flight – the North Sea or the channel depending on where we're heading. Mac calls out GUNNERS, TEST YOUR GUNS. So Hank fires off a burst from the rear turret & then I fire one off from the mid upper. Then we use our hands to feel the breaches & check that the guns

A Hally with crew

fired properly & reloaded. We have to get used to doing it by feel because it'll be dark when we're actually out on an op. Can't relax for even a second. 4 hours in daylight. First overseas entry in my flying logbook!

Jan. 30, 1943

2nd training flight today in R for Roger. More local flying & air to sea firing practice. I test fired my guns over the North Sea & then we dropped bombs on targets in the sea. Harry reports BOMBS GONE when he drops a bomb. 3 hours daylight flying this trip. Bombing specific targets accurately at night will be next to impossible. First RAF daylight raid on Berlin today.

Jan. 31, 1943

3rd training flight today. O for Orange. Cross country flying & more air to sea firing practice. 5½ hours in daylight. Low ceiling.

Feb. 1, 1943

4th training flight. R for Roger again. More cross country flying & air to sea firing practice. 4¾ hours in daylight.

The BBC news reported on February 2, 1943 that the fighting in Stalingrad had finally ended with a German surrender. It was considered a huge defeat, the casualties on both sides and civilian enormous. The German 6th Army commander had given himself up days earlier. Stalingrad was reportedly destroyed. The BBC reported that the Red Army had 90,000 Germans soldiers in custody – all that were left after hundreds of thousands of them died of starvation, sickness and frostbite after being trapped inside the city with little food after their supply was cut off in November. Hitler would not allow them to surrender.[5]

Feb. 3, 1943

5th training flight. E for Edward this time. Every A/C is a bit different & takes a bit of getting used to. More local flying & air to sea firing practice & height test using oxygen. Went to 16,000 feet. Have to wear an oxygen mask after 10,000 ft. Plugs in up in my turret. It hisses. 2¾ hours in daylight.

Feb. 4, 1943

Bad weather today so 6th training flight cancelled. Seems to me the weather here is mostly bad so when the weather cancels a flight I know it's REALLY bad. Learned about the GEE radio navigation system. Auto pilot is called George.

Feb. 5, 1943

Rescheduled 6th training flight & my first night flight. H for Harry. 5 hours cross country over England. Poor visibility & rain on top of it being dark. Just as dark inside the A/C & have to move around by touch & feel. My turret is a lonely & cold place at the best of times & worse at night I now realize. But Hank's got it even worse in the tail end of the A/C. Pitch dark up there, couldn't see anything. I don't know how I'll ever be able to spot German fighters. On the way back over Liverpool we flew too close to a barrage balloon. I heard Mac & Bill K. saying we were going to fly into it & they were in quite a dither. Our IFF was going crazy with the signals from the balloons & getting louder & louder as we got closer. It sounded like the end of the world in my earphones. They were able to take evasive action. So much for the heated flying suit. It didn't work & I near froze. Like an icebox in there. Wires must be broken. It's extra clothes from now on just in case. Thank God for the extra sweater Aunt Jean sent me.

Feb. 6, 1943

I took my flying suit back & told the quartermaster it was

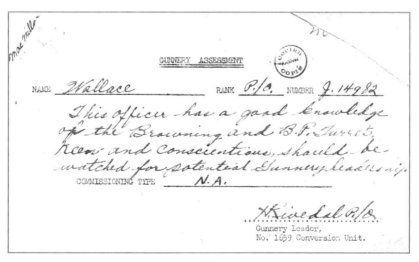

a dud. Didn't bat an eye. He gave me another one for my 7th & last training flight but I'm not optimistic it'll work either. R for Roger. Pilots McMillan & Sgt. Palmer. More local flying & air to sea firing practice. 2¼ hours in daylight. I'm getting pretty good with the BP turret. Ping pong tourney tonight.

Feb. 8, 1943

So that's it, that's all the training I'm getting. 22 hrs 15 min daylight flying & 5 hrs night flying. Off to Middleton St. George tomorrow - about 25km from here.

Feb. 9, 1943

We & another crew arrived today at the rail station. Short drive to the base. It's quite rural & the most northern station in 6 Group which will make all our ops a little longer. Two squadrons based here – us & 420. Squadron's in a stand-down at the moment so no ops going out. Big place & better than I expected. It's a permanent air force base so it's got some nice officer quarters. But they're all taken right now so I have to live in a nissen hut temporarily off site. It's just a steel shell with lots of bunks – at least 20 – & a big cast iron stove at the end. Surrounded by mud. Sad thing is that I'm waiting for some poor devil to go missing from an op to take his spot in the permanent quarters. At least I get to eat in the officers' mess. The meals are good except that I'm again separated from the rest of the crew other than Harry. Might as well get used to it. The English lose all their sense once they become officers. Us Canadians are more relaxed about that stuff. And from what I hear we're paid much more than them so we have the last laugh. But it's a quiet laugh since the Canadian government pays us at the RAF rate while we're here & puts the difference in our bank account back home. Ma's looking after my money for me while I'm here. That's one good thing about being over here – I'm still getting paid but hardly spending. I've never been such a good saver! Pub just outside the gates. WAAF living quarters are just outside the station. Known as the "waafery"! Separation of quarters is pretty strict business around here. No funny business tolerated.

The Pub

Feb. 10, 1943

Nice breakfast this morning in the mess. Good food. Have to remember not to call my napkin a serviette. We're called the Moose squadron & our badge has an attacking moose on it. Very Canadian I'd say. Makes us Moosemen! Our motto is "Moosa As-wayita". Heard it's Cree for BEWARE OF THE MOOSE. Named for the first CO, W/C John "Moose" Fulton - a Canadian, RAF. Very distinguished – DSO, DFC, AFC.[6] He bought the farm last July in his second tour & there's been a string of COs since. I'm told the City of Kamloops in British Columbia just "adopted" 419 squadron on account of Moose Fulton having grown up there. Our code letters are VR - V for Victor & R for Roger.

Feb. 11, 1943

I put my name up on the board in the flight room to volunteer as a spare gunner. Might as well get the show on the road. The sooner I complete my 30 trips the better. My new morning routine is to check the flight board to see if I'm up for an op. Sometimes takes until noon or so before it's posted. They also post any crews from last night's ops that didn't make it back. Issued my escape kit. Packed it into my own little goody bag in an old gas mask bag I scrounged – my escape kit, a flashlight, orange juice, chocolate bars, fags.

419 Badge

Feb. 12, 1943

Ate my breakfast on edge as I imagine I will every morning as I wait to find out if we're on tonight or not. Air Gunners orders are that I have to inspect my turret every day right after morning roll call & then sign the D.I. Record Book in the Gunnery Office. Except I don't yet have a turret I can call my own. The perspex has to be spotless & the rest of the turret thoroughly clean before every op.

Feb. 13, 1943

Mail here for me already. Picked it up in the mail room. Couple of days of lectures. Good library here too with a news-room that has war updates from around the world, plus news from Canada. Orders are that I'm responsible for cleaning & maintaining my guns in the A/C I'm detailed to fly in. Air Gun-ners orders are that guns have to be cleaned by 16:00 hours on the day after an op. Have to harmonize the guns every 2 wks, change the ammo once a month & record it in the charts in the Gunnery Office. F/L Ley Kenyon is the Gunnery Leader.

Feb. 14, 1943

Early this aft a fellow came looking for me to tell me I was up for an op tonight. Went to check out the flight board & sure enough there it was with the 14:30 hours briefing time. 11 crews. Filling in as MU gunner with F/O Snider & his crew because their usual AG is sick. Mac's up with another crew too. My first air op & not even with my own crew. These guys are on their second tour so I'm flattered they'd be willing to take a sprog like

WOI Glen Allan (Mac) McMillan, Skipper

me along with them. Happy too that they're so experienced. I'll be glad to finish one tour let alone push my luck for a second. The briefing room is just a barracks with a stage & lots of chairs. Roll call first. Huge map on the stage, covered up. W/C Fleming came in & we all jumped to our feet. Gave us a pep talk & told us our target was Cologne – first time the squadron's been back to Cologne since mid October. Then someone pulled the cover off the map. It had a red line marking where we're going & it showed where the armies are on the front line. Then other men took over & told us departure time, how many waves there would be, which wave we'd be in, where we'd be dropping our bombs, the Pathfinder TIs would be green, what our bomb load would be. The Met. Officer stepped up & told us about a weather front over the North Sea, that the target would be cloud covered. Told us about the winds but didn't seem so sure about take-off wind. An Intell Officer told us what anti-aircraft defence we could expect & to beware of dummy fires meant to mislead us from the target. It was for real but I still didn't know what to expect. Snider & the nav went off to put their heads together to plan our course. Then we all went to the mess for dinner – bacon & eggs is what they serve us before we head out on an op. Good old bacon & eggs are always a treat when eggs are so hard to come by these days, for civilians anyway. Civilians are lucky to see an egg a month. They told us there's another egg waiting for us when we return from our op – IF we return, only no one actually said that last part. At least no brussels sprouts. Lots of joking – it helped to hide that we were all thinking about it being the last supper for some of us – maybe me too but I can't think that way. I'll be one of the lucky ones, right? Then it was waiting around for the sherabang to drive us out to our dispersal point. Emptied my pockets in case I'm captured & searched. Nothing incriminating. Anxious. Better to be busy than to have the time to stand around thinking about what's coming next. Truck finally picked us up & drove us out to where our A/C – VR-T for Tommy, DT-798 was parked & waiting for us. The ground crew greeted us. Aircraft are all spread out over the airfield to minimize the damage in case of an air raid. We stood around some more waiting for our signal. We thoroughly checked her out. The bomb bay doors were open so I could look up & see all the bombs, the incendiaries in their canisters, all suspended and armed just waiting to be dropped – 2 x 1,000lb, 990 x 4lb & 16 x 30lb incendiaries. Then we all had a pee on the rear wheel. Either that or take a can along but there's no room to swing a cat in my turret anyway. We boarded & I plugged in my flying suit & this one worked so at least I was toasty. I was so nervous even tho I know how to do my job. We each did our final checks & reported into the skipper. What if we don't make it to the target? What if we miss the target? We took off at 18:20 hours. A bit nervous – all that fuel, all those bombs. If we lost an engine it would be certain death. 10/10 cloud up to 10,000 ft. I constantly rotated my turret on the lookout for night fighters but it was intense & pitch dark. I was scared as hell. The meteorologist was right – the clouds moved in as we approached the target. No lights in the bomber stream but I could see the red hot burning exhausts of a bomber next to us. Amazing there aren't more midair collisions but I better not speak too soon. We bombed on the PFF markers. There were areas over the target where there was a lot of ground flak. Could feel it hitting the fuselage & see the bursts. Scary as hell. Our A/C vibrated when the flak got close. We were successful as much as we could tell anyway. I didn't see a single enemy aircraft although the skipper reported in at 19:58 hours that he did around 16,000 ft. No attack. I was so focused, the 5½ hours passed quickly but I felt drained. Non-stop stress. My hands were sore from white knuckling my guns & one of my thumbs had a mind of its own & was twitching. A truck picked us up as soon as we landed & took us back to the base for a debriefing. Coffee with a shot of rum. We all sat around a table & an Intell Officer sat there with his file getting our rundown & asking us questions about what we saw that could be useful. Then back to the flight room to get rid of our gear. Now I know the drill. One op down & only 29 to go to make my tour. Then we got to enjoy another egg at our operational breakfast. Boy did it taste good.

Feb. 15, 1943

Squadron stand-down so nothing going on. Saw the Padre & another officer going through & packing up a lad's stuff – a sure sign he's not coming back. Didn't take long for the next guy to move in. Went to the Oak Tree public house to celebrate my first completed op. It's walking distance away from the airfield & eliminates timing buses into & back from Darlington. I've heard of guys going into Northallerton & having to walk 20 miles to get back to the base if they couldn't find transport. Lots of locals & always a few drunkards. Met a nice local girl. Her name is Wynne. Lives with her family in Darlington. We talked a lot & danced a bit. I walked her home & we made another date. Sorry Aileen but I never did want to get serious. Life gets complicated when the future is all blurry. Didn't stay out late – never know when I'll be up again for an op.

P/O Harry Enever, Bomb Aimer

Feb. 16, 1943

Still living in the nissen hut & it's bloody cold sometimes. Doesn't have any insulation & the darn stove is hard to light & always out. Doesn't throw off much heat anyways though the coal shortage shortage doesn't help. Seems like I'm the only one who ever lights the thing. Must be hellishly hot in the summer & hopefully I'll be in better quarters by then. At least the meals are good. Must have done okay the other night because I'm on the job tonight with F/O Snider again. To Lorient in occupied France – a double whammy since it was hit only 3 nights ago & F/O Snider was on that op too. Lorient is the major base for the U-boats that are beating up our Atlantic convoys so the sub pens & surrounding area are a hot target. We're flying VR-T for Tommy again, DT-798. Took off at 18:25 hours. 4 x 1,000lb, 18 x 4lb & 16 x 30lb incendiaries. We had 2 homing pigeons in a box in case we had to ditch in the channel. Wouldn't want to be counting on those pigeons I can tell you. Lorient wasn't hard to find – it was still burning from the raid on Sat. night & with bright moonlight, visibility was near perfect. We bombed on the PFF flare markers. We're trying to liberate the French but killing some of them in the process. We were coming out of the target & I just happen to have the turret swung around facing parallel with the port wing. And all of a sudden for a split second there was a Focke-Wulf 190. I thought maybe I was seeing things at first. Guess he was on his way into the target. Seemed like we were only feet apart & he was right at the end of our wing tip. I could see the German crosses clearly on his A/C & I could actually see the pilot. Scared me almost speechless but I managed to report it to Snider. Close call. He'd never be able to turn around & find us again thank God. We won another one tonight but I think I aged years. A tour of 30 ops is starting to sound really daunting. Life is not going to be too long at this rate. Back on the ground at 00:22 hours. Logged 6 hrs. All our crews returned to base safely.

Feb. 17, 1943

We've got 7 days leave coming up. Saw a notice on the board that Lord Nuffield will sponsor airmen on leave. He's a rich Brit who likes to help the war effort. All I have to do is apply & he'll pay for my hotel. Don't have to ask me twice! There's a cinema in Darlington too. Went on a date with Wynne. The nissen hut is depressing to go back to. Bloody cold.

William Morris, later Lord Nuffield, was a British car manufactur-
er (Morris and MG cars) and philanthropist. He formed the Nuffield
Trust for the Forces of the Crown in 1939 to personally help those who
were giving up their home life to serve their country. He started the
Nuffield Aircrew Leave Scheme in 1943 to support bomber crews who
were under great strain at the time. They could spend their leave at a
hotel, chosen from a list of some thirty located all over Great Britain,
at little or no cost to themselves. They could take a relative or friend
with them, and these were put up at special rates. The scheme ended
with the War.[7]

Sgt. Bill Howell, Flight Engineer

Feb. 18, 1943

Parade this morning at 08:00 hours for a respirator carrying drill. Ran into a bit of trouble afterwards when I left the parade square & walked past HQ. Next thing I knew some guy was
running up behind me calling "suh, suh". It was the Adjutant's
assistant telling me ever so politely that "the Adjutant wishes to

speak to you". That can never be a good thing & sure enough it wasn't. The Adjutant dressed me down for walking past the flag without saluting it & penalized me with Orderly Officer duty for 2 days. Gave me no lenience for being a sprog who doesn't know any better. All but called me a colonial. At least he assigned me an NCO Orderly Sergeant to help. I had to go back to my room & pick up my kit since I have to sleep in the orderly room to be on call for whatever comes up. My first OO duty was to visit the airmen's mess while they were eating. The OS announced ORDERLY OFFICER. ANY COMPLAINTS? Usually there's not a peep & all the guys keep on eating. Just my luck that today a smart aleck NCO complains his food was served cold. They all looked at me expectantly & I knew they were playing me. So I said I'd investigate. Had no idea what to do so I went into the kitchen & made some noise looking in the huge containers of food. Tried to look official. Filed my report.

Here we go again - first gardening op & finally with my own crew. We had VR-M for Mother tonight, DT-548 & she looked after us good. Took off at 17:53 hours. 2 x 1,500lb mines. We were 1 of 7 crews mining nectarines in the shipping lanes off the Frisian Islands. Target was easy to find – bright moonlight & almost perfect visibility. We could clearly identify Juist Island. Over the garden at under 600 ft. Sowed our vegetables successfully & then flew over 2 mine sweepers with flak cannons & they fired at us. From my turret I could see all the tracer flying up between the wing & the tail plane. I was ducking! My days are numbered for sure. At 20:42 hours & roughly 1500 ft Hank sighted an enemy fighter astern & fired a short burst on it. It broke away without firing a round & we didn't see it again. On the ground again at 22:53 hours.

Feb. 19, 1943

One of our mining crews didn't return last night. Another crew was attacked by an ME-110 but they fired back & at least made it back to base safely. Heard their A/C has 3 cannon holes & 6 machine gun holes in it. We're on the Battle Order again tonight.

Night op with the crew to another hot U-boat target, Wilhelmshaven the German naval station on the North Sea. 13 crews. Tonight we had VR-S for Sugar, W-7869. Took off at 18:10 hours. 3 x 1,000lb, 720 x 4lb, 24 x 30lb. Bright moon on the city but ground haze – 7/10 cloud but then visibility was good above

8,000 ft. Still, the PFF ground markers were easy to see & we completed our op. Ran into a little trouble on our way back to the base. Bill K didn't realize our course was taking us directly over London – prohibited airspace. All of a sudden all these searchlights were in front of us & swinging through the sky. We didn't think they had anything to do with us so we didn't pay any attention at first. Then the anti-aircraft started exploding in front of us & that sure got our attention. Howell about crapped himself getting into the astrodome to fire off the colours of the day with the Very pistol to show them we're friendly. Seems the searchlights were trying to show us the way to go but we were too daft to get the message. I'd say we'll know for next time but there better not be a next time. Back on the ground at 00:29 hours. We had to explain this one to the CO.

Feb. 20, 1943

Before I could start my leave today I had to report to the Gunnery Office & state that my turret & guns are clean & in good order. Then I had to conduct Saturday inspection of the NCOs as my last OO duty. The OS announced me ORDERLY OFFICER HERE FOR INSPECTION & I inspected all the kits laid out on their beds for uniformity & cleanliness & then inspected the NCOs at attention for their uniform & personal grooming. Glad to be done with that. Finally caught the train to London to start my leave – after saluting the flag of course. I considered saluting it a second time for good measure but decided against it in case the Adjutant was watching & thinking I'm a smart ass colonial. I'm staying at the Strand Palace Hotel in London. It's all arranged that Lord Nuffield is paying my way so I don't have to pay the hotel anything out of my own pocket. There's a dance tonight in the officers mess & I'm missing it.

Feb. 22, 1943

The Strand is in the west end of London. I'm enjoying just walking around even though the weather is bad. Visited St. Paul's Cathedral today. Quite the place. Saw a lot of the city from the top. Whispering gallery is swell. Lot of famous folks buried in the crypt. Interesting. I like stuff like that. Walked to Leicester Square. Walked along the Thames. Lots of bombing damage but still beautiful. I slept half listening for an air raid siren.

Sgt. Bill Klein, Navigator

Feb. 23, 1943

Saw Buckingham Palace & Westminster Abbey. Rode the Underground too – it was pretty easy to get around on. Great place to be in case of an air raid.

Feb. 24, 1943

Piccadilly Square. Saw the Parliament Buildings today. Totally different city by night. Hardly any light – everything's blacked out. Easy to get lost in the dark so took a cab back to the hotel. Think I'll just stick to daylight touring from now on.

Feb. 25, 1943

I'm walking my feet off. So much bomb damage in London. Visited Hyde Park today. It's huge.

Feb. 26, 1943

Trafalgar Square, Pall Mall & Covent Garden today.

Feb. 27, 1943

Returned to the base from London & back to my turret. A parcel was waiting for me - a warm sweater Mrs. Baird knit for me. Bless her heart. It'll come in handy in this miserable weather. Finally I moved into the officers' quarters. Like a hotel compared to Nissenville. Central heat. I'm sharing a room on a lower floor

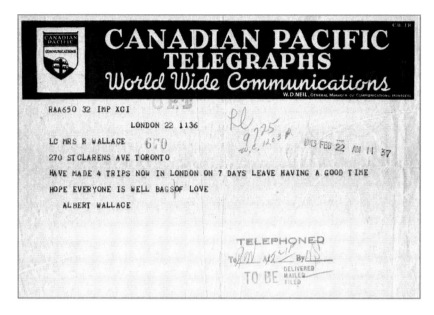

RAA650 32 IMP XCI

LONDON 22 1136

LC MRS R WALLACE   670

270 ST CLARENS AVE TORONTO

HAVE MADE 4 TRIPS NOW IN LONDON ON 7 DAYS LEAVE HAVING A GOOD TIME

HOPE EVERYONE IS WELL BAGS OF LOVE

ALBERT WALLACE

with another fellow P/O Russell Harling, a rear gunner. He's Canadian too - from Winnipeg. Been with 419 since last May so he's doing pretty good in the luck department. Most aren't around that long. I don't know anything about the guy whose spot I'm taking but I don't have to ask to know that he just didn't come back from an op. I try not to think about it & that one day some other fellow may be taking my spot. Only a matter of time. Sister Bett's birthday – all of 17 today. Happy birthday little sis. Sent her a telegram.

The squadron base at Middleton St. George is today known as Durham Tees Valley Airport. The officers' mess still exists as the St. George Hotel.

Feb. 28, 1943

Only 1 day with Russ my new roommate & his crew are missing after last night's gardening op to the Frisian Islands. Hope they're OK. You know your thinking is all upside down when you're hoping they're POWs. Better than dead. We're on the Battle Order for tonight. Last op of the month & we're up with R-Roger. Op number 5 for me. Dave is under the weather tonight so Sgt Coburn is filling in as wireless op. I knew the op was a big one when a groan went up after the CO announced it at the briefing - St. Nazaire, another top spot where the Germans hide their U boats in the harbour now that Lorient is destroyed. We had VR-R for Roger, DT-641. Took off at 18:15 hours. 2 x 1,000lb, 810 x 4lb, 36 x 30lb. Haze & smoke at the target but visibility still pretty good with green markers. Couldn't tell for sure if the smoke was from decoy fires or our incendiary fires. Identified the river north of town & also the Loire River. We ended up with engine trouble & had to jettison our bomb load (safe) & return to base early. We got lost again over England. We saw the ground beacons but the Gee signals didn't correspond to the ones we had so Bill still couldn't figure out where we were. Sgt Coburn went on the air & broadcast "darky, darky" to tell the ground operators we were lost. A female operator came on the air & told him where we were & gave him a course for the base. Was embarrassing to admit in our debrief but at least we made it back to our own base. I've heard of lots of other crews getting lost, landing at other bases & then having to find their own way back to the base. We had the pigeons with us again & at one point during a violent manoeuvre their box crashed into the bottom of my turret. Those things won't live long enough to carry a rescue message! Back to base at 02:00 hours. 7 hrs 45 min tonight & 30 hrs 55 min flying time this month. All our crews made it back to base safe.

Mar. 1, 1943

Here at the base we have a batwoman instead of a batman! What a nice surprise after my first night in officers' quarters to be woken up with a gentle shake of my shoulder & a pleasant female voice asking if I'd like "a cuppa". Good news came in about Russ & his crew – they were hit by flak the other night & had to ditch in the North Sea. A sea search found them all safe this morning after they floated in their dinghy for 22 hours. None the worse for wear other than some exposure. Apparently W/C Fleming himself spotted their dinghy. That was a rough op. Another of our crews was hit by a flak ship & night fighter cannon on the same op – the FE & RG were killed & the 1 of the navigator's legs was badly injured. The navigator had to look after his own duties plus the FE's to get them back to England while the rest of the crew put out a fire in the fuselage. They crash landed in Coltishall, England still carrying their mines but are OK.

Night op to BERLIN as spare RG with Sgt. Jackson & his crew. VR-D for Dog, DT-672. It's Berlin we all want to bomb the most, the Nazi heart especially too because Goering boasts that no one will ever bomb Berlin. It's also the most heavily defended target so we release at higher altitude – from 17,000 to 21,000 ft. The German fighters all have cannons. They can fire quite a distance so I never see them but boy do I hear them exploding. The odds are against us. My .303s are like peashooters against them. At least the weather was about perfect. Took off at 18:49 hours. 2 x 1,000lb, 630 x 4lb, 24 x 30lb. We could see the Havel & Spree Rivers & visually identify Berlin without the PFF flares. Lot of searchlights. We were hit by flak but not seriously. Lot of fires that we could still see burning from 150 miles on our trip home. It was an 8 hour trip – a long haul & an even longer time to be a target. Pretty lonely back there as RG. Back at the station at 02:47 hours. We all got a lot of satisfaction out of bombing Hitler's town & everyone was pretty excited at the debrief. Another crew's RG had his turret door blown right off its hinges by flak on the way into the target. He's OK aside from having a pretty cold trip home. I'll take my M/U turret any day to being Tail End Charlie.

Mar. 2, 1943

Squadron stand down. I've heard about quite a few ops where the crew couldn't get their aircraft to altitude & got hit by friendly munitions from above. An incendiary or bomb right through their wing. Heard that our op last night was a success – several hard hits to Berlin's industrial area. One of our crews didn't make it back & they were flying the same kite we had only the night before. Must have been another one of our lucky days. I wonder how many we have.

Mar. 3, 1943

Funeral service today at RAF Coltishall for the 2 lads killed in the mining op the other night. Russ & the rest of his crew reported back to base today. Got the gen from Russ about their ditching the other night. They'd already planted 1 veg when they developed engine trouble, began losing altitude & couldn't work their hydraulic system. Couldn't close the bomb doors & the drag did them in. They ditched without a problem & everyone made it out & into the dinghy without any injuries. Then Russ told me this was his SECOND ditching. First time was last September. 419 has only had 2 successful ditchings & Russ has been part of both of them. Amazing. I'd be getting a horseshoe or angel tattoo if I were him. Or maybe 9 cats.

P/O Harling was indeed a lucky man. He was one of the few in the RCAF to hold a "dinghy badge and bar". After his first encounter with the sea in September 1942, he became a member of the unofficial "Goldfish Club" and was awarded a dinghy badge for ditching in the sea, spending time in a lifeboat and being rescued. When, against all odds, he did it again in February 1943, a bar was added to his dinghy badge. P/O Harling went on to complete a tour of operations and earn a Distinguished Flying Cross.[8]

Mar. 3, 1943

Our crew is up again tonight to Hamburg. Dave is back in charge of the wireless. We had VR-M for Mother again, DT-548. Target heavily defended. Back to my own MU/AG position. No more pigeon passengers. Took off at 18:15 hours. 2 x 1,000lb, 810 x 4lb, 36 x 30lb. Good visibility, no moon. We lost an engine when we were 70 or so miles from the target, close enough to see it burning. Mac came on the intercom and said, "Well boys, we just lost the starboard outer. What do you want to do?" We all yelled out TURN BACK! So back we went. Then next thing I knew at 21:05 hours & 15,000 ft Hank was firing but I didn't know at what. All I could see was his tracer. He reported in that it was a single engine A/C but couldn't identify it. Red light in the nose & white at the rear. About 500 yds away starboard beam flying parallel to us & then it closed in to about 400 yds. Hank fired 200 rounds & then lost sight of it. He couldn't tell if he damaged it or not. Could've been a decoy except we didn't spot any other fighters. At 21:25 hours Harry jettisoned the incendiaries live & the H.E.'s safe so they wouldn't explode when they hit the ground. We landed fine on 3 engines. Back at 23:37 hours. We might have been able to carry on to the target with 1 engine u/s but who knows. We don't need to be heroes, not today anyway. We won't get credit for this op.

Mar. 4, 1943

I'm surprised we didn't get challenged in our debrief for turning back from the Hamburg op for "lacking in moral fibre" or some such rot. If Mac got challenged separately he hasn't said anything. Ping pong challenge tonight. Won 2 games & 2 shillings. Heard that 1 of our crews last night was attacked by a JU-88 AND an ME-110 destroyer & the 2 gunners shot them both down. Jolly good!

March marked the beginning of Bomber Command's second major bombing campaign against the Ruhr area, known for its highly defended industrial cities. Key bombing targets included Essen, Duisburg, Bochum, Dortmund and Düsseldorf. The "Battle of the Ruhr" would last five months.

Mar. 5, 1943

Short practice session this morning with T-Tommy. Air firing on the drogue just like we did at Jarvis. I did OK. All my skeet shooting over the years helps too. First raid on the Ruhr industrial region – Krupp Works in Essen but we're not on the Battle Order for it. Everyone calls the Ruhr "Happy Valley".

Mar. 6, 1943

Another crew didn't return this morning from the raid on Essen. Heard otherwise it was a good night. Squadron stand down & a good reason to go into Darlington or Stockton to the pictures.

P/O Russ Harling – my roommate

Mar. 8, 1943

Not much to do here in the off hours. Took the bus into Darlington with the crew & went to the pub. I'm not much of a drinker. I think dad drank enough for both of us at home. Couple of beers & that was it for me. Caught a taxi back to the base. The rest of the guys stayed on. Mac can put it away pretty good.

Mar. 10, 1943

Heard one of the crews returned early last night from their op to Munich when they discovered their wireless op wasn't even on board!

Mar. 14, 1943

Had dinner with Wynne & her family. Very generous of them to share their rations. Her folks & sister are really nice. They treat me like family. Makes me miss home even more.

Mar. 16, 1943

Went skeet shooting. Just like old times back at the farm.

Mar. 22, 1943

Signed up for the squadron softball team but we have to wait for some decent weather. Shouldn't be too long – it's been pretty mild, dry & sunny. Till then skeet shooting & ping pong will have to entertain me.

Mar. 24, 1943

Air Vice Marshall Edwards visited the station. Rain.

Mar. 25, 1943

Rain. I have another leave coming up & I think I'd like to see Edinburgh this time so I applied again to Lord Nuffield. Hope I never see another brussels sprout in my life.

Mar. 28, 1943

George Sweanor's crew didn't return this morning from their op on Berlin. Hope they're ok. Some of the crews have nicknamed their aircraft based on its call letter & even painted something comical on the fuselage. So far we haven't flown the same kite long enough to call it our own let alone paint it. Too bad because they're all different & some are definitely better than others. Bit of rivalry in that the ground crew consider that THEY own the A/C & we aircrew just "borrow" it from them.

Mar. 29, 1943

One of the crews didn't make it back from St. Nazaire this morning. Tonight it's back to Berlin for me. Flying tonight as spare MUG with Sgt. John Morris & his crew. First time I met them. He's a nice guy – Canadian, from Alexandria. We flew VR-N for Nuts, DT-689. Our load was 2 x 1,000lb, 450 x 4lb & 40 x 30lb incendiaries. We took off at 21:30 hours & as we were going up through the cloud I saw the reflection of our navigation lights in the clouds. Damn if we didn't still have our lights on. Talk about being a target ourselves! I chimed in on the inter-com & told the Skipper but he still didn't turn them off. He's the boss, what could I do. Then when we were at about 7,000 ft over the North Sea, we couldn't get altitude. I heard the FE telling the Skipper to give her more boost but he still couldn't get her over 10,000 ft. I couldn't see a darn thing from my turret so the FE stuck his head up into the astrodome to have a look. I heard him tell the Skipper we were covered in ice. No wonder it seemed colder than usual in my turret. So the Skipper took us down to a lower altitude to melt off the ice. Then I heard all this crashing on my turret that scared me silly. Thought we were under attack. But then I realized it was just the ice flying off in huge chunks & hitting my turret. Very nerve-wracking. I thought it was going to knock the turret right off the A/C. We recovered but too late to join the bomber stream. So we aborted the op, jettisoned our bomb load in the North Sea & headed back to base. Back on the ground at 00:29 hours & logged only 3 hours. We hadn't even made it to the French coast so another op we won't get credit for. 3 other crews had to abort too because of icing. Another crew crash landed at the base. All OK. Total flying hours for March are 1 hr 15 min daylight & 16 hr 5 min at night.

Apr. 1, 1943

Won our softball game.

Apr. 3, 1943

We all started our leave today. Harry & Dave went home & the rest of us went our own ways. I took the train to Edinburgh with another guy from the base. 7 whole days! I'm staying at the Royal British Hotel thanks to Lord Nuffield again.

April 5, 1943

My hotel is right next door to the train station on Princes

Street known here as the Royal Mile. Edinburgh Castle is at one end & the Holyrood Palace is at the other end. I can see the castle from my room & I can walk everywhere. It's quite the place. The only castle I've ever seen before is Casa Loma at home in Toronto.

April 8, 1943

Visited the palace & parliament today. Mostly I just like to walk & look around. Hard to understand some of the Scottish accents.

Apr. 10, 1943

Back in my turret & we're on the Battle Order for tonight. While we were on leave the squadron passed the 1000 sortie mark with a raid on Duisburg April 8th. Sgt. Morris & his crew were on that op & didn't return. Hope they're safe. Other than my own crew & the ones I've spared with, it's hard to get to know anyone here very well. It's depressing that no one's here long enough. 1 hour bombing practice this morning with the crew. Gave the Ruhr a break & headed to Frankfurt with VR-R for Roger, BB-323. Took off at 23:47 hours. 502 A/C total – biggest raid for me yet. 2 x 1,000lb, 540 x 4lb, 36 x 30lb incendiaries. Target was completely cloud covered (10/10) & we relied on the track flares. No markers. Back at the station at 07:43 hours. 8 hours & 5 min – my longest trip yet. All our crews made it back to base safely.

Apr.13, 1943

Warm & sunny – softball game!

Apr. 14, 1943

Bought a bike from one of the fellows here at the station. Easiest way to get around aside from the bus. Air test this morning with Mac to make sure our A/C for tonight was okay after some maintenance – same one we had the other night - VR-N for Nuts, DT-689. We were short Bill K. He has a cold so F/L Russ Lowry filled in as our navigator. Russ is from Hamilton. Stuttgart tonight. Took off at 21:36 hours. 2 x 1,000lb, 540 x 4lb, 56 x 30lb incendiaries. We were over France somewhere when I heard Russ tell the Skipper that we had the turn for Stuttgart coming up in 15 seconds & that there'd be yellow markers in the sky to mark it for us. Sure enough in 15 seconds yellow markers burst in the sky. Russ sure knows his stuff. Weather was clear of clouds over the city so we could visually ID the Necker River & the red PFF markers on the ground. Dense smoke & a lot of fires concentrated in the marked area, so hazy. Successful op & all 13 crews returned. Back home at 04:53 hours.

Apr. 16, 1943

Night op with the crew & VR-Q for Queenie, JB-923. Russ filled in for Bill again as our nav. I knew it was going to be a long night when I heard the target at the briefing – the Skoda armaments factory at Pilsen. A round trip of 1800 miles or so & a lot of it over well defended enemy territory. When we got out to the dispersal point the gas overload tanks between the main spars confirmed a long night ahead. Took off at 20:48 hours. Good visibility worked for us – full moon. We identified the target visually from the Beroun River & the PFF markers were right over the factory. Fire & black smoke covered the target. The fires were still visible from 100 miles on the way home. Back on the ground at 06:57 hours. Longest trip yet – 10 hours & 10 minutes. It was daylight by the time we were over France returning to base so we were still a target. Survived another one along with all 15 of our crews on this op.

Apr. 17, 1943

Still pretty warm & sunny. Softball game.

Apr. 18, 1943

Fighter Affiliation exercise this aft in N-Nuts again. Used a gun configured with a camera & test fired at a Hurricane fighter. I think I did okay. Like the cine-camera we used at Jarvis.

Apr. 19, 1943

We & 13 other crews were warned for an op on Turin but it was cancelled.

Apr. 20, 1943

No op.

Apr. 21, 1943

Rain.

Apr. 24, 1943

1 hour & 15 min. of daylight bombing practice this morn-

ing as RG with FS Johnson. Bunch of us went skeet shooting again this aft for fun. All my practice back home has served me well. I'm the best shot.

Apr. 26, 1943

Back to work. Finally, a night op with the crew in VR-Q for Queenie again, JB-923. Second pilot with us tonight – Sgt G. Adams, an RAF lad. Still short our nav & Russ wasn't available to fill in tonight either so Sgt. Ernest Pope helped us out – met him on my very first op with F/O Snider. RAF lad. Target Duisburg - an industrial area at the western entrance to the Ruhr Valley. Very heavily defended. 2 x 1,000lb, 630 x 4lb, 48 x 30lb incendiaries. Took off 00:40 hours. Took us about 2 hours to get there. Bad weather. We were early but lots of flak once we arrived. Was like a firestorm with all the searchlights. I was scared to death. Target identified by ground markers. We evaded being coned by the searchlights – no small feat thanks to Mac considering they surrounded the city with up to 20 in a cone. Huge concentration of fires at the target – masses of orange glow. Successful op & all crews made it back. On the ground at 05:31 hours.

Apr. 27, 1943

Night gardening op with the crew in VR-Q for Queenie JB-923 again. 3rd op in a row we've had the same kite. That's some kind of record for us. Still no Bill so Sgt. Simpson filled in as our nav. Back to the Frisian Islands. Took off at 01:22 hours. We got our coordinates from the Navy as usual for our drops but tonight the weather made it impossible to be sure. 10/10 cloud. Flew over the North Sea at 2,000 ft. Terrible visibility & our GEE all but useless with the Germans jamming it up the second we hit the coast of France. Mac had us down to 400 ft but still couldn't get our position right. Had to return to base with the mines still on board. Howell was all in a fuss about landing with so much fuel & the extra weight so he adjusted the engines to burn more fuel to lighten our load. We made it just fine. We weren't the only ones - 6 out of our 10 crews returned to base with mines still on board. Back home safe & sound at 05:27 hours.

Apr. 29, 1943

Air test this aft with the crew to test check out VR-X for Xray, JB-791. She's brand new & we just might be able to call this kite our own. We all went to the pub & I had 1 beer. Heard that

Taken by the camera on board as we bombed Duisburg

Q-Queenie didn't come back from a mining op last night. She was lucky for us 3 ops in a row but not for the lads who flew her next.

Apr. 30, 1943

Night op with the crew to Essen in the Ruhr Valley with VR-X for Xray, JB-791. Bill is still out of action so P/O Hendry subbed in as our nav. Took off at 00:15 hours. Target was covered in cloud 10/10 at 15,000 ft. Had to completely rely on the skymarkers to drop our load from around 18,000 ft. We couldn't tell if we were accurate or not. Our kite sustained some damage from heavy flak. It was Harry's lucky day. When he returned to his nose turret after dropping the bombs there was a bullet hole in the perspex & shrapnel buried in his seat. If he'd been sitting there he would've been a goner. Very cold in my turret. All crews got back okay. On the ground at 05:53 hours. My flying hours for

April are 5 hrs 35 min daylight & 40 hrs 30 minutes night.

According to 419 squadron history, statistics later showed that for the month of April, "the Moose squadron was top dog of 6 Group in point of most sorties, lowest losses, and best early return, non-starters and accidents."[9]

May 1, 1943

5 crews had to turn back last night on account of the lousy weather. Heard today that Sgt. Morris & 4 of his crew are dead. They bought the farm on their Duisburg op April 8. Word has come back that only 1 of them (a Canadian lad) is a POW. No wonder it's so hard to get to know anyone very well here. They go off & don't come back. Hardly enough time to even learn names. And since we could be next, we went to the pub, drank a toast to them & tried not to feel callous about it. Trouble is, the callousness is all around us. Their names were erased from the crew board just like that. The show must go on. If you're not available to fly an op then it feels like you just don't matter any more.

May 2, 1943

We were briefed with 12 other crews for another op on Duisburg & were all ready to go when the op was scrubbed at 21:00 hours. It's a good night when an op is scrubbed even tho it slows us down making our tour.

May 3, 1943

On the Battle Order again. Op scrubbed again (Essen).

May 4, 1943

Bought a .32 Savage Revolver #15 from one of the guys to use for target practice. Back to the Ruhr tonight with the crew on the first major attack on Dortmund steel factories & docks. Bill finally back on board as nav. 18 of our A/C – best effort for the squadron. We flew VR-X for Xray again, JB-791. Took off at 22:47 hours & we were all airborne in 18 min. 2 x 1,000lb, 630 x 4lb, 48 x 30lb incendiaries. Visibility was good, no clouds & Harry had no trouble seeing the red TIs. Slight haze over the target. 20 big fires & 30 or so smaller ones seen & several huge explosions. Didn't see any night fighters. Back at the station at 03:50 hours.

May 5, 1943

2 crews didn't make it back this morning.

May 6, 1943

Squadron stand down so practice bombing this morning with the crew & X-Xray again.

May 8, 1943

Good news out of Africa today – Tunis captured. Shouldn't be long now before we hit Europe. Hoping for Christmas 1943 at home.

The North African Campaign had been going on for close to three years. On May 13, all Axis forces in North Africa would surrender, ending the desert war.

May 11, 1943

Glen & another fellow got themselves into a spot of trouble tonight for getting oiled up & raiding the waafery! I heard the gals didn't take it too well.

Shot Down
Wednesday, May 12/13, 1943

May 12, 1943 began the same as any other day for Dad and the rest of the McMillan crew, as they were known. The Battle Order showed they would be heading back to Duisburg in "Happy Valley". The squadron suffered another double loss that night – Halifax JB-861: Skipper FS J. Palmer, and JB-791: Skipper WO1 G. McMillan. Both crews were roughly halfway through their tour and considered to be experienced. For the McMillan crew and Halifax JB-791, the 419 squadron Operations Record Book noted:

> *"Nothing further was heard from this aircraft after take-off, and its failure to return to base is presumed to be due to enemy action."[1]*

A third double loss of aircraft in three successive operations would occur the following night on a raid to Bochum. By then, in one way or another, the war would be over for over 40 Moosemen, including the McMillan crew.[2]

May 12, 1943

Parade first thing this morning so the killjoy WAAFs who complained last night could pick out the 2 culprits who raided their barrack. Of course they did & the lads are in big trouble now. They'll be written up on their service conduct sheet & be scheduled to appear at a hearing to determine their punishment. The RAF doesn't have much of a sense of humour either.

A night I'll remember as long as I live although started out like any other. Night op with the crew to Duisburg – our 2nd trip to Duisburg & our 3rd op in VR-X for Xray, JB-791. Strike 3?? We were targeting the port & industrial areas including the Thyssen steel works. Still cold at night & since I can't rely on my flying suit to work, I wore 2 sweaters. Thanks Aunt Jean & Mrs. Baird. When we arrived at our A/C at 21:30 hours we discovered that mechanics had removed my turret & covered the opening with metal without even telling us. Better for air speed they said. Worse, they'd cut a hole in the floor of the A/C about 15 ft in front of Hank's rear turret & installed a blister! Apparently my new job was to be a lookout. Lie down over the blister on my belly, watch out the floor of the A/C for night fighters & give Mac instructions if I spotted any. No guns. Great except that I felt very vulnerable – a flak target if there ever was one. I think I'd prefer to not see it coming right at me. And if it's my turn to get the chop I'd rather it happen in a more active way.

We took off at 23:18 hours & everything else was normal – climbed & set course in the usual way. 2 x 1,000lb, 630 x 4lb, 48 x 30lb incendiaries. Mac got us up to 20,000 or so feet. Encountered some flak over the Dutch coast but nothing bad. Took us about 2 hrs to get to the target. Bill K. reported we were right over the target but the raid hadn't yet started. We were 5 min early. Skipper had to orbit north until it was time to rendezvous & it's hard to rejoin the bomber stream. On the way back into the bomber stream the big blue searchlight coned us & then all the white ones zeroed in on us. Frightening. The searchlights were blinding & Mac apparently couldn't even read his instruments but he got us out with a violent corkscrew manoeuvre. Pretty slick. We ended up east of the target so when we made our bombing run it was from west to east instead of north to south as we'd been briefed. When we were over the target, I could see the flares. Heard Harry call out his usual BOMB'S GONE & the view from my new lookout position was spectacular. I watched the 1,000 pounders drop out of the bay & followed them as they whirled their way down. Hundreds of incendiaries scattered in the air like matchsticks until I lost sight of them. Camera on board automatically takes a picture when the bombs are dropped. I could see huge shock waves as the bombs hit & then flashes of flame. Incendiaries went off like sparklers. It was quite a show. That birds-eye view shocked me. Made me realize for the first time how awful it must be for the poor people on the ground. And you know it's all women & children because the men are all at the front. Hope they're all in their shelters. We fin-

97

ished dropping our load & Mac closed the bomb bay doors. Then Bill called out that we had a hang up – 2 clusters of incendiaries hadn't dropped. So Mac opened the bomb doors again & flew us straight & level to repeat the run. In a split second after the bomb doors were closed, we got hit - heavy flak in our starboard wing & forward fuselage section probably from a .88 shell.

Mac's canopy burst & he reported that he was OK but had to put on goggles to protect his eyes from the airstream. Must have been 200 mph or more in his face. No one was injured luckily & it seemed like our A/C would be able to limp home. But after a few minutes I saw what looked like a blow torch coming up through a hole in our starboard wing. Blue flame. Obviously we had a leak or leaks in one or more of our fuel tanks. Howell called on the intercom & asked me to close the valves on No. 5 & 6 tanks. Looked like the fire was around our starboard outer engine. Mac used the fire extinguisher but it didn't do any good so he feathered the starboard outer but we were starting to lose altitude. Then a new fire began by the No. 1 tank & Mac accidentally feathered the port inner instead of the starboard inner. He still managed to keep us straight & level while Howell went forward to unfeather the port inner & feather the starboard inner. Mac & nav Klein discussed us maybe being able to reach the Zuyder Zee & ditch but then I heard Bill tell him we wouldn't make it because the fire was burning right on the main spar of our starboard wing & it could fail any time. Took only a second for us all to know this was it.

The Skipper gave the ABANDON THE AIRCRAFT order that I never wanted to hear. I yanked off my earphones & oxygen mask & hurried back to the rest position for my parachute. I clamped her on with fumbling hands, grabbed my goody bag, went to my escape position at the rear hatch & plugged back in. Then Mac countermanded the bail out order to do a roll call & make sure we were all OK & accounted for. We each chimed in on the intercom except Hank so Mac asked me to go back & check on him. When I got to his turret I saw it was turned around & the two doors were wide open & flapping. Hank was gone. He didn't have to be told twice – he'd already bailed, brave soul. I hurried back to the rear hatch & after Howell bailed I sat down at the edge with my legs dangling over but it was pitch dark & I couldn't get the nerve to go. Frozen to the spot & scared silly. I guess I'd naively hoped this minute would never come. Then I started to panic that if I jumped I'd hit the ground. Maybe I was hallucinating from a lack of oxygen or something. So I plugged my intercom back in & asked the Skipper how high we were. He shouted 12,000 feet. WALLY, GET OUT GET OUT. He sounded so afraid but at the same time calm. I said a prayer and I'm not a praying man, unplugged, & wiggled my butt a little closer to the edge. The slipstream did the rest & just sucked me out into the night. I had one hand on my goody bag & the other on my D ring as I went. I remembered the instructor at Bournemouth telling us to count to 5 before pulling it but I sure didn't wait no 5 seconds. It all happened so fast. There was a great cracking sound & a jerk like an explosion as the chute released & screamed up past my face. The harness dug into my crotch but that was the least of my worries. I'd forgotten to close the flap on my bag & everything flew out of it & just disappeared into the night sky. So much for my escape kit. It was black all around me, no horizon & so quiet. I never felt so alone in my life. I just floated in the pitch dark & it seemed I was up there for so long I thought they'd have to send up a fighter tomorrow to shoot me down. Very disorienting & very cold. Glad I wore the extra sweater. Last I saw of our A/C was a ball of fire falling through the sky & I hoped Mac wasn't in it. Doesn't even seem real that I'm writing this. Like a bad dream.

Finally I saw the horizon glowing & knew I was on the way down. Then the earth came up under me fast. Thank God I could hear that instructor back in Bournemouth talking in my head. It all came back to me just like it was yesterday. I held my breath, closed my legs, bent my knees, hit the ground & rolled over. Happened just like he said it would & I was alive & not injured, not that I could tell anyway. I pulled in that mass of beautiful silk that had just saved me. I could see in the moonlight that it looked like I was in a field. There was a barn about 20 ft away that I hadn't even seen as I came down. Miracle I didn't hit it. I thought there was a chance I might be in Holland but not sure why I thought that mattered seeing the Germans have control of it. Not thinking straight. I unbuckled my chute & looked around. As I looked up to see if I could find the North Star, I saw some woods about 100 yards away & made a plan to run there & hide until I got my bearings. But then I spotted some movement by the barn. People were watching me, probably saw me come down. They started walking towards me & I could see they looked like regular folks, probably farmers, 2 men & a woman. I put my hands up to show I was unarmed & surrendering. I wasn't about to fight them. They came over & helped me up. Took me into the barn & through it into a farmhouse. Not rough with me or anything. Took me into their kitchen & sat me down.

They were talking very fast to each other but I didn't know if it was German or not. I got up the nerve to ask if they were Dutch & they nodded & answered JA, DEUTSCH. Oh boy. I don't speak or understand German but that was enough for me to know I was in trouble. At least they were friendly types & gave me a cup of coffee at their kitchen table. Worst coffee I ever tasted but they were kind so I smiled & thanked them. I think I was in shock. They didn't speak any English. They seemed to be asking me questions but I just shrugged. I pointed to the word CAN-ADA on my shoulder patch. No one else was around. At least it was warm in their kitchen. One of them left for a while maybe a half hour & then came back.

About an hour later, there was noise out the front & I stood up to see 2 Military Police on a motorcycle with a sidecar. I guess I don't blame them for turning me in. Probably too afraid not to. They'd be as good as dead if they were caught hiding or help-ing me. The police searched me & didn't seem too alarmed. I guess they could see I was pretty harmless. All they took from me was my Mae West. One of them said in English FOR YOU, THE WAR IS OVER. That's the only English I heard out of them. They took me outside & got onto the bike. Made me get into the motorcycle sidecar. They left my parachute behind. I guess the silk was the farmer's reward for turning me in. We drove to a town & I nearly froze my arse off sitting in that sidecar in only my battledress. They pushed me into a building. Spent what was left of the night sitting & dozing in a chair between their 2 desks. I think it was a civilian police station. They just kept doing their work & let me sit there & stew in my thoughts. I'd thought about the possibility of being killed or wounded but not about being taken prisoner. No post op bacon & egg breakfast for me that's for sure. I was hungry too. Best I got was a coffee, a piece of dry bread & an escort to the toilet.

May 13, 1943

This morning the officers took me to a cell & when they opened the door, who was sitting there but Harry. I was never so glad to see someone in my life. I hope the rest of the crew are safe too & that we're separated from them only because we are officers. We shared our shot down experiences. Harry found out we're in a town called Kleve near the Dutch border. Later, 2 armed guards came to our cell & walked us outside to a green army truck. One of them made a big show of waving his pistol under our noses. His way of telling us that if we tried to run he'd shoot us. Didn't have to worry about me. I wasn't going anywhere. In the back of the truck we could see bits & pieces of A/C equipment & 2 rough boxes that looked like coffins. We wondered if the equipment was from our A/C & hoped the boxes didn't contain 2 of our crew. We drove for awhile to a building that turned out to be a mortuary. Harry & me had to carry the boxes inside. Then they drove us to a Luftwaffe air force base & put us in a cell in the station jail for the night. I took the upper bunk & Harry took the lower. By now they'll know at the base that we we're not coming back. Mom, Dad, El & Betty will soon be getting that dreaded MISSING telegram. Poor Ma. I wish I could save her from that. And I wish I hadn't added Aileen to my next of kin but I did so they'll send her a telegram too. Wynne will find out from the lads at 419 soon enough.

May 14, 1943

Our boys bombed in the night & I was scared that we were under attack. Some of them hit very close & Harry & me could feel the explosions shaking the building. All I could think was that now the tables were turned & we could be killed by our own guys.

May 15, 1943

This morning the Germans drove Harry & me to a train station. We got on a regular passenger train & a few civilians stared at us but most just ignored us. I guess they're used to seeing armed soldiers & prisoners. We sat in a private compartment with 2 armed soldiers. At least they didn't handcuff us. Saw a lot of bomb damage out the window. After a couple of hours we stopped at a large station. Sign on the building said Frankfurt. Last time I saw Frankfurt it was from the sky & we were bombing the tar out of it. Small satisfaction. The guards transferred us to a smaller tram that took us to a town called Oberursel. They marched us a short distance to a big gated place surrounded by barbed wire, guard towers, searchlights & all, a prison camp for sure. Once we passed through the gates they separated us. German officers searched me, confiscated my RCAF ID tag, took my picture, filled out some papers & took me to a cell. Very small,

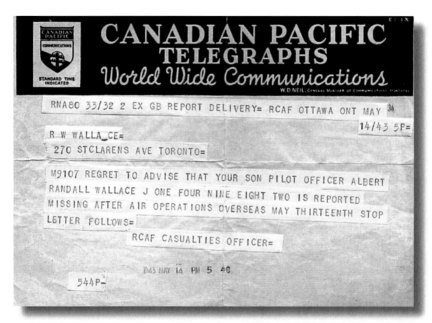

maybe 5' by 8' with 1 small window that was too high to see out of, bare hanging light bulb, solid wood door. A narrow wooden cot, no mattress, a blanket, small table. The door had a peephole in it about 6 ft off the ground & occasionally a guard opened it & peered in at me. All I could see was one of his eyes. He could look in at me but I couldn't look out. I had to pound on the door & holler to get his attention when I needed to use the toilet. Not even a slop bucket. A guard finally came when he was good & ready & escorted me to a washroom at the end of the corridor. They gave me a package from the Red Cross - a toilet kit so I could wash & shave, some clothes, a kit bag & a greatcoat. Bless the Red Cross.

One of the roles of the Red Cross organization was to facilitate communication between individuals and families separated by war, through governments and the International Red Cross Committee in Geneva, Switzerland. Four kinds of parcels could be sent to prisoners of war:

(1) Weekly food parcels (11 pounds) from the Canadian Red Cross society (not addressed to individual POWs),
(2) A "Capture" parcel from the Overseas Office of the Canadian Red Cross, once the identity and camp of a prisoner was known (to tide the prisoner over until next-of-kin parcels began arriving

from Canada),

(3) Quarterly parcels from next-of-kin, and

(4) Gift parcels of tobacco, cigarettes, books, games and music from any civilian. Such parcels had to be bought and shipped directly from a government-approved firm.

Bulk parcels were also shipped to camps with British prisoners by the British Red Cross. They could include: clothing, including uniforms and footwear; medical supplies; recreational and educational books; games and sporting goods; musical instruments and sheet music; plays.[3]

May 16, 1943

Still in solitary. Nothing to eat, nothing to do, nothing to see, nothing to read, no one to talk too. The light in my cell never went out so it was hard to sleep. My mind was racing anyway. I hoped being a prisoner of war would get better than this. I kept repeating to myself – name, rank & service number. That's all I have to provide. Drummed into my head at lectures. A guard finally escorted me to a washroom so I could wash up. A cup of coffee or something that resembles coffee anyway & a thin slice of black bread. Tasted good. I paced a lot. A German civilian came into my cell & said he was from the Red Cross in Geneva, Switzerland. There was a red cross on the front of his hat & several more on his tunic. TRUST NO ONE. He spoke English & told me I was at Dulag Luft. Gave me a form that looked official & a pencil. Beside a red cross at the top it said International Red Cross Committee, Geneva, Switzerland. He told me to answer the questions on it so he could notify my next of kin that I was alive. In addition to name, rank & service number, it asked for a lot of other information - family details, where & when I was shot down, our A/C details, crew member names, my squadron information, you name it. I didn't believe for a minute that he was from the Red Cross so I didn't answer any of it except my name, rank & service number. Crossed all the other questions out so they couldn't fill it in for me. We'd been warned about German interrogators pretending to be from the Red Cross. Tricky & skilled at getting you to give them information that seems innocent until they have enough to put together a bigger picture. So he stood up, snatched up the form, then shrugged & said something about me not caring that my poor family back home must be thinking I'm dead. Then he banged on the door to be let out & stomped out. A second meal of black bread, potatoes & watery stinky soup, maybe cabbage. Food, at least.

The first stop for captured airmen was Dulag Luft, a *durchgangslager der Luftwaffe* or interrogation camp, at the town of Oberursel not far from Frankfurt. It was essentially an interrogation centre run by the Luftwaffe. An airman's stay typically began with a few days in solitary confinement, longer for some. Germany had signed the 1929 Geneva Convention, in which Article 5 stated:

> "Every prisoner of war is required to declare, if he is interrogated on the subject, his true names and rank, or his regimental number. If he infringes this rule, he exposes himself to a restriction of the privileges accorded to prisoners of his category. No pressure shall be exercised on prisoners to obtain information regarding the situation in their armed forces or their country. Prisoners who refuse to reply may not be threatened, insulted, or exposed to unpleasantness or disadvantages of any kind whatsoever. If, by reason of his physical or mental condition, a prisoner is incapable of stating his identity, he shall be handed over to the Medical Service."[4]

May 17, 1943

I'm just sitting here in my cell. Nothing to do. They're not mistreating me but I guess they're letting me sweat before interrogating me. Mom will be worried sick. Me too but it's better than dead. I'm so lucky. I have no idea how long before anyone at home will find out I'm a prisoner & at least alive. I hope I get all my stuff at the base back. Strange the trivial things I find myself thinking about.

May 18, 1943

Today a guard took me to an office to see a Luftwaffe officer. He was pleasant enough & spoke very good English. He shook my hand & even offered me a smoke. One of those too nice to be trusted types if you ask me. His office was very messy, full of books. He just started talking & told me the names of our crew & their aircrew positions, our squadron, what our target was. Told me that Mac & Dave were in the 2 coffins. Just like that. He said that Sgt. Alison had been thrown out of the A/C when it crashed & died in hospital & that WO McMillan was found dead in the A/C. He asked me about the rest of the crew but all I gave him was my name, rank & service number. He asked me a lot of questions about 419 squadron & when I didn't answer he told me all sorts of stuff about it instead. If he was trying to impress me with his intell he did. Truth is he seemed to know as much about the squadron & our A/C as I did, maybe more. He told me the CO's name & how many A/C we could send out at maximum effort. Then he asked me about a new gunsight that I've never even heard of. Where does he get his information? Finally he stood up, shook my hand & left. The guard took me back to my cell. All I can think about are Mac & Dave. Mac was a good friend & a great pilot. Dave I never got to know too well. He was older than the rest of us, married & kept more to himself. But what I can't understand is why Dave didn't get out of the A/C. Maybe he didn't want to bail out & leave Mac behind alone. They didn't teach us that stuff. Makes me feel numb thinking about it but we'll never know. I wonder where they'll bury them. So far from home especially for Mac's mom back in Saskatchewan. Rest in peace boys. You served your country well. I won't ever forget you as long as I live.

The following notification card is one of the many "Missing" communications my grandparents received from various government sources. Its heavy card stock, embossed coat of arms, formal script and elegant handwriting intrigued me; they seemed more fitting to a party invitation.

To Mr. and Mrs. Robert William Wallace
I have learned with deep regret
that Pilot Officer Albert Randall Wallace, R.C.A.F.
has been reported missing.
The Government and people of Canada join
me in expressing the hope that more favourable news
will be forthcoming in the near future.

Charles G. Power
Minister of National Defence for Air

According to 419 squadron history, the five surviving McMillan crew members completed post-war POW questionnaires to determine the sequence of events on May 12/13, 1943. (See Appendix 4 for transcripts.) "The explanation for the failure of McMillan and Alison to leave with the others may be found in the words of Sgt. Klein, who reported "...Shortly after I bailed out I heard an explosion which I believed to be our aircraft..." As it so often happened, the captain had probably remained at the controls just a little too long for the others to bail out. As for Alison's failure to get out, that will forever remain a mystery, especially in view of Sgt. Klein's statement, which read "...The wireless operator was ready with his chute on to follow me out...".[5]

May 19, 1943

I think the Germans are done with me. They know I have nothing of value to tell them. Not senior enough I imagine. Thank goodness because I'm no match for them. This morning they moved me out of my cell into the main compound with other prisoners until they ship us all out to POW camps. What a relief. I'm so happy to be alive even though still worried about what comes next. There are a lot of men in the compound, some in RAF uniform, some in the brown US Army Air Corps uniform, some RCAF. All just milling around. Nothing to do but gab nervously to each other. The compound is just a big square of dirt with 3 long narrow huts all surrounded by barbed wire, searchlights & guards armed with machine guns. I stopped & stared at the barbed wire. This is my new life. I'm allowed to write 2 letters so I can let Ma & Dad know I'm okay. The Germans will censor what I write of course. I wonder how long it takes for mail to get through. Don't know what I expected but treatment so far is decent & the Red + is here for us. Helps to be an officer I imagine. There must be at least 100 prisoners here, some I know from home & some from 419 too. We're all so relieved to see friendly faces after having survived being shot down & interrogated. Everyone is sharing their experience. I bumped into Harry & we heard the rest of our crew are here too although I haven't seen them yet. Sure glad they're safe. That's 5 of us anyway. Full moon tonight.

Bumped into Art Hawtin this aft! He was shot down the night after me – it was a raid on Bochum & only his 2nd op. Might have been the raid that shook the walls when Harry & me were in jail at the Luftwaffe base. I don't know what's coming next but gee it's great to be alive.

19/5/43 (from Dulag Luft)
Dear Mom,

Well first of all I am quite well and healthy. This camp is a swell place, good food and treatment to us. 5 of the crew are here. 2 were killed. I bailed out and landed beside a farmhouse. All I do all day is play cards or read or lay in the sun, a lazy life. To find out what you can send me go to the Red Cross and they will tell you. I can only send 2 or 3 letters a month but you and the others can send lots more. We are to be moved to another camp soon, this is only temporary. But this is a swell place. How is everyone at home. All well I hope. Dont you be worrying about me cause things are okay. Send everything youre allowed. I never got the chance to eat the chocolates or smoke the cigs that I received in England but I am alive & thats more important. Save all my money cause Im going to buy a car after I get back. The weather here is marvelous. Use this as a community letter and pass it around cause you wont get many. The Red + is a wonderful outfit. If it wasnt for them, it would not be so hot. I believe there is a return address on this sheet. Bye. All my love. Albie

May 20, 1943

Still waiting to be purged to a POW camp. Art's already gone. Rest of us just put in time while we wait our turn. Still haven't seen the rest of the crew. The Germans aren't making us work.

In my conversations with Dad and Art Hawtin while writing this book, both told me they'd met while in Stalag Luft III; however, the following letter suggests they already knew each other from home. The proximity of Art's home town in Beaverton, Ontario, and my grandparents' country home in Bolsover, Ontario suggests a possible connection, but neither Dad nor Art's memory could explain the reference in this letter. Dad is still friends with Art and his wife Noreen and visits them regularly.

> ***20/5/43 (from Dulag Luft)***
> *Dear Mom,*
> *Well here goes the other letter. We are leaving for the next camp soon. One of the crew that is here, Bill Howell, I want you to phone his Mom and find out how he is and tell me in the letters you send me. All the food we get in the Red + parcels is put into the mess's hands for our meals and all we get is the chocolate & ciggs out of them. That is the best way. Send me smokes the same way you did before. You had better write Aileen and tell her what I say cause all Im sending her is postcards. Howells address is 6 Hugo Ave. Toronto. Also phone Jessie Turnbull 1531 Bathurst St. and tell her Art Hawtin from Beaverton is here too. The weather is marvelous and I have quite a sunburn already and its sore. You can write to this address till you get a letter from my new camp. The mail will be sent on. Hope all are well at home. Say hello to everyone for me. Ill be back with bells on after its over. We are treated very well and I am fine. Bags of Love write soon. Love Albie*

May 21, 1943

Last night I dreamed again about that night, more like a nightmare. I can't stop thinking about Mac hanging onto our A/C with only 2 engines working long enough for the rest of us to get out & then not getting out himself. Did he decide to sacrifice himself to save the rest of us or was the decision made for him? What did it feel like to know he was going down with the aircraft? Thinking about it torments me. He was the same age as me. I feel guilty for being alive when he's not especially when he's the reason I am alive. Hope I can be even half as brave as him.

May 23, 1943

Back at 419 they'll be packing up my stuff like I'm dead & some new guy'll be moving into my room with Russ. I'm just happy to be alive.

May 24, 1943

This morning the Germans piled Harry, me & some other prisoners into an army truck & drove us to a train station. Said they were taking us to a prison camp that's for officers only so I don't know where the 2 Bills & Hank will end up. It was just a regular civilian train that pulled in. Very small private compartment with hard wooden seats, an armed guard who wouldn't let any civilians into the compartment, lousy food & not much of it. A 2 day trip they said.

May 25, 1943

Slowest train trip I've ever taken. We keep pulling off onto sidings & stations & just sitting to let other trains go by. Or so we could relieve ourselves. All I know is that we're going deeper & deeper into enemy territory. It's good to see the bombing damage we've done. Lot of civilians curious about us seeing there were so many armed guards around.

The following letter sent to my grandparents by the R.C.A.F. doesn't reference P/O Enever or Sgt Alison, because they were R.A.F.

ADDRESS REPLY TO:

The Secretary,
Department of National Defence for Air,
OTTAWA, Canada.

OUR FILE J14982 (R.O.4)

REF. YOUR

DATED

ROYAL CANADIAN AIR FORCE

OTTAWA, Canada, 24th May, 1943.

Mr. R.W. Wallace,
270 St. Clarens Ave.,
Toronto, Ont.

Dear Mr. Wallace:

It is my painful duty to confirm the telegram recently received by you which informed you that your son, Pilot Officer Albert Randall Wallace, is reported missing on Active Service.

Advice has been received from the Royal Canadian Air Force Casualties Officer, Overseas, that your son was a member of the crew of an aircraft which failed to return to its base after a bombing raid over enemy territory on May 13th, 1943. There were four other members of the Royal Canadian Air Force in the crew and they also have been reported missing. Since you may wish to know their names and next-of-kin, we are listing them below:

Warrant Officer G.A. McMillan,
Next-of-kin, Mrs. G. Mitchell, (mother)
Antler, Sask.

Sergeant H.G. Bees,
Next-of-kin, Mr. H.B. Bees, (father)
Kelwood, Man.

Sergeant H.W. Howell,
Next-of-kin, Mr. A.E. Howell, (father)
6 Hugo Ave., Toronto, Ont.

Sergeant W.J. Klein,
Next-of-kin, Mr. Michael Klein, (father)
211 Douglas St., Stratford, Ont.

This does not necessarily mean that your son has been killed or wounded. He may have landed in enemy territory and might be a Prisoner of War. Enquiries have been made through the International Red Cross Society and all other appropriate sources and you may be assured that any further information received will be communicated to you immediately.

Your son's name will not appear on the official casualty list for five weeks. You may, however, release to the Press or Radio the fact that he is reported missing, but not disclosing the date, place or his unit.

May I join with you and Mrs. Wallace in the hope that better news will be forthcoming in the near future.

Yours sincerely,

J.W. Westman F/L

(W.R. Gunn)
Flight Lieutenant,
R.C.A.F. Casualties Officer,

Prisoner Of War
Stalag Luft III: 1943

Stalag Luft III had opened in March 1942 with the East Compound. Centre Compound came soon after. The North Compound, where Dad ended up, opened a year later, and by the end of 1943, South Compound had been built. The West Compound followed in July 1944. In time, the camp grew to over 60 acres and over 10,000 Allied prisoners. To thwart tunneling attempts, the Germans had specifically chosen the camp site for its sandy, yellow soil, which would readily stand out once disturbed. Hermann Goering, head of the Luftwaffe, would perhaps later regret proclaiming the camp was escape-proof.

May 26, 1943

I lost count of how many times the train stopped before we got to a town where we finally got off in a small station. Sign said Sagan. We may be in occupied Poland. From there we marched maybe a couple of miles, to the camp. In the middle of some pine woods. Feels like the middle of nowhere. Welcome to Stalag Luft 3 North Compound. It's for Allied air officers only. Camp is run by the Luftwaffe which I hear makes it better than the camps run by the German army. First off the guards searched us & our kit bags, took our picture, fingerprinted us & deloused us. I'm POW #1338 according to the ID tag I have to wear around my neck from now on. Maybe that's how many of us are here. Issued me 2 blankets, 2 sheets, a pillow case, a bowl, a cup, knife, fork & spoon. Made me sign for the stuff too if you can believe it – & warned me NO replacements. Then they escorted us through a big gate into the compound & told us we would have to be interrogated by our own people! I was annoyed – aren't we on the same side? Had to be 40 or 50 prisoners standing around inside the gate. They were greeting us & studying us, looking for familiar faces I suppose. Didn't see anyone I knew at first. Everyone's wearing something different & some look pretty scruffy. Beards too. Doesn't look like anyone cares much how we look or dress so that's good. I had to wait around until I was called into a room to face 3 Allied senior officers (2 RAF types & an RCAF) who said it was their job to make sure I was the real McCoy because the Germans try to infiltrate the camp all the time to spy. Spy on prisoners?? I obviously have a lot to learn about being a prisoner. The RCAF officer asked if I know anyone in this compound & I said how would I know when they won't let me in. Felt like I was on the hot seat. Not what I expected. They told me I would have to be "validated" by at least 1 other prisoner otherwise be grilled about the ops I've been on, my squadron and so on. Anyway, Harry couldn't vouch for me since we came in together but then I saw George Sweanor, a navigator from 419. Don't know him well but he knew me to see me & that's all that matters. Last I heard of George he'd gone missing on an op so it was really good to see him alive & well. So he spoke up for me. Then I saw Bruce Baker from home so he vouched for me too. Pretty strange to be in a prison camp in Germany & running into a chum from bible class back in Toronto.

I was escorted to the closest barracks block - hut 101. I met the Block Captain or "Hut Fuhrer" as he's known. He's the most senior officer living in the hut so he gets his own room at the end of the corridor. He took me to my room. 6 of us bunked in together. Told me not to talk to any of the guards & to ignore anything unusual I see or hear going on in the camp. Not sure what that means. My roommates are 5 South African lads who yak at each other in some language that sounds like German. Haven't heard a word of English out of them yet. Great. The camp seems pretty big from what I've seen so far, lot of barbed wire. Intimidating.

On May 26, 1943, when the McMillan crew was still officially classified as missing, the 419 squadron Commanding Officer wrote a letter to Grandma saying *"He [Dad] was one of the most popular men in the Squadron, always cheerful and willing to fly with any skipper. His ability in the Squadron softball team was a great help to us, and he*

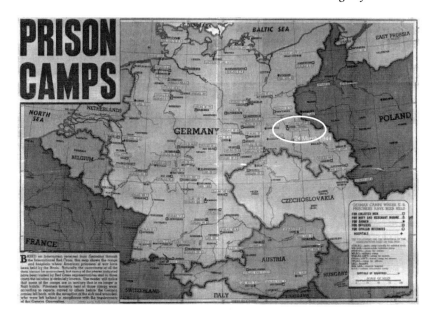

was our best skeet shot. We certainly miss him badly....Your son's kit and personal effects have been collected and forwarded to the Central Depository, Colnbrook, Slough, Bucks., who, after completion of necessary details, will communicate with you regarding their disposal. May I extend my sincere sympathy on your loss and express the hope that better news may follow."[1] He must have had to write a lot of these letters.

May 27, 1943

Well I slept like a baby last night. The bunk has wood slats & the palliasse on top isn't bad - stuffed with wood chips. Our room is decent enough – 2 windows with blackout shutters, 3 bunk beds, locker for my gear, a big table in the centre where we eat, 4 stools, 2 chairs, a smaller table, a stove in the corner that sits on a tiled base. 1 bare light bulb hanging that throws pretty weak light. 18 rooms in the block on either side of a corridor that runs the length of the hut. 3 of the rooms are smaller for 2 guys only. Must have to be more senior to get one of those. The hut is made of wood. No insulation. I'm guessing it's going to be pretty cold come winter if we're still here. We call ourselves "Kriegies" – short for KRIEGSGEFANGENER or something like that - German for "war prisoner" I'm told. At least I'll learn some German. We refer to the German guards as "goons" & they don't seem to mind a bit. They think it's a compliment or a show of respect or something. Most of them look middle aged & not in tip top shape.

We can send 3 letters & 4 postcards a month but the cards are puny so no space to say much. The letter form isn't much bigger. I'm not much of a writer so that's not so bad. And everything gets censored, incoming & outgoing, here in Germany & at home in Canada, as if I'm going to say anything worthy of being censored. No limit on the number of letters we can receive but only 1 personal parcel allowed from home every 3 months. I hear it takes a letter from Canada about 4 months to get here.

May 26, 1943
Stalag Luft 3
My new number is 1338.
Dear Ma,

I am only allowed 3 letters a month so heres a list of what I need the most. First see Eatons & Simpsons about games parcels with sports clothes, windbreaker, sweat shirts etc. also shirts, socks, T Paste, razor B, pajamas, pair scampers, scarf, gloves. There is no ban on cigarettes so send some weekly or every two weeks. There is some type of food you can send. Get labels & information from Red +. Send as much stuff as possible. The Red Cross is swell to us and there is no need to worry. We are well looked after. Have good billets. Phone bible class and tell them Bruce Baker is here. Bill Howell is at another camp. So that is 3 of us that are P.O.W. Some of this stuff will be rather expensive so use my money as you see fit. I am not going to get married as soon as I come home cause Ive changed my mind. Got to have a little fun first. Well hope everyone is well. Give my best to everyone & tell them Im doing all right and keeping fit. Tell dad to take it easy on the car. I want to drive it when I get back. But Ill be buying one of my own. Write me often as you can & tell the others to do the same. Dont worry. Bye. Love to all Albert W.

By the time Dad arrived at Stalag Luft III, fellow POW and RAF Squadron Leader Roger Bushell had already masterminded the idea to build three major escape tunnels in north compound at the same time. The thinking was that should one of the tunnels be discovered, the Germans would never imagine there could be two more on standby. Amongst the POWs, an escape committee became known as the "X Organization" led by "Big X" (Roger Bushell). Secrecy was of the highest order. Only a handful of the prisoners knew the three tunnels even existed and where the trapdoors were located, let alone from which huts they originated. It was safer that way. Roger Bushell is said to have claimed, "They're [the three tunnels] are all to be known by their names, and by their names only. If any bastard in this camp ever utters the word tunnel carelessly I'll have him court-martialled."[2] One tunnel would begin in one of the huts farthest from the German compound and closest to the perimeter - hut 123. It would go out to the woods under the wire on the west side of the compound and be code-named "Tom". The second tunnel would originate in hut 122, an inside hut and therefore less likely to be suspected. It would also travel westward and be known as "Dick". The third and most famous tunnel would go from block 104 and travel under the northern wire. Known as "Harry", it would be the boldest of the three tunnels for its length, its audacious pathway running under the German compound, and for eventually being the tunnel of the Great Escape. A fourth tunnel, George, would come along later.

May 27, 1943

I'm learning the ropes. There's a pecking order of prisoners in the compound that seems to be led by the Brits who seem to make up most of the prisoners here. Starts with the Senior British Officer – Group Captain Wilson, Royal Australian Air Force. Haven't met him. He's the go-between for the prisoners & the German camp Kommandant. A South African fellow, Roger Bushell, seems pretty important too. A Spitfire pilot. He was a big shot lawyer in London I heard. Known around here as "Big X". All his cronies are part of the "X Organization" but I don't know yet what they're all about.

Each block has a little kitchen with a small coal stove with 2 burners, a small oven & sink but all the rooms in the block have to share it to prepare meals so there's a timetable. We get about 20 minutes to cook our meal but I gather there's not always anything to cook & not much to cook it in other than pots & utensils the boys have made themselves. Either that or cook bully beef in its own can. The stove in our room isn't good for much beyond warming up as long as there's any coal for it. There's a main cookhouse that stands by itself. We go there for our German rations once a week, hot water for our brew, coal for the stove, mail, hair cuts. Sometimes watery soup. Not good for much else. They're stingy with the coal. Doesn't burn very good anyway. Hopefully we won't still be here next winter. From what I've seen so far the Reich issue food rations per man are slim & I hear quite unreliable – sugar, margarine, 1 loaf of black bread that's as heavy as lead, dry & hard. Must weigh 5 lb. Vegetables twice a week I'm told but not much & so far only some root vegetable called a swede. Looks like turnip. I hate turnip. There's something that's supposed to be jam except there's hardly any fruit in it, a few puny spuds & the worst smelling cheese ever. Terrible stuff. How the heck can cheese smell like fish I'd like to know? I'd have to be desperate to eat it but lots of the fellows really like it. Today there's sausage too. One of the boys said it's made of congealed blood. No thanks. I guess Ma spoiled me. There's coffee too but different than any brew I've ever tasted. Tastes the same as what they gave me at the farmhouse & the jail. One of the boys says it's ersatz coffee made from ground up acorns. Better than nothing. All of us in the room pool our rations, store them in a locker & share. More economical that way. We portion everything out carefully to keep it fair. No one's getting full here let alone fat. We have a set of ration cards, just ordinary playing cards, 1 each with our name written on it. We use them to divvy up rations like spuds where there are different sizes. We also get food parcels from the Red Cross but mine won't start until next week. Then there's whatever we get from home but who knows how long it'll be before I get anything from home. Mom & Dad won't even know I'm here for a while yet I imagine. One of the lads said his parents didn't find out he was a POW for 3 months. Lunch today was 2 thin slices of black bread, some of the stinky cheese & a brew. I can't even be in the room when they're eating that cheese. We cook & stooge in pairs for a week at a time. There's a schedule for the room. But the guys who like to plan & cook & do it well do it more often. Every few weeks is enough for me. I guess I'll learn but I'm sure not used to doing my own cooking. Cleaning up is easier. There's a notice board outside the cookhouse too where the goons post war news or should I say Goebbels propaganda since it seems to portray the Germans on top. It's all in German but some of the boys can read it & translate.

May 28, 1943

There's a curfew long before dark when a guard comes around & locks our hut door & closes the shutters for the night. Nothing quite like the sound of the door being barricaded with a wood bar from the outside. Hope there's never a fire. And the shutters can't be closed until the window is closed so it gets stuffy in here especially if there's a lamp lit. I don't know what it's burning for fuel but boy does it stink & smoke the place out. Lights out at 11 but at least then we can push open the shutters & windows for some fresh air. The searchlights are on all night flashing back & forth on the camp. A guard walks around with a big dog running around loose. Everyone calls him the "Hund Fuhrer"! Sure need to like your roommates & I can't say as I do just yet.

There's only 1 washroom in the block for the 100 or more of us to share – concrete floor, sinks, urinals & a shower – ice cold water. Must be spring fed. Will be hellish come winter if we're still here & there's no hot water. The showerhead is just a tin can with holes punched in it. There's a small abort that we're allowed to use only at night when we're locked in. Otherwise during the day we use one of the 2 aborts outside. They're just giant outhouses - open sided huts perched over a pit with a railing you sit on. That's a lot of shit or SHEISSEN in German. No bumf so bring your own if you have any. An outhouse to beat all outhouses I'd say. Makes the one out at the farm back home look downright fancy. Next to walking the perimeter, it's a good place to hear the latest gossip & rumours except that it stinks like a polecat in there so I don't stay any longer than I have to. Hope to heck I never fall in. Some of the lads have trouble with the lack of privacy. Well who doesn't but there's not much choice. Better get used to it.

May 29, 1943

The only routine around here I can see so far is appell every morning around 09:30 hours & again late afternoon so the Germans can count heads. There's actually a rule that says we can't smoke or read during roll call. Other than that they don't seem to care what we do. The goons barge into our hut & stomp down the corridor banging & yelling RAUS RAUS! SCHNELL! to get us out of our rooms & outside for appell. GET YOUR BUTT OUT OF BED & DO IT FAST is my translation. Lots of voices from up & down the hall yell back the likes of GODDAMN KRAUTS & ARSEHOLE SQUAREHEADS & other imaginative cusses that the goons don't understand. That gets us all laughing so it's a good way to start the day. We take our time & line up on the parade ground in 3 rows according to our block number. No military protocol. Wear whatever you want, shave or don't shave – there aren't enough razor blades anyway. We don't even have to stand at attention. Just show up, have a pulse & be counted. *Hauptmann* (German for captain) Hans Pieber walks in front of us & counts. Pieber's a little guy, pleasant enough. *Oberfeldwebel* (German for sergeant) Glemnitz counts us from behind. Seems like a tough nut but with some sense of humour so okay for a German anyway. I wouldn't cross him though. Then they compare numbers to make sure they agree. I think they just like counting.

There are 2 or 3 English speaking Germans in the compound who seem to do nothing but sniff around for signs of escape activity. We call them ferrets behind their backs. Glemnitz is in charge of all the ferrets. They can search the huts whenever they want. They wear coveralls except for Glemnitz & carry a long metal probe that they're always sticking somewhere. We're not supposed to even talk to them. There's a particularly mean one called Greise with a very long neck so everyone calls him Rubberneck. Even looks like a ferret. He's Glemnitz's right hand man but he's just a *gefreiter,* German for corporal, so he knows we're all more senior than him. I think that makes him hate us all the more. I wouldn't look at him the wrong way I can tell you.

I walked around the compound today & boy this is some place. There are 2 barb wire fences going around the perimeter, 9 or so ft high, about 5 ft apart. The space in between is filled with more coiled barb wire. Pretty nasty looking. Outside the fences the trees are all cleared for about 30 yds & then beyond it's all bleak woods. There are guards with mean looking dogs walking the perimeter. And every so often there's a guard tower with a ladder & a guard up top with a machine gun, a rifle & a search light. We call them goon boxes. About 25 or 30 ft inside the fence there's a warning wire that's about 18 inches off the ground. Stepping over it is grounds for being shot no questions asked! Well they don't have to worry about me trying to escape. I wouldn't get 10 ft. I heard that Goering says the camp is "escape proof" anyway. How does he know? Even the Titanic was supposed to be unsinkable. Seems to me he also said that no one would bomb Berlin. Anyway I'll just wait the war out. The odds of making a home run are next to impossible anyway. Inside the warning wire is a dirt track that runs around the perimeter of the compound. It's a social gathering place where we can get some exercise & talk. I met Russ Lowry from my squadron out there today. His crew was shot down on a raid to Bochum the night after we were – the same raid that Art got shot down on. Being in the latest purges, we were pretty popular. Lots of questions about 419, where & when we were shot down, any news at all about England. Everyone has a story & everyone's homesick. Some of the goons don't seem very smart but the officers are armed so that's good enough for me. Some of them carry cameras too. Always snapping pictures of one thing or another & especially us.

I counted 15 barrack blocks - long skinny wood buildings - lined up in 3 rows plus the cookhouse which is between hut 110 & 112. The blocks are all raised off the ground a couple of feet so the goons can crawl underneath to listen in on our conversations. The stove in each room & the hut washroom sit on concrete foundations that extend down to the ground so that's all you can see underneath each hut. Must have been a dense forest before they built the camp. There are a few pine trees left between the barracks blocks but mainly there are loads of stumps everywhere. Other than pine trees I can't see a darn thing outside the camp, not even a road. I can already tell it's enough to make us go crazy in time. There are 2 more compounds aside from this one – East & Centre. This camp only opened at the end of March & the first POWs to move in here came from East compound. Some of them tell stories about how they actually helped to build this camp! I guess it was a way to pass the time but I heard they had their own reasons.

While families at home anxiously waited for news, misinformation was known to make its way through. Wynne, the local girl whom Dad had met while stationed at Middleton St. George in England, had written a no doubt, well-intentioned letter of sympathy to my grandparents based on information she'd been given (or perhaps misunderstood) by lads at the squadron. Grandma – not yet herself in receipt of any official RCAF news beyond the "missing" telegram - was understandably upset to hear from a complete stranger in England that her son was dead.

270 St.Clarens Ave
Toronto, Ontario
May 29, 1943

JUN 1 AM 10.16

Casualty Officer
R.C.A.F.
Ottawa, Canada.

Dear Sir: - Telegram No. M-9107 -

In reply to telephone conversation with Flt.Lt.
Richards, R.C.A.F. Toronto, I am quoting below letter received
from England with reference to my son, Albert Randall Wallace,
Pilot Officer, air gunner overseas:

"Dear Mr. and Mrs. Wallace -

I know you will be feeling very distressed
and upset over the terrible news of Albert. Why I
am writing is to let you know that he was quite
happy here, my parents, my sister and I, did all in
our power to give him the home he was missing. He
used to say that it was like his second home.

I met him just a week after he was stationed
at Middleton St.George and we have been together ever
since. It was our distant dream that we could go on
sharing each others company.

You may think I am being callous using a past
tense when he crashed so heroically only four nights
ago.

Tonight I was talking to one of his friends.
He rang up and arranged to meet so that I could know
just really what happened. Albert was in one of the
bombers that was in the raid on Germany. It was the
biggest raid every made. He died like a hero, he is
a hero. The boys from the mess send their deepest
sympathy along with my own.

I feel so terrible at the moment I do not
really know whether I am expressing myself coherently.

His personal belongings will be sent home to
you. One thing I would like to ask, would you please
let me have a picture or snap of him, I haven't one,
but if you will reply to me I shall be only too glad
to write back. Sincerely, "

I feel sure that Albert would not want to get anyone
into trouble regarding this but think it is to the best interests
for all concerned that information of this sort should not come

---

-2-

through if it is not true and that we should be informed if it is.
It seems rather strange that this information should be available
at the station and is not to us.

Trusting that you will be able to tell us something
definite on this shortly, I am,

Yours sincerely,

Mrs. R. Wallace

P.S. This letter was received from
England by air mail May 25.

May 30, 1943

The men here come from all the Allied nations – Canada, Britain, United States, Poland, Czechoslovakia, South Africa, Australia, Holland, Norway, you name it. Fleet Air Arm aircrew too. Majority seem to be Brits. I found out it's Afrikaans my South African roommates are speaking. I don't care except that they can't or won't speak English so I feel like a foreigner in my own room. Sometimes when they're talking they laugh & look at me. Maybe I'm paranoid but I asked the Hut Fuhrer to be moved to another room with some Canadians.

The Fleet Air Arm was an air branch of the Royal Navy.

May 30, 1943

Outside the main gate where we came in the other day is the German compound called the VORLAGER. It's where the cooler is (the jail), the sick quarters & storage sheds for coal & the Red Cross parcels. I don't plan on seeing the inside of the cooler. There's a secret radio somewhere in the compound but it's VERBOTEN to talk about it. I think some of the boys built it but from what I have no idea. They listen to the BBC news every night. At least we have some idea of what's really going on in the war other than what we get from Hitler's minister of propaganda a.k.a. the German "news". We gather in the hut corridor every day outside the Hut Fuhrer's room & listen to him read the latest BBC news report about what's happening in the war but only as long as there aren't any goons around. A couple of the boys stand guard at the hut doors. There are a couple of German newspapers that circulate around the compound - the Deutsche Allgemeine Zeitung is one of them, Voelkischer Beobachter is another. A few of the boys know German. I guess I should try & learn some.

May 31, 1943

No sleeping in around here. Got to be up for appell & then at the table when the bread is cut to make sure I get my fair share. It's funny – we all watch like hawks while it's sliced. Every crumb gets allocated. Lot of pressure on the slicer. 1 slice of toasted black lead bread for breakfast with a skimpy layer of marg & phoney jam, brew. Nothing like Aunt May's jam that's for sure. It was my job this morning to haul the jugs up to the cookhouse & get in line for hot water – 1 jug for our brew & cooking & the other for washing & shaving. The one for washing & shaving is metal & has a tag on it that says KEIN TRINKWASSER. The lads who know German say it means "not drinking water" so I guess we better not mix them up. Stalag is short for STAMMLAGER. The camp Kommandant is oberst (German for colonel) von Lindeiner. Haven't met him & don't even see him around but he sounds like a decent chap. Speaks good English apparently. Won the Iron Cross for bravery in World War I. An old timer.

June 1, 1943

Red + food parcels distributed today & full ones too although I hear that's not always the case. Full means about 10 lb. Each of us is supposed to get 1 parcel every week but I hear sometimes they get hung up in transport. The Canadian, American & Brit Red + parcels all have different contents. Consensus among the boys is that ours is the best on account of the butter. Today we got 1 lb tin of Klim powdered milk, 1 lb of butter, ½ lb of sugar, ¼ lb of coffee, a tin of bully beef, York Meat roll, a tin of salmon, a tin of sardines, 15 oz raisins, a box of prunes, 5 oz of Neilsons Jersey Milk chocolate!!!, 1/4 lb of cheese, jam, a box of biscuits, soap, salt.[3] We squirrel away the odd thing & splurge now & again for a special bash or Sunday dinner. Have to resist the temptation to overeat our grub right away so we don't starve the rest of the week.

June 2, 1943

The sooner we clear the stumps out of the compound the sooner we can have a sports field. There's some sports equipment from the YMCA & the Red + plus whatever we can get from home in personal parcels. Badminton & volleyball, cricket, baseball, the Brits love their rugby. I already signed up for baseball. Bread, goon jam & tea for lunch. Heard 2 Americans escaped under the south fence.

June 3, 1943

The Germans are actually letting some of our fellows build a theatre behind blocks 119 & 120. I'm sure we must be paying for it somehow. They must be trying to keep us busy. I can just hear Ma saying "idle hands are the devil's tools"! Anything to help pass the time is fine with me. It's boring & they don't make us work because we're officers except for a few NCOs who are

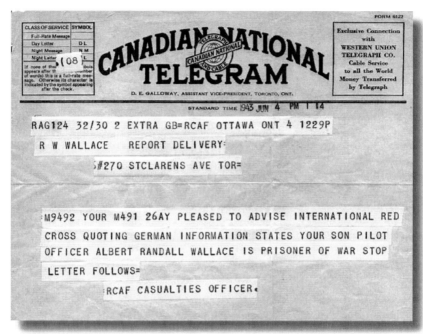

here as orderlies. A new prisoner arrived in the latest purge today & no one could identify him. I hear some of the senior guys are watching him like a hawk until they're satisfied he can be trusted. What a place.

June 4, 1943

Tried out the dhobi stick today to wash some of my clothes. It's just a tin can on a stick but works pretty good. Ma would be impressed. There's actually a goon rule that says we're not allowed to hang washing on the warning wire. They must think we're DUMMKOPFS.

June 6, 1943

Sunday today & since we have the grub on hand dinner will be a bit better than usual. Another new purge of prisoners arrived. My turn to pick up our weekly bread issue from the cookhouse. The goons ration it exactly for the 15 huts & it equates to about 3 slices per man each day. Not a crumb more. It's terrible bread, tough & dry, but can't afford to turn it down.

June 7, 1943

We get paid a stipend out of our air force pay in "lagergeld". It's just camp money & not worth the paper it's printed on if you ask me. Nothing to buy anyway. I heard we're supposed to have a

June 6/43
Dear Ma.

Am writing my 2nd and last letter for this month. Hope you have some word about me by now. You had better thank all the people who sent me cigarettes & stuff while I was in England cause I cant thank them now. Dont forget in my clothing parcels you send lots of chocolate. And heres a few things I forgot. Bottom & tops summer underwear, soap, gum. How is Aunt Rae, Ed & Mary, Uncle Al, Eleanor, Betty. Tell them all to write. And anybody else who will write. You can write as many as you want. Dont forget to put my P.O.W. No. 1338 and Stammlager Luft III on all the letters & stuff you send. Send photos of all the family & folks. Guess Ill be a lot of trouble here for you. All Im telling you to do is send stuff. I only get 3 letters & 4 cards a month so I try and write everybody I can. I had the sweaters Aunt Jean & Mrs. Baird knit for me on when we were shot down so theyll be handy when the cold weather gets here. Some of the fellows here are building a theatre & we expect moving pictures in about six weeks time. (Send a scarf and some needles and thread too.) Well Mom this is about the end. Say hello to all for me and bags of love to you, Dad, Betty & Eleanor.

Be home soon. Alb

canteen but that'll be the day. Some of the lads are obsessed with trying to escape.

Back home, the Canadian Red Cross, along with its counterparts in other British Commonwealth and American Red Cross societies, offered humanitarian aid to wounded, captured and sick troops.

June 9, 1943

Breakfast of fried potatoes, toast, Red + jam & brew. Today I moved a couple of huts over to Block 104, room 23. No more listening to Afrikaans thank goodness. Guys are always changing rooms to be with friends anyway. One of my new roommates is Pat Langford - from Edmonton. Suffered a lot of burns when he bailed. Doesn't say much. Another is Brian McFarlane from South Africa. Nice fellow. Strange request today from Big X through the Block Captain. Imposed a "2 board levy" from our beds & he went to every room in the hut to collect. That's a lot of bed boards. They're about 6 in wide & 30 inches long. Something's going on. Didn't ask any questions but I'll ask out on the perimeter.

Although Dad's new room at first seemed more hospitable, he would find out that it came with its own unique story and accompanying challenges. Unbeknownst to him, it was the room from which Tunnel Harry was being dug, the tunnel of the Great Escape that would take place the following year. The trapdoor to Harry was under the stove in room 23, and any time tunneling was in progress, the room would be off limits to its inhabitants. Blankets would be spread out to catch any wayward sand. Any information or activity concerning any tunnel was on a strictly "need to know" basis. Dad had no idea he was living in the tunnel room until much later.

June 10, 1943

Everyone I talked to on the circuit today got hit up for bed boards too. Something big is quietly going on.

June 11, 1943

The goons are all in a flap over a possible lice infestation & are marching us in parties out to a delousing station for shower baths. 33 boys used it as an escape cover & managed to walk right out the main gate with guards in fake uniforms & everything. You have to give some of these fellows credit. Pretty smart or maybe stupid some would say. Bold at any rate. Then more tried the same trick but were caught & the rest of us had to pay for it with a 5 hr. appell in the pouring rain, photo check & everything. The Kommandant & Glemnitz looked angry & Rubberneck stood there pointing his pistol at us looking half cocked himself. Something to do on a dark old day since the goons don't give us any electricity during the day. The goons threw the escapers into the cooler but the cooler isn't big enough to hold them all! It doesn't change anything. The boys who are bent on escaping will keep on trying. The goons like to learn our slang & now they use the word "cooler" too. They seem to like the sound of it so they use it a lot.

The news back home would always lag behind events at the mercy of the German authorities, leaving family members anxiously waiting for word of their sons and hoping for the best. As the weeks passed, crew members' families turned to each other for support. Information often changed hands through word of mouth. The "Air Force Casualties" column had become a regular, much-read feature in the local newspaper.

CANADIAN RED CROSS SOCIETY

PRISONERS
WOUNDED, MISSING
SICK

Red Cross Enquiry Bureau
18 Rideau Street
Ottawa

Telephone 3-9378

DECEMBER, 1942

June 12, 1943

Planted a little garden outside the hut with seeds we got in a Red + parcel but I'm not sure why we bothered. The ground's all sandy so I don't know if anything will grow. It's the only way we'll ever see fresh vegetables other than the awful turnip the goons give us. I think I understand now why they think the camp is escape proof, from tunneling anyway. The sand below the surface is very yellow so it would be tough to hide it. Strange that it's such a different colour. Never seen anything like it.

June 13, 1943

We always know when something's going on in the compound because the goons get jumpy. Either rumours of escape or an actual attempt. Once the count is done at appell they keep us out on the parade ground, all lined up with their guns drawn while they search every room in every hut. Doesn't matter if it's pouring rain. Some days there are so many appells. One no sooner ends before they call another one. Sunday dinner of scal-

Is the British Red Cross still sending any parcels to prisoners?

Yes. The British Red Cross is still supplying food to approximately fifty per cent of the total number of British prisoners, and sends the clothing, medical comforts, and drugs needed by all "British" prisoners to the prison camps. The clothing, drugs and medical supplies are generally sent in bulk consignments to the camps to be given out as required. Uniforms are sent to prison camps for British prisoners of war by the British Government through the British Red Cross.

Have you any proof that the prisoners really get the Red Cross food parcels?

In the Red Cross Enquiry Bureau there are filed more than 400,000 postcards signed by "British" prisoners of war in Germany, Italy, Algeria and France, acknowledging the receipt of Canadian Red Cross food parcels sent from Canada. These cards were enclosed in the parcels when they were packed in Canada, and returned by the prisoner who received the parcel. But the most satisfactory evidence regarding the efficiency of the system and the value of the parcels is that given by released prisoners and internees. They are free to speak frankly on both points. Their testimony to the value of the parcels is unanimous and enthusiastic.

Are you sure the prisoner gets the food? Perhaps he is forced to sign the card without getting the food.

If that system were to be tried it would soon be reported to the Inspectors of the International Red Cross Committee and representatives of the Swiss Government, who are allowed to visit the camps and talk to the prisoners and report on conditions.

How do you know the prisoners really sign the cards?

Because in many cases the wife, mother, or other relatives of the prisoner have recognized his handwriting on the returned postcard.

How do Canadian Red Cross food parcels get to Geneva from Canada?

The parcels are packed in Toronto and Montreal, Hamilton and Windsor—10 lbs. of food ingredients in a parcel—16 parcels in a big plywood box. These boxes are sent by sea to Lisbon in Portugal and thence by sea, on Red Cross ships, to Marseilles, and thence by train to Geneva where they are taken into the great warehouses of the International Red Cross Committee, but these arrangements may, at any time, be changed by new war conditions affecting transportation.

How do the Red Cross parcels get to the individual prisoners? Is each parcel addressed to a prisoner?

No; these food parcels are not personally addressed. They are all uniform in size and contents so that it is only necessary to see that there are enough parcels sent to each camp for each British prisoner to get one. At Geneva the parcels are put on board trains or trucks with a Red Cross representative in charge, and on arrival at the prison camp they are given over to the British prisoner chosen as "Spokesman" by his fellow prisoners. He gives a receipt to the International Red Cross Committee for the parcels received at the camp, and is responsible for seeing that each British prisoner gets a parcel each week unless difficulties of transportation make this impossible.

In each parcel when it is packed in Canada, there is placed a postcard addressed to the Canadian Red Cross in Toronto. This card is signed by the prisoner who receives the parcel and these are the cards which are now coming in thousands to the Red Cross Enquiry Bureau, Ottawa.

Do the food parcels go to officer prisoners as well as privates?

Yes. They are distributed to prisoners without distinction of rank—or even sex—some of these parcels have gone to Canadian women when interned in Germany and France.

What goes into a food parcel?

Here is the list of the contents, which are all (except the soap) selected for their food value in proper proportions by Dr. Fred Tisdall, a well-known authority on nutrition, and a committee of food experts.

16 oz. Whole milk powder	8 oz. Dried prunes
16 oz. Butter	8 oz. Sugar
4 oz. Cheese	16 oz. Jam or marmalade
12 oz. Corned beef, or other meat.	16 oz. Pilot biscuits
10 oz. Pork luncheon meat	8 oz. Eating chocolate
8 oz. Salmon	1 oz. Salt and pepper
4 oz. Sardines or kippers	4 oz. Tea
8 oz. Raisins	2 oz. Soap

Why do you not send vegetables in the parcels?

Because the food furnished to the prisoners by the Germans and Italians include vegetables, such as turnips and cabbage and vegetable soups; and our parcels supplement this diet.

How much does a parcel cost?

It is difficult to give the exact cost because of the fluctuations of prices of food, transportation rates, and so on; but the Canadian Red Cross reckons it costs about $2.50 to "lay down" each weekly parcel of food in Geneva. This is becoming one of the chief items of Red Cross expenditure; and the bill would be a great deal bigger if the Red Cross had to pay for the

8

9

loped potatoes, corned beef, prunes & coffee. Sure tasted good. The Red + parcels are a lifesaver.

June 14, 1943

A work crew of Ruskie prisoners are cutting down trees & digging up the ground on the south side of the compound. Don't know what that's all about. The goons treat the Russians & Poles worse than dogs & obviously think they can make their own rules about applying the Geneva Convention but then again Russia didn't sign it. Poor guys have no Red + to watch out for them either. I watched a goon yell ACHTUNG SCHWEINEHUND to a Russian officer, make him get down on his hands & knees & use a small hammer to break up rocks on the walkway to the abort. It was pointless & humiliating. I felt sorry for him.

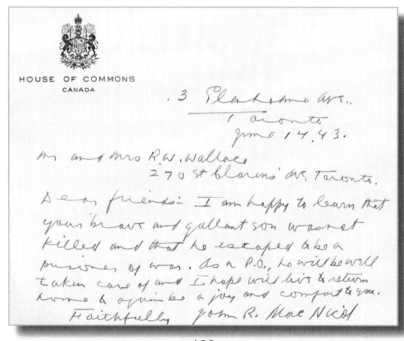

211 Douglas St.,
Stratford Ont.
June 11, 1943.
Dear Mrs. Wallace,-
We have just
had a cable from one
of Bill's friends in
Edinburgh. This is
what it said, "Heard
from Bill, Prisoner
in good health, Camp
Dulag Luft, Germany."

2.
We have not had any
official word from
Ottawa as yet. We
hope that you will
get good news from
your son too.
sincerely
Mrs. M. Klein.

June 16, 1943

Heard from guys in the latest purge that Hildreth & Richmond from my AG class got the chop. Cliff was shot down the same night as me & John a couple of nights later. Cliff was with 428 Ghost squadron. Only 21. I hope he didn't suffer. We had some good times chumming together. My first classmates gone that I know of. Rest in peace boys.[4]

HOUSE OF COMMONS
CANADA

3 Plahsmo Ave.,
Toronto
June 14, 43.
Mr and Mrs R.W. Wallace
270 St Clarens' Av. Toronto.
Dear friends: I am happy to learn that
your brave and gallant son wasn't
killed and that he escaped to be a
prisoner of war. As a P.O., he will be well
taken care of and I hope will live & return
home & again be a joy and comfort to you.
Faithfully John R. Mac Nicol

Kelwood Manitoba,

June 15th 1943.

Mrs R. Wallace,

Toronto Ont.

Dear Mrs Wallace

In reply to your letter of the 12th June, we have
had no word of our son Henry since the first telegram that he was
missing on the 13th.of May. I am very glad that three of the crew
have been heard from, and it begins to look as if they all had a chance
to land safely.

Cannot figure out what it means that we have not heard anything
of our son, as apparently the Germans had reported one member of the
crew as dead. Maybe Henry is in a different prison camp from the
rest, or it may even be that he is down there and is in hiding, though
this is hardly likely.

Would welcome any news of him whatever, and perhaps later on
when some of the rest are heard from the mystery will be cleared up.
In the meantime we are hoping for the best.

Thanking you for your letter,

Sincerely,

Henry B Bees.

June 17, 1943

The goons searched the whole compound last night.
Matched each of us up to our ID card & then searched our room
too. Made a mess of it too but logbook well hidden. Didn't get
back to bed until around 03:00 hours. It's happening more &
more. Turns out the camp is growing again. The Germans are
building a new compound to the south of us. That's what all the
clearing & digging were about. Heard they're going to move all
the Americans into it in the fall. That'll be 4 compounds – east,
centre, north & south. Full moon tonight.

Air Force Casualties

Ottawa, June 13 (CP). — The R.C.A.F. in its 600th casualty list of the war containing a total of 20 names yesterday, reported three men killed on active service overseas, and seven missing on active service after overseas air operations. Following is the latest list of casualties with next of kin:

HEREFORD, Winston Isaac, Sgt., killed on active service overseas. B. E. Hereford (father), Nordegg, Alta.
NABORS, James Cannon, Sgt., killed on active service overseas. Zebedee Nabors (father), Paul's Valley, Okla.
WARD, Leslie, Sgt., killed on active service overseas. Mrs. James Ward (mother), Winnipeg.
ELLIOTT, William Gerald, PC missing after air operations overs: W. D. Elliott (father), Moncton, N.B.
FARRELL, John Alexander, Sgt., missing after air operations overseas. Steven Farrel (father), 128 Colborne Street West, Brantford, Ont.
HOLDEN, William, PO., missing after air operations overseas. Nathan Holden (father), Senlac, Sask.
KENNEDY, Elmer Earl, PO., missing after air operations overseas. Mrs. E. E. Kennedy (wife), Winnipeg.
McINTOSH, John William, Sgt., missing after air operations overseas. G. R. McIntosh (father), 771 Manning Avenue, Toronto.
MENZIES, George Douglas, Sgt., missing after air operations overseas. Mrs. R. W. Menzies (mother), 935 Bathurst Street, Toronto.
METCALFE, Hugh Morland, PO., missing after air operations overseas. L. R. Metcalfe (father), 453 Woburn Avenue, Toronto.
OLIVIER, William George Marcel, FO., previously missing on active service, now reported prisoner of war (Germany), E. F. Olivier (father), Sherbrooke, Que.
SPIECE, Gordon Thomas, Sgt., previously missing on active service, now reported prisoner of war (Germany), A. G. Spiece (father), 26 Aldergrove Avenue, Toronto.
WALLACE, Albert Randall, PO., previously missing on active service, now reported prisoner of war (Germany), R. W. Wallace (father), 270 St. Clarens Avenue, Toronto.
HODGINS, Adam Kidd, Sgt., previously reported missing on active service overseas, now for official purposes presumed dead. H. K. Hodgins (father), Carp, Ont.
MARONEY, Paul James, Sgt., previously reported missing on active service overseas, now for official purposes presumed dead. J. E. Maroney (father), Angola, N.Y.
VAUPEL, Raymond Ernest, PO., previously reported missing on active service overseas, now for official purposes presumed dead. E. W. Vaupel (father), Port Elgin, Ont.
WADDELL, Woodrow Wilcox, Sgt., previously reported missing on active service overseas, now for official purposes presumed dead. Mrs. W. W. Waddell (wife), Stourbridge, Eng.
WADDLE, Ward Ralph, Sgt., previously reported missing on active service overseas, now for official purposes presumed dead. R. B. Waddle (father), Tavistock, Ont.
WALLAND, Allan Clarence, Sgt., previously reported missing on active service overseas, now for official purposes presumed dead. T. B. Walland (father), Watrous, Sask.
NEWALL, Harold John, Sgt., seriously ill overseas. Mrs. H. J. Newall (wife), Winnipeg.

June 18, 1943

Out on the perimeter today I heard that some of the X lads lost important stuff in the search the other night. I imagine their hiding skills are about to get a lot better. Heard a couple of boys tried to escape the other day in the back of one of the trucks hauling pine branches out of the compound. Good try but they didn't get far. Two weeks in the cooler helps to break up the monotony around here. Lot of the Brits live to plan their next escape & some think it's their duty as an officer to try even if only to upset the German war effort. King & duty & all that stuff. I don't ever remember being told that. I'm not the escape type anyway. Just as well – all escape plans have to be presented to & approved by an "Escape Committee". Red tape even here.

Although many ex-POW officers have said it was their duty to try to escape, Dad doesn't recall it that way. I reviewed The King's Regulations And Air Council Instructions For The Royal Air Force 1943 – a 1,500 page tome, essentially the airman's Bible – without finding any direct reference to a duty to escape.

Laundry day

June 21, 1943

Another search last night. Saw the SBO talking to the Kommandant today. In his sixties I'm guessing & very sharply dressed. Saw the Iron Cross on his tunic pocket. Walks with a cane.

June 23, 1943

Searched again last night. Was weighed today. 143 lbs so that's okay.

June 27, 1943

Everyone here gets along pretty good. I walk the perimeter a lot with Bruce & Art. Helps to pass the time & keep us fit. We figure

131

one circuit is half a mile or so & we did 10 of them today. Gives me something to do when the room is off limits. Visit Art too - block 120 room 114. We talk about what's going on in the war, home, girls, what we're going to do after the war, swap jokes & what not. Also great for hearing any camp gossip. Heard today on the circuit the goons have microphones buried underground around the wire to listen for any sounds of digging. Isn't stopping anyone from trying! The goons underestimate Air Force officers. Can't believe everything you hear out on the perimeter. Lots of boys with interesting stories for sure but lots of lineshooters too. Met a fellow walking the circuit – face badly burned. His name is Scruffy Weir, Canadian, pilot.

June 28, 1943

Went for a hair cut today in the cookhouse. For just about anything we need there's a Kriegie here who can do it.

June 30, 1943

I'm on stooge duty again this week. I'm not much of a cook so lucky I don't have to do it too often. My cooking hasn't killed anybody yet. But the cleaning up isn't as easy as I first thought. The German soap or whatever they're passing off as soap won't get rid of grease. Sand from the garden works better. Might have been the corned beef incident that got me off the hook from cooking. Last week a Polish fellow who I see all the time on the circuit gave me a head of garlic that he got in his parcel from home. So I chopped it up & cooked it with our tin of bully beef & potatoes. How was I supposed to know not to cook the whole thing. Anyway we all stunk to high heaven after that. Ha. Ha. He's teaching me a few words in Polish. JEAN DOE-BRAY PAN-YOUR-AY or something like that. I like the way it sounds. Means good day or good morning. I think all the Poles in the compound live together in the same room. Just like the rest of us I suppose, we tend to want to stick together with our own. We had kohlrabi again at dinner last night but it was so stringy. You could boil it forever & I don't think it would help.

July 1, 1943

Heard a shot fired last night after lights out. Some of the boys have a gramophone & it's swell to hear music in the camp even tho sometimes it's the same song over & over again. Grows on you. I'm going to ask Ma to send me one & some records too.

July 3rd
Pilot Officer A. Wallace
Prisoner of War No. 1338
Dear Ma,
This letter is mostly things to send me. Dont send any heavy clothing because the Red + gave all we need. But you can send socks. Well here goes. 1 pipe & tobacco & pipe cleaners, cigarettes as many as you can they only cost $1.90 a thousand, summer underwear, razor blades, handkerchiefs, leather belt, tooth paste, good nylon tooth B. Dont send sweaters. Lots of pictures of you & family and everyone else. In the second clothing parcel you send put 5 lbs of chocolate at least, milk if possible, 1 can opener, tin of Yardleys Brilliantine. You can send as many sports parcels as you like so dont forget if I am costing you too much take it out of my bank acct. Send running shoes & shorts in sports parcels. How about buying me a small portable gramophone, hand wound, and send it in 2 pieces by sports parcels. Also a bundle of the best records. Well I am in good health. Getting fairly tanned. Run around in bare feet a lot. We eat plenty so don't think Im starving. I hope everyone is well and the war is over soon. Anyway dont worry. Im hale & healthy. Give my regards to all. Bye.   *Love Albie*

It's Dominion Day back home. Not much celebrating here.

July 2, 1943

Someone escaped yesterday. I doubt he'll get very far. Maybe that's what the shot was all about. Cut some pants down to make a pair of shorts.

The following letter Dad wrote home contains the first of several references to a gramophone, records and gramophone needles. At this point, I suspect his request was entirely innocent. After all, the lads were always looking for new ways to entertain themselves and pass the time. Later on in the year and into 1944, his requests may have had an ulterior motive.

July 3, 1943

Finally got the courage today to write Aileen. Wanted to tell her the engagement is off but chickened out & told her we should wait & see. In a postcard too not even a letter. Not a very nice way to break the news to her but what else am I supposed to do. Who knows when I'll get home, maybe never. And then there's Wynne...

July 4, 1943

All the American lads celebrated Independence Day today. Lots of noise & Yankee Doodle Dandy singing & parading through the huts complete with a marching band. 2 of them even dressed up like a horse. Stars & stripes everywhere. Some of them were drunk on home brew they made by fermenting raisins or prunes with sugar. I heard it was pretty potent stuff too. That's a good use for the prunes if you ask me. God knows we get enough of them in our Red + parcels. I don't care if I never eat another one. I'm not sure this room is much better than the last. There always something secretive going on & I get kicked out & can't get back in for hours on end. Mostly I end up bashing a lot of circuits which at least is keeping me fit in this lazy joint. Pat Langford just sits on his top bunk & watches everything going on in the room & out the window like a hawk. At least the weather is good. I joined a minor league baseball team so I'm playing all the time – 3rd base. There are a lot of teams & plenty of talent for 3 leagues – minor, intermediate & major. Bill Paton is on one of our teams – a navigator from Toronto, shot down at Mannheim & an excellent pitcher. He strikes me out every time. We always get a good turnout to watch our games. Sometimes our ball ends up between the warning wire & the fence. We all wave & shout at the goons in the 2 towers to get their attention & I sure as heck don't put so much as a toe in there to get it until I get the green light from them. Some of them would shoot for less. Once they both give me their OK, I slowly step over the wire. It's liberating to cross the wire but scary at the same time. I'd hate to bite it at the hands of a trigger happy goon. Still haven't received any mail or parcels from home. You know you're bored when you write to your mother twice in 1 day.

July 5, 1943

The goons have posted a new rule that says "The manufac-

July 4th
Dear Ma,
Hope you are all well at home. I am fine here. The weather has been swell lately and Im as brown as a nut. I go around in a pair of pants cut down to short pants, no shirt, no shoes. Hope you have phoned Loblaws about me. Tell me when did my first letter arrive? Have you sent off a parcel to me yet? How soon did you find out I was a POW? Our camp was covered with trees when I got here but the Germans are cutting them all down now. We have a fire pool here where we can swim. Its small but six feet deep. I hope you have told everyone to write me. Tell me Ma how much money have I in the bank now. The theatre in the camp is nearly finished. I got weighed the other day and I weighed 143 lbs so I'm not losing. You had better use your discretion in sending stuff to me but send lots of fags and chocolate in the clothing parcels. I hope you have put tooth powder & brush in. Well Ma hope youre not worrying cause all is well. How are Betty, Dad and El. I wrote El a card last month. It sure will be nice to see Toronto again so heres hoping its soon. Bye for now Mom.
Bags of Love Albert.

ture of alcoholic drinks is forbidden". Ha! They're always at least one step behind! Searched our room again last night.

July 6, 1943

Watched a rugby match today. Crazy game. Starts with 8 guys from each team in a tight huddle – called the scrum. The ref throws the football into the centre of the huddle & they all go crazy kicking it & anything in their way. It's a free for all. Eventually the ball gets kicked out & whoever gets to it first grabs it & tries to run for the goal. You can't throw the ball forward but you can kick it. Play at your own risk.

July 7, 1943

Today some heavy trucks drove around the compound in-

> **4th July**
> Dear Ma,
>   Well another letter to you today. All the Americans are celebrating today. Hope you are getting my letters. The is the ▇▇▇ one Ive written you since I came down. I want you to send a sports parcel from Eatons for one of the fellows in my room. Buy the stuff from my money. Heres what he wants. 1 pr running shoes boot type size 8, 1 pr blue basketball shorts size 32, 1 white sweatshirt size 40. Thats all. Address it to LT. B.L. McFARLANE P.O.W. NO. 1430 the same address as Im at. Hes going to pay me. The weather is pretty good here. Use your discretion in regards to sending stuff if you think the war is going to end. I hope everyone is well. Hows El and Betty and dad? Tell them all to write. I still have my watch. I hope youre not worrying because were not too badly off at all. I wrote Aileen and told her I would not be getting married after the war for a year at least a year. Hows the car running? Still got enough gas to rip around on? I am not expecting any mail from Canada for a month or two yet. Say hello to everyone for me. Aunt Rae, Uncle Ed & Aunt Mary, Uncle Al, Aunt Jean, everyone. Guess this is all for now.
>   *Bags of Love. Albie*

side the wire trying to collapse any escape tunnels. Good luck to them. The goons don't give our boys enough credit. They found nothing of course but they wrecked a lot of gardens. Not much was growing anyway.

Dad wasn't keen on escaping himself. He felt he'd done his part for the war and was satisfied to wait it out. Too, without at least one other language and a risk-taking personality, it would have been difficult if not impossible to move around in Germany. On the other hand, Dad was happy to support the escape efforts of others, and was about to find out what it meant to have volunteered to be a "penguin". All the sand that was coming out of the three tunnels had to go somewhere. The X Organization devised an ingenious contraption from long underwear and pajama pant cord that allowed the men to carry two bags of sand slung around their neck and down their pant legs. String held onto from inside pant pockets allowed the men to pull a nail out of each sand bag to release its contents in a trickle at an opportune moment. With a bag of sand down each pant leg, the men's gait became penguin-like.

July 8, 1943

The Germans have lots of orders for us & they're all posted. One of them says "Foodstuffs issued to POWs and not consumed by them are to be returned".[5] Seems the goons have a sense of humour after all. Got called back to the hut this aft to start my new job as a "penguin". Beats the boredom. X has all the ferrets shadowed so the coast must have been clear. There were lots of us in the corridor all lined up waiting to pick up our cargo. It's a good use for the bloody long underwear the Red + sent in July! I shuffled out to our little garden & dumped my load. A little swiveling of my feet & it was done. Bare feet so my boots didn't catch any. Thank God. I was sweating bullets. Some of the others dumped theirs on the sports field in the middle of a rugby scrum.

July 9, 1943

Some of the boys are suffering from barbed wire insanity especially the ones who've been prisoners for years already & came here from other camps. Anything & everything to get out of this joint – tunnel under the trip wire, under & through the barbed wire with homemade wire cutters, they'll try anything. Takes guts to get past the sentries, I'll give them that. And that's the easy part. Once they actually make it out they hardarse cross country with not much more than the clothes on their back & whatever they can carry. Even the thought of getting to the wire at night without getting caught in the lights & shot at or attacked by one of the dogs is enough deterrent for me. I guess if you're on the verge of going crazy some time in the cooler is a small price to pay for a couple days of freedom. Could end up dead though. I hear the Kommandant has ordered that the sentries can shoot at us at night if we're outside our hut.

July 10, 1943

Another night search. German radio today announced the British, Canadian & American troops had landed in Sicily so it was a good day for us.[6] Saw another lad on the circuit today with serious burns. Larry Somers, Canadian. His A/C blew up.

July 11, 1943

I heard some of our more mechanical boys built the camp radio from odds & ends & parts they bribed some of the goons to smuggle in. And there's more than one too. They take them apart every night & hide all the parts separately. It's better not to know too much. But thanks to our radio sometimes we know more about what's going on in the war than the purge coming in. An invasion can't be far off now. Searched again tonight.

July 13, 1943

It's Ma's birthday today. Hope they're treating her extra nice at home. The ferrets are searching all the time now, day & night, poking & prodding everywhere with their probes. Something's up. I heard one of them spotted yellow sand around the camp & are sniffing out where it came from. There's 1 appell after another – we had 4 today. Searches & appells - it's the only time I ever see Pieber & Glemnitz. For a goon, Pieber is a friendly sort. Most of us like him.

July 15, 1943

Another 2 escaped yesterday & another search last night. Took hours. Air raid during the search so no lights. The goons cut the power as soon as the air raid siren goes off so the lights won't guide our bombers. Made us stand out in the hall while they turned all the rooms upside down. What a mess. Dug up our garden too & I was hopeful for some tomatoes.

July 17, 1943

The news improves every day. We're betting on when Italy surrenders. I say another month. Maybe I'll be home by Christmas. Red + parcel delivery is late & we have to cut back on our meals. The Russians are keeping the Germans busy on the eastern front & the Allies on the western & Italian fronts but likely buggering up transportation of our parcels at the same time.

July 20, 1943

Red + parcels cut in half. I hope not for long. Means we have to continue belting up. Watched a football game today. The Allies bombed Rome. Locked out of our room again this aft so I killed some time in Art's room.

July 21, 1943

Another search in the early hours this morning. Very thorough. The theatre is moving along & a bunch of the arty types are getting ready to stage a play. We've got actors, directors & everything here – some real professionals from London. We'll have movies too except I can't imagine there'll be much to choose from. The boys are doing a swell job building the theatre I must say - seats, projection room, stage, orchestra pit, dressing rooms. They made the seats from the plywood crates the Red + parcels come in. I tried one out & it was pretty comfortable too. Even has arm rests. Sloped floor like a regular theatre. They built extra rooms too. Heard one will be used for classes. We've got a few teachers here & lots of highly educated guys. I didn't like school the first time so I'm not much interested in going back even to pass time. I'd much rather read. One of the fellows is a doctor back home & he lent me a medical textbook to look at. Didn't understand much but lots of interesting diagrams.

July 22, 1943

Our room was searched again last night. Hope Ma has received my kit from 419 by now.

July 24, 1943

Big search early this morning – 4 of the American huts. Some of the lads were still locked out at lunch time.

July 25, 1943

Mussolini has quit.[7] Hitler can't be too happy about that. We hear they're dancing in the streets in Italy. Heard a shot fired & later that 2 escaped over the west fence. Over the wire, under the wire, through the wire. It's all been done. I would have said it's impossible but where there's a will there's a way.

July 28, 1943

It's really hot. Had to make another pair of shorts. Thank goodness for the fire pool. Not the cleanest but at least we can cool off in it. Saw Big X walking the circuit again today. Walks a lot always wearing his old RAF tunic. Looks very intense. Heard he's been in different camps & escaped twice. The 2nd time I heard the Gestapo recaptured him in Prague & executed the family who were hiding him. The whole family. Brutal.

July 29, 1943

2 got out last night under the wire. Very long appell this morning to pay for it & all the other escape attempts of the last week or so. Huge Bomber Command raid on Hamburg last night. Major civilian losses. Not a good time to get on the wrong side of the goons. Full 10 lb Red + parcels again thank God. 6 parcels for the room warrants a feast including Prem & corned beef! I sure miss home cooking.

Aug. 1, 1943

Another search last night. VERY hot. Still having 4 appells a day. Summer heat is making the aborts really stink. Watched a Polish prisoner come in with a honey wagon pulled by oxen to pump out one of them. The abort stinks at the best of times but it REALLY stunk when he stirred it all up in this heat. The best part was he calmly ate his lunch the whole time he was doing it!! We call his cart the "shizenpanzerwagon". When we don't know

Camp orchestra

the German word for something we just make one up with the bits & pieces of German we do know! Shizen = shit. Panzer = tank. Wagon = wagon. See Ma, I'm learning something in this joint after all.

Aug. 3, 1943

Today was the hottest day so far. More swimming in the fire pool. Water fights everywhere. This letter writing business is a lot of work. I have nothing to say & thankfully no room on the forms to say it anyway.

Aug. 4, 1943

No spuds in our goon ration this week.

Aug. 5, 1943

Heard today about another boy gone from my class at Jarvis. Norm Notley & his Hally crew from 427 squadron.[8]

Aug. 6, 1943

Strange turn in the weather today – much cooler & a sand storm blew up. Tom, Dick & Harry are producing too much sand for the penguins to get rid of so some of it's going in Red + parcel boxes under our bunks. Risky business. May end up in the cooler yet. Bashing a few circuits every morning after appell. It's the best way to visit with some of the lads, hear the gossip & get some exercise.

Aug. 8, 1943

It's boring most of the time so some of the boys are always looking for ways to have fun. They'll jump around at appell just to mix up the count. Red Noble, a Canadian fellow, is one of the worst. He really upsets Glemnitz some days & Rubberneck can't stand him. Shag Rees (RAF) is another one who loves being a burr in Glemnitz's ass. Between the 2 of them a 30 minute appell can turn into 2 hours. It's something to do at least & good entertainment. Those 2 spend a lot of their time in the cooler.

Aug. 9, 1943

Appells cut back to 3 a day. Fried spuds, toast jam & coffee for breakfast.

> *Aug 13th Monday*
> *Dear Ma.*
>
> *Well as I dont expect any mail from Canada this month Ill write my last letter to you. Hope you are all well at home and writing me lots of letters. Things are okay here. Im getting browner all the time. I do hope youre not worrying about me. I play ball here in one of our leagues. I play 3rd base. Hows Betty, El and Dad? I hope youve sent me a parcel by now. Dont forget 1 every 3 months. There are lots of Toronto boys here. This is all officers at this camp though. I hope the Red + informed you I was a P.O.W. quickly. Our theatre will be ready in about 2 weeks. With our Red + parcels our meals are fair enough. Are you sending cigarettes? Have you been up to the country lately? How is everyone up there? Are you sending lots of pictures with the letters? Well I have lots of time on my hands here with very little to do. But heres hoping its all over soon and I can come home. Say hello to everyone for me. Tell them all to write. Hope youre still not working. How is Lloyd and El. Dont forget to send lots of stuff. So long for this month. Lots of love to all and a quick end to this war. Albert*

Aug. 10, 1943

We had a camp sports day today. Our baseball team made it to the league final & we won! Big crowd for the game – even some of the goons although lots don't even understand the rules. Glemnitz is a big fan. Wrote to Aileen & broke the engagement off for good. Dirty trick but I can't even consider marriage right now. Every time a new purge arrives at the compound we all go to the gate to see if there's anyone we know.

Aug. 11, 1943

Penguin duty called today. Only 1 ferret in the compound. There are about 150 of us now. Scattered my load on the circuit once the guard passed. Lots of us out there so didn't take long for it to be tracked in.

Aug. 12, 1943

A few spuds in our goon ration but pretty slim pickings.

Aug. 15, 1943

I put in for another move with the Hut Fuhrer. I don't want to be seen as a troublemaker but this room is impossible to live in. I'm always getting kicked out & then I can't get back in. Can't hardly count the time I'm allowed to spend in the room as living here anyway. Still haven't received any parcels from home. Sure would be nice to have some family photos. Full moon tonight.

Aug. 16, 1943

Air raid as Berlin bombed again. It's close enough that we get a bit of vibration in the glass in the windows. Orders are we have to stay in our huts until we hear the ALL CLEAR signal. We have no other bomb shelter to protect us.

Aug. 17, 1943

This is some kind of place alright. There's one boy who walks around the compound wearing only his jock strap. Even comes to appell that way. No one looks twice at him any more. He obviously doesn't care about the goon rule that says "The dress and bearing of the POWs shall be consonant with military dignity. Dress shall be governed by the usual military regulations."[9] Ha! Maybe he's loony or pretending to be & bucking for repatriation. Not that easy to get I hear. Have to go in front of boards of German docs & convince them. Wouldn't be too hard for some of these guys I can tell you.

Aug. 19, 1943

Finally some mail from home that was sent in July so that's not so bad. When I saw Ma's handwriting I almost cried. She

---

POSTKARTE
August 19th, 1943
Dear Ma,

Received your first 2 letters today. Glad everyone is well. Sure was good to hear from you. Write lots more than one a week. I will send a picture in a month or so. Had it taken the other day. Have been in swimming in the fire pool twice today. This is my last card this month. Cant write till Sept. now. Send lots of pictures, sports parcels, pair running shoes. Well Im okay. Write lots. Bags of love Albert W.

said the minister announced in church that I was missing. They do that. Poor Ma. Must've been hard not knowing & listening to everyone praying for me. Ma found out I was a POW from a total stranger 2 weeks after we were shot down. Good thing because she said the telegram from the RCAF advising I'm a POW came almost 3 weeks after they told her I was missing. That's a long time to worry & imagine the worst. Seems the Germans broadcast the names of captured airmen on the radio. Folks back home with short wave radios listen in, look up the families & write to let them know. Pretty decent of them. She also received a letter from Wynne saying how sorry she was that I'm dead! Wynne must've got her info from the boys at 419. Shows you that nothing has changed – they assume that MISSING more likely means dead than POW. Of course Ma wants to know who the heck Wynne is. Last she heard it was Aileen. She has no idea how many lives I've lived since she saw me last. She said she got a nice letter too from W/C Fleming at the squadron. Letter from El too with bad news. She says Don Kelly from my AG class was killed in a freak accident. He'd just returned to 432 base from an op, got out of the A/C & walked into the moving prop of a Wellington. I'd rather be shot out of the sky than go like that. Only 21 years old. They said he'd shot down a JU-88 too.[10] Letters from home make all the difference.

Aug. 21, 1943

The goons discovered over 150 Red + boxes full of sand under the bunks in my old hut 101. Now for sure they know something's going on & pressure will be on to find out what. One of the Canadian lads here – Bob Buckham - is quite an artist. He's always sketching something. He drew a portrait of me today & it's pretty good.

Aug. 22, 1943

Compound searched today. No spuds issued again but extra turnip in their place. Oh joy.

Aug 24, 1943

Ma says she got a letter from Spud's wife Flo Hiscox in Guelph. I stood up for them at their wedding last year. She says Spud's been overseas since May/42 as a Wireless Op. I lost track of him. She didn't know I'd left Jarvis until she read in the paper that I'm a POW. Ma gave her my address & she said she's going to

Aug 27
Dear Ma.

This is my last letter this month so I decided to write it to you. First of all I am fine and eating pretty good. Havent had any mail for a long time. Seem to have got all the July letters but none after that. Have written Aileen and told her I definitely wont be getting hitched after the war. But she'll probably write you. ▮▮▮▮▮▮▮▮▮▮ *This is a hell of a life. Im getting lazier every day. I wont be able to work when I get out of here.* ▮▮▮▮▮▮
▮▮▮▮▮▮▮▮▮▮▮▮▮▮▮▮▮▮▮▮▮▮
▮▮▮▮▮▮▮▮▮▮▮▮▮▮▮▮ *Well I got the clothing parcel also a few cartons of smokes. Thanks a million. I also got six books, cribbage board & a deck of cards that I think came from Loblaws. Well its getting cold here. They tell me it gets about 40 below here in the winter. Hope youre sending lots of photos. I am now in a room where we are all Canadians, five of us. Hope everything is okay at home and all are well. I sent a Xmas present to you through my bank. Hope you get it. Well this is all for now so lots of letters. Love Alb*

write me & send the odd parcel. That's sure okay with me. Spud wants to write me too. The more letters the better. She's sending me a picture.

Aug. 25, 1943

Moved again, this time to Block 107, room 2. There are 5 of us Canadians & no lockouts so already it's much better. Al Matthews, Joe Glover & Don Middleton are Canadian RAF. They've been POWs for years already. Spud ration issued.

Aug. 27, 1943

My first personal parcel arrived from home today & 1 from Loblaws too. I was like a kid at Christmas. Ma sent some warm clothes that'll come in handy soon & some fags to top up my supply. Books & games from Loblaws. Anything to help pass the time.

Aug. 28, 1943

    The extra rooms in the theatre are all up & running now. There's a library that has more & more books all the time from the Red + & personal parcels too. There's also a War Room with a huge map of Europe on the wall where some of the boys chart the front lines & armies & the latest bombing targets with tacks & yarn according to the German news. The goons study them as much as we do. There's a chapel too although I won't be a regular customer.

Klim cans containing powdered milk were a staple in Red Cross food parcels. (Klim is "milk" spelled backwards.) The more resourceful Kriegies, such as fellow Canadian John Colwell, diligently scrounged the cans, and any cans for that matter, to turn them into useful articles: plates, cups, pails, kettles, coffee pots, wash basins, dhobi buckets, baking pans.[11] Klim cans would later be used to make a pipe under the floor of Tunnel Harry through which a pump would force air to the tunnel face.

Aug. 31, 1943

    Extra long appell this morning while the goons searched every hut & seized all kinds of stuff. They took hundreds of Red + boxes so we can't hide sand in them but we can't make things

Class schedule

Sept 5

Dear Ma,

Up to now I have received 5 letters from you, 4 from Eleanor, 1 from Uncle Al and D Sproule, Loblaws and Nadine Anderson. Im glad everything is okay at home. In a few days its my birthday. I hope my parcel gets here this month. Put a little food in my clothing parcels. We get enough to eat but some nice things for a change and dont forget candy. Well I cant write everybody that writes me so if I cant answer them Ill tell you and you can phone them. Sept 9th. Today is my birthday. Glad you had a good time on your holidays. My mail is coming through very good now. The weather is pretty good here. I guess I wouldnt send too much stuff Ma. Send a few games in the sports parcel for our long winter nights & cards. Our minor league softball team won the league. Did you ever get those shells I asked you to get for me? Well we eat in about half an hour now. Tell El thanks for the letters. I wont be able to send her more than a card. But it might be over soon. I have received 8 letters from W. Hands in Eng. She is the only person in Eng I know who writes. Dont know what Aileen thinks about my not getting married when I get back but now I dont want to. Give my love to Betty, Eleanor, Dad. Keep writing. Lots of love Albie

from them either. Some of the guys are pretty good with their hands & imagination. They've made stools, bookcases, shelves & all kinds of things from the Red + boxes & crates, until now anyway. And that's nothing compared to what guys like Johnny Colwell are making out of Klim & other food cans. Johnny's a master at tin bashing. He's from B.C. & lives in the same room as Art Hawtin. He makes pots & pans from the empty Klim cans, clocks that actually work & even a cooking stove for their room. All kinds of stuff. Amazing! I'm going to try my hand at some pans for cooking.

Sept. 3, 1943

The theatre opened on Wed. The first play they're putting on is a musical called "Turn Back the Clock".[12] Not that I'm a theatre type but I couldn't get in anyway even with 400 or so seats. All the seats had to be reserved & the goons got first dibs! To heck with turning back the clock anyway. I'd like to turn it ahead to when we're finally out of this joint. I heard the play was pretty good. Props, sets, costumes, make-up – the whole works. Apparently the fellows who dressed up as women got a lot of whistles. No end of talented men in this compound that's for sure. Most of the Americans are moving to the south compound. We can see it now that the trees are all gone.

Sept. 4, 1943

We hear the bombing raids in the distance. Tonight was a long one. Had to be Berlin. We waited it out in the dark. Allied troops invaded Italy mainland yesterday.

Sept. 7, 1943

Thanks to the SBO the Kommandant extended curfew to 22:00 hours so we can visit each other after dark. So he's not that bad. Our shutters still have to be closed at dusk but at least we can get out & walk & actually look at the night sky.

Sept. 8, 1943

Great uproar in the compound. Glemnitz found Tom's trap while he was searching hut 123 next door to us. I heard he dropped his probe & it chipped away a piece of the cement. Rotten luck. We watched as the goons surrounded the hut & ordered everyone out. Glemnitz & Rubberneck are wearing big smiles. Now they've got guards on the doors while they investigate I guess. Big news - Italy surrendered & declared war on Germany.[13]

Sept. 9, 1943

Happy Birthday to me – 23 today. Cake & tea this afternoon to celebrate. The goons won't let any of the boys from 123 back into the hut so they all have to bunk up in other rooms.

Sept. 11, 1943

Johnny Colwell is making an artificial leg for Don Morrison, another Canadian lad from Orillia, and a Spitfire pilot shot down over France. That's how good Johnny is. He can make anything out of anything. Don's leg was badly injured when he bailed out & had to be amputated.[14] That was the second time he had to bail out too! Once was enough for me. The goons are guarding 123 around the clock but they don't seem to know what to do about the tunnel. Too long & too sturdy to flood I imagine. They must be impressed with the workmanship! Probably afraid to go down it.

Sept. 12, 1943

We heard the goons finally sent Charlie Pfelz down Tom. He's a likeable goon & just a little guy so he can easily maneuver in a small space. And I guess he's not claustrophobic either. More like it that he's their sacrificial lamb. He's also just a private so he gets all the crumby jobs. The Kommandant was apparently quite upset when Charlie was gone over half an hour & that was before he found out that Tom goes down 30 ft! Then past the west fence & all the way out to the trees. That means Tom is hundreds of feet long. Impressive except there'll be hell to pay. Some ferret heads will no doubt roll. I don't know how the lads managed to dig such a tunnel. I'd be so afraid of it collapsing in on me. I think I'd rather be shot out of the sky than suffocate in sand.

Sept. 13, 1943

I made a soldering torch that uses boiled margarine as fuel & a pyjama cord for a wick. It works pretty good. I run when we're dismissed from parade to scrounge old cans from the garbage to melt off the solder. Lot of competition for raw materials these days. I'm working up a nice little supply of solder so I can start to make a few things.

Sept. 14, 1943

We saw an army type going into 123. Little guy. Seems the Kommandant has brought him in help to figure out how to deal with Tom.

Sept. 15, 1943

The guy they brought in must be an engineer. He's spent 2 days going in & out of the hut. Looks like he's going to use explosives to blow Tom to kingdom come. Should be a good show. Anything for entertainment to offset the gloom on account of Tom being discovered.

Sept. 16, 1943

Today a bunch of us stood around watching as the army type set up his detonator. When he finally pushed the plunger we heard a dull bang & all of a sudden something blew right

Backstage crew at the theatre

through the hut roof. It was the concrete trap blown sky high! We laughed our asses off for ages. So much for their expert. Rolling on the ground in tears we were laughing so hard. We'll be telling that story for a very long time. The shizenpanzerwagen showed up & dumped a load down Tom. THE END punctuated with a big stink.

Sept. 19, 1943

It's getting cold at night. We don't get enough coal to generate any decent heat but at least we're allowed to burn stumps from around the compound. Heck of a lot of work to dig them out though. The Germans lend us tools & equipment on the parole system so we have to return them. Rummy tournament this afternoon. Made my first pot out of a Klim can with my little

---

POSTKARTE

Sept 25/1943

Dear Mom,

Glad you liked your first plane ride. Nice isnt it. Well nothing new here. Havent had any mail for months, but itll come I suppose. The weather has changed here, cold now bleak looking as hell. I sure hope this war ends before Xmas. Well bye for now. Lots of love to all Alb

---

Sept. 25
Dear Mom,

Have decided to write my last letter of the month to you. Hope everyone is well. Its starting to get cooler here now. You had better not send all that stuff I asked for. But use your own discretion in sending things. If you send any clothes try and send them in sports parcels and save room in clothing parcels for little extras of food and candy. Tell El I got Nadine's letter. Also a couple from Dot Sproule. I hope youve sent lots of tooth powder and a good T. brush. Well I hope its all over soon as I want to do some hunting & fishing. Well time is creeping along here. Im playing a lot of softball these days but thats about all. I see Hawtin and Baker every day and we walk around camp a lot. Well this is all for the night. Next day. Today I got 2 letters from Wynne. So its a good day. How is the car running? Not much gas now I suppose. I have met a fellow who knew Uncle Al in Moncton. Used to work with him. If you get this before you send my next clothing par. put a blanket in it but if you can send it in a sports parcel. This is about all so say hello to everyone for me. Be home soon. Bye.

Lots of love Albie
P.S. When sending cigarettes send "Export" Brand.

torch & solder. My mail has dried up.

Sept. 21, 1943

Heard 3 Americans escaped from south compound last night right after lights out.[15] South compound is so close to us that some of the boys are communicating by semaphore through their room window in 120. Just a playing field away. Another call for bed boards – 2 boards this time & so soon after Tom's demise. Our bunks are getting risky for sleeping.

Sept. 24, 1943

Finally saw a play at the theatre last night called "George and Margaret".[16] One of those Brit comedies. I like that kind of humour. Big X was in it too. He's in a lot of plays. These guys are really good. The goons think so too – there were a few officers right in the front row! Things seem quiet in the camp now that Tom's gone kaput, for awhile anyway. Harry & Dick all quiet.

Sept. 30, 1943

I bash a few circuits regularly these days with Slim Larlee. He's from New Brunswick. He's a skinny bugger like me so he comes by the nickname honestly. I haven't had a meal yet that actually filled me up. Slim & me munch on chocolate & shoot the breeze about the war or about home mostly. He showed me some pictures from home. I don't have any yet so I told him about Mom & Dad's place in Bolsover & about hunting & fishing with the uncles. It's good to talk about home but makes me miss it more. Slim says he'll take me to a whorehouse when we get back! So much for getting married. I've got too much living to do yet. Just have to survive this place first.

Oct. 2, 1943

Big news from southern Italy – the Allies captured the port of Naples.

Oct. 4, 1943

Turned the clocks back 1 hour last night – just what I need, an extra hour in this joint. Time means little and everything to

Mom & Dad   *Betty & El*

Aunt May giving the cat a drink

me now. Sold my Gruen watch today to Skinner, a Brit. Hated to part with it but it's not doing me much good here. I still remember paying $25 for it many years ago when I was delivering groceries on my bike for good old Mr. Nimmo. Bought it at Peoples Credit Jewelers for $1 down & 24 payments of $1. Ma signed for me to help out. Skinner paid me 15 D bars plus a cheque on his bank account in England that he wrote on a scrap of paper. Only time will tell if his cheque is any good. He must have traded with one of the Americans to have all those D bars. They're good too, about an inch thick. Ma would be disappointed that I didn't get anywhere near the $400-500 the watch must be worth now but those D bars are like gold to me right now. Slim & me will thoroughly enjoy them while we bash circuits.

Oct. 8, 1943

Received a birthday card from Ma & finally some pictures of everyone. No gramophone though. It'd probably never arrive in 1 piece anyway. There's 1 being passed around from room to room in our hut that we're all sharing. Maybe it came from the YMCA or got left behind by 1 of the repats. All I need now are the records. We can borrow in the meantime & there are lots around the compound. No word from Aileen. I guess she got the message. We're supposed to have some sort of canteen but it hasn't happened. I heard some of the lads have set up a racket they call Foodacco for bartering - mostly food & some clothes. Stuff that guys get in parcels that they're willing to trade. Haven't checked it out yet.

Oct. 9, 1943

No spuds issued but some barley instead. Ma sent this picture of Aunt May milking one of the cows out at the farm. I think she figured it would make me smile every time I look at it. She's right. That old barn cat always used to find Aunt May at milking time. He'd sit himself under the cow & Aunt May would squirt one of the teats right into his mouth. It's a game between them. Aunt May's the funny one always doing stuff like that. I remember the time she called me out to the barnyard with her to catch a chicken for dinner. She caught it easy & lopped off its head before you could wink. Then we both laughed like heck while it ran around headless.

Oct. 10, 1943

Undated, but postmarked
Oct 16, 1943
Dear Ma,

I have received quite a few letters & the parcel you sent from Simpsons with moccasins & sweat shirt. Thanks it was swell. Have not received the personal parcel yet. Got your birthday card this morn. Tell Aunt Rae & Aunt Jean thanks for their letters. Hope you had a great time at Bolsover. I am not doing any studying here of anything cause I havent the ambition. The Red Cross paints too rosy a picture for you. Have received letters from Aileen but apparently she doesnt know I wont be getting married when I get back. But I have written her. The pictures in the card were good. Send more. Send me a pair of heavy warm gloves. If youre sending any books send good novels and stories of Canada. You can tell people who write me I cant answer cause I don't have enough forms. So you can thank them for me. Dont forget in my next personal parcel to put a lot of food, soup mixtures, dried apples, gum, mixed candy and other things you can think of. I have a bad cold right now. Keeps me busy washing the few hankys I have. Dad and Betty how are you? All working hard? Well lets hope its all over soon. I would like to see Toronto & the country again. Bye for now. Love to all Alb.

Cousin Dorothy

Now that the theatre is in full swing the goons want in on the action too. They're bringing in their own films & the Kommandant has supplied a projector. He's a pretty reasonable fellow. They played a goon film last night. I'll wait for an English one. The Red + has supposedly sent some. Bet making on the World Series tonight.

Oct. 12, 1943

We heard the New York Yankees beat out the St. Louis Cardinals to win the World Series 4 games to 1.[17]

Oct. 13, 1943

Whole compound searched first thing this morning. Not a great way to wake up.

Oct. 14, 1943

News is bad for the US 8th Air Force bombing ball bearing factories in Schweinfurt. 60 B-17s lost & hundreds of casualties.

Oct. 15, 1943

I can't keep track of time around here – day of the month, day of the week. At this rate, pretty soon I'll forget what year it is.

It's like living in a big black pit. Maybe it'll help if I start including the day of the week in my log book dates. Every day is as boring as the one before & it bothers me that I've been sucked into this lazy life & don't have the energy to do anything about it. Who'd think that doing nothing is so exhausting. It'll be worse come winter. Have a cold & that DOESN'T help my mood.

Oct. 16, 1943
Word has come down from the SBO that any 'offence against the Reich' can result in court martial along with some unreasonable amount of time in the cooler while you wait for a hearing.

Sunday Oct. 17, 1943
Don Morrison was repatriated today on account of his bum leg. Lucky stiff. He wasn't even here long enough for Johnny to finish making him the new one. Last night saw my first English film here - Fred Astaire & Ginger Rogers in "Shall We Dance".[18] Films are scarce. I hear that all the compounds have a theatre now except the south & that ours is the best. From the back of the theatre looking forward, it's just row on row of seats with the big red cross on the back of each one. There's a new purge practically every day now. Some of the rooms are being bumped up to 8 boys. That's another whole bunk. Still no spuds in our ration. The goons say we are fed better than they are so we shouldn't complain.

Mon. Oct. 18, 1943
Received 300 fags from Ma today. Can't have too many. The American Red + parcel actually has smokes in it! Al & Joe are the only ones who will eat the stinky cheese we get in the goon ration. They say that when you've had as little to eat as they had at Colditz Castle, you don't turn ANYTHING down. I'm hungry but hope I'm never THAT hungry. New SBO is G/C Wilson. He's RAAF. Shot down in June.

Wed. Oct. 20, 1943
Watched a raid to the west of us – must be Leipzig. Bumped into Ley Kenyon the Gunnery Leader from 419 out on the perimeter today. He was shot down Sept. 16 on an op to the rail yards at Modane.
Thurs. Oct 21, 1943

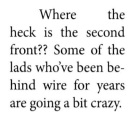

Where the heck is the second front?? Some of the lads who've been behind wire for years are going a bit crazy.

Mon. Oct. 25, 1943

The Brit Red + food parcel has oatmeal in it & sweet condensed milk too. Maybe we can trade. Other than that, the Canadian parcel is the best, better even than the American one. Still no spud issue.

El & Betty

Tues. Oct 26, 1943

Heard that someone made it out past the wire last night. Not sure how he did that without getting cut to shreds. Must have gone under.

Sat. Oct 30, 1943

We're giving the gramophone quite a workout. Need more records since it's not looking good for being out of here by the end of the year. Some Harry James records would be good.

Ma & Betty

Nov 4th

Dear Ma,

> *Got a letter from you the other day. Im doing okay on mail but where are all the photos? How is everyone at home? All well I hope. So Roly is near home now. Thats swell. Tell him to write or Ill have to bash him when I get home. Dont send any winter stuff off to me later than Jan cause it wont get here till summer although we hope to be out of here by summer anyway. I hope so. Sorry to hear about your accident. Glad nobody was hurt. I hope you havent let the Red + talk you into sending only 1 letter a week cause thats a lot of malarkey. Hope you have sent lots of gramophone needles. The weather here is getting colder. You can tell all the people who write me if they dont get a reply its not my fault but only because I havent got the letters or cards to write. I will give my personal thanks to all when I get home. I got 2 pictures from you taken at Bolsover. Have received quite a few cigarettes now from everyone so thank them all. Got a letter from Aunt May in California. Was good to hear from her. Well its 11:30 just about time for lights out. So Ill close now. Hi Dad, Betty & Eleanor. Lots of love Albie*

Mon. Nov. 1, 1943

Heard out on the circuit today about a rather ingenious escape from east compound the other night. Seems 3 of the lads used Red + parcel crates to build a hollow vaulting horse for gymnastics practice. It was carried with them inside it to a spot near the wire every day last summer. While some fit types practiced on it, they dug a tunnel under the wire from inside it. Brilliant!

These three lads, Eric Williams, Richard Codner and Oliver Philpot, posing as French workers, hit "home runs", the expression for successfully escaping and actually making it back to England. After the war, Eric Williams told the story in a book called *The Wooden Horse.*

Wed. Nov. 3, 1943

From a play at the theatre.
"She" looks pretty good
doesn't she?

One of the lads on the circuit today heard in a letter from home about a German officers POW camp in Canada. Nice grounds, good treatment. They play tennis in white flannels! They don't need food parcels either - they get a choice of cereals for breakfast, bacon, eggs, toast & coffee. For dinner – roast meat and veg. Beer always on hand. How'd they get so lucky?

In the following letter, Dad looks for assurance that Grandma has sent him "lots of gramophone needles". I wondered why he would need so many; Dad could not recall when I asked.

Nov. 6, 1943

Now that it's too cold for sports, some of the boys are teaching classes in the theatre. You can learn just about anything at the University of Sagan as it's known – practically any language, math, economics, English literature, science, exams included. The escape types are all learning German. I'd have to be pretty desperate to study Greek or Latin. I can't believe how tiring it is doing nothing at all.

Mon. Nov. 8, 1943

We're now 6 Canadians in our room. Al Matthews is from Calgary. He sleeps in a nightshirt, right down to his ankles! Joe Glover is from Toronto. He's in the bunk over me. Penn McLeod is from B.C. Doug Wraith is from Vancouver. Don Middleton is from Manitoba. First snow yesterday & a first for the South African boys. We showed them some true Canadian snowball warfare. There's a goon rule that says "Snowballing must cease ½ hr before Roll-Call."[19] We'll see about that. Stew for supper tonight.

Tues. Nov. 9, 1943

Don told me some of his story. He was sent to Colditz Castle near Leipzig in November 1940. It's where they send the repeat offenders & it really is an old castle. He'd escaped from another camp with 2 other Canadians & told he was being sent to Colditz to be shot. Was just a scare. Then he pushed his luck & tried to escape again in '41.

Wed. Nov. 10, 1943

> *Nov 12/1943*
>
> *Dear Ma,*
>
> *Heres another letter to you. I am sending a photo we had taken in the summer. Pretty bleak looking joint or what. Well I don't know whether Ive told you but Im in an all Canadian room now, six of us. None of the fellows in the picture are in the room though. I hope youre sending the odd sports parcel to me. I got a parcel from the Canadian Red + in London the other day which was very welcome. Dont let the Red + talk you into only sending 1 letter a week. Look Ma if you can get food parcels sent to me from the States do so by all means. How are Betty & El & Dad & yourself? All well I hope. As I told you I wrote Aileen & told her I wanted the engagement busted. I know its a lousy trick but this joint has changed all of that. I wouldnt get married after coming out of here. Im almost too lazy to write. How is my pay coming through? Okay I hope. Am getting quite a few letters now. Hope you like this picture. Dont forget lots of food in my parcels, clothes in sports parcels. Well Ma this is all for now. Lots of love Albie*

Me with the skinny legs

A few of us Canadians – *Ted White (Midland) George Smith (St. Catharines), Ross Gillespie (Kitchener), Jim McCague (Alliston), Heije Schaper (Holland), me in the short pants*

Following the war, Heije Schaper, standing next to Dad in the above photo, ultimately rose to supreme commander of the Dutch Air Force. In the early days of the war, he won the "Militaire Willemsorde der 4e klasse, a Dutch decoration equivalent to the Victoria Cross."[20]

Received a personal parcel postmarked from an address in London England with no sender's name on it. Aside from guys still around at 419, the only person I know in England is Wynne & I'm sure it's not from her so maybe it's from the Red +. Contents are a bit odd - some ping pong bats that I haven't asked for mainly because we don't have a ping pong table although now we'll improvise one like some of the boys have. A few hairbrushes – how many do I need? A sweater made from shiny rayon or some such fiber, not wool & so heavy I can't imagine wearing it. I gave it to Harry who lives 2 rooms up the hall. He's Ukrainian from western Canada. Nice guy.

Thurs. Nov. 11, 1943
Remembrance Day. Went to a service in the theatre. Hope everyone at home is remembering us.
Sun. Nov. 14, 1943

161

Workmen repaired a loudspeaker outside the cookhouse so we can be enlightened with a radio broadcast of German news, music if we're lucky. Heard that Red Noble & another prisoner managed to lift quite a bit of electrical wire the workmen left lying around outside the kitchen. There'll be hell to pay by those electricians for their carelessness if it's found out. Haven't the goons figured out yet that anything left unattended is fair game to a bunch of scrounging Kriegies??

Wed. Nov. 17, 1943

I heard today that my old pal Huck from Jarvis is dead - he & 4 other guys in his crew. Happened a few weeks ago. They were with 405 squadron.[21] Shot down on a mission to Hanover. He was only 21, younger than me. That's 5 of my best pals from AG training (that I know of) gone plus Mac & Dave from my own crew & so many others from 419. Easier to just be a loner.

Thursday Nov. 18, 1943

Couple more of the boys have received Dear John letters from their girls back home. As if this place isn't bad enough without that. But I guess I can't talk. Berlin was bombed again heavily. We sat & listened to it in the dark.

Mon. Nov. 22, 1943

Berlin got it again.

Tues. Nov. 23, 1943

We're all hoarding supplies from our personal & Red + parcels so we can make a bash on Christmas Day. I don't know what we'd do without the Red +. Penn never stops going on about B.C. & how great it is. We call him the "B.C. Booster". Enough already. It's starting to get pretty cold at night & daytime too for that matter. I see McFarlane out on the circuit & he's all bundled up like he's at the North Pole. And he's not out there for long before he's back inside huddling around the stove. These South Africans aren't used to the cold. I'm not even wearing my greatcoat yet if I can help it. Berlin bombed again tonight for 45 minutes or so.

Fri. Nov. 26, 1943

Berlin bombed again tonight. The windows rattled. Can tell by the sound of them that they're Mossie bombers probably on nuisance raids just to disrupt things or create diversions. They probably end up dumping their bombs any old place.

Sun. Nov. 28, 1943

South compound's American band lined up as close as they could get to us this morning just before appell & played "God Save The King" for us. We saluted them in thanks. The goons were not impressed.

Mon. Nov. 29, 1943

We heard the goons confiscated the Americans band in-struments for a month to punish them for serenading us yester-day. Another new purge arrived at the compound. I walked out to the gate even though I doubted I'd know anyone. Most of my old friends are all dead.

Tues. Nov. 30, 1943

Al is teaching me to play chess. Takes me forever to make a move. Al says he can take a nap while I'm planning my next move…zzzzzzzzzz. He ALWAYS wins too.

Wed. Dec. 1, 1943

Heard that another boy from my AG class at Jarvis is dead. Doug Storey & his whole crew from 100 squadron.[22] Shot down on an op to Leipzig a few weeks ago.

Fri. Dec. 3, 1943

Happy 25th Birthday El, sorry I'm missing it. Berlin bombed again last night. More bombing tonight but to the west of us so maybe Leipzig again.

Sat. Dec. 4, 1943

I bumped into Harry on the circuit, the boy I gave that strange sweater to that came in that anonymous parcel from London. He told me he unraveled it & rigged up a hammock! He says it easily holds his weight & is way more comfortable to sleep in compared to his palliasse that was falling through the missing bed boards. Not sure who would have wanted to wear it as a sweater. It was heavy as lead.

Sunday Dec. 5, 1943

Heavy snow. The boys formed a skating rink from Red + parcel crates on the sports field & flooded it. The Canadian

YMCA sent skates enough for 2 hockey teams. There are some keen players, mostly Canadians. I'm a lousy skater. Weak ankles.
Tues. Dec. 7, 1943

To Canadian Prisoners of War in Europe

Arrangements have been made to forward to all Canadian prisoners of war a Christmas gift from the "People of Canada". It is hoped that in spite of the difficulties and uncertainties of transportation these will arrive at the camps in time for Christmas.

Each Canadian prisoner will receive a small parcel for his personal use, but the greater part of the gift will be of a collective or communal nature, comprising articles such as gramaphone records and cooking utensils, which will be delivered in bulk to the Spokesman at every camp in which Canadians are interned, with the intention that their use might be shared as far as possible with all prisoners in the camp regardless of nationality.

In the past Christmas cards have been responsible for considerable congestion in the prisoners of war mail service, with the result that ordinary letters arrived only after considerable delay. Since the prisoners themselves have expressed the view that the prompt arrival of these ordinary letters is preferable to the receipt of Christmas cards, postal regulations do not permit their despatch. It is hoped therefore that the enclosed card from the Prime Minister will be regarded as representing those which prisoners might ordinarily have expected to receive from their friends.

I told the boys about Harry's hammock which got us talking more about that parcel from London so I dug out the stuff I hadn't given away. Sure enough the handle of one of the hairbrushes came off & tucked inside were some packets of dye. Another one had some German money in it. It's an escape parcel! Don't know why I didn't think of that sooner. Wasted on me since I have no intention of trying to escape. I'd last about 15 minutes on a good day with my limited German. I'll stay put until the war's over. Just glad to be out of it. I gave the stuff to one of the "X" Security guys. They can put it to better use than me. Then I heard that other boys have received the same kind of parcel with maps & a compass.

Fri. Dec. 10, 1943

We all received a Christmas card from Canada signed by old Mackenzie King himself. Not often I get mail from the Prime Minister. A personal parcel for each Canadian POW is supposed to be on its way and also a group parcel for us to share.

Wed. Dec. 15, 1943

We have our own dental surgery in the compound. One of the New Zealand POWs is a dentist so he's doing work on any of the boys who need it out in the sick quarters in the vorlager. He filled a cavity for me today. Feels a lot better. Too much chocolate & candy & not enough tooth powder I guess.

Thurs. Dec. 16, 1943

POSTKARTE
Dec 17th 1943
Dear Ma,
Got 2 letters from Betty this AM. Glad you have sent my 2nd parcel. Please accept my apologies for my letters of Dec. which you will get soon but thats how I felt at the time. All well here. How are you all? Have you sent any blankets? Send clothing in sports parcels. How about a few good books. Well its pretty cold here. I have written Aileen to tell her the engagement is off. This is all for now.
Love Albie

Berlin hit again tonight. The hut shook. Watched a hockey game today. The goons are pretty big fans. Received a Christmas card from the Canadian POW Relatives Assn. 300 fags & 2 lb of chocolate are on the way. Merry Christmas to you too.

Christmas 1943

To Canadian Prisoners Of War

Our Christmas gift of two pounds of chocolate and three hundred cigarettes has been despatched to you and we trust will arrive safely and in good time. The thoughts of your friends and relations and of all your countrymen are with you this Christmas time. The message we send you is one of hope and faith. Hope that the New Year will bring a speedy end to the separation and hardships of war. Faith in the future that we will build together. May the coming year bring you back to us and restore peace to the peoples of the World.

A Happy Christmas and A Happier New Year

Beatrice John Amelin.

President

The Canadian Prisoners of War Relatives Association

Sat. Dec. 18, 1943

      Some of the boys are very artistic & have terrific sketches of the camp & the lads in their logbooks. Guys like Bob Buckham are happy to share their talent & draw in the books of the artistically ungifted like me. I couldn't even draw a straight line in drafting class back at Central Tech.

Dad remembers the drafting teacher at Central Tech looking at his work and announcing in front of the class, "Wallace, these lines look like they were made with a whitewash brush".

Fri. Dec. 24, 1943

      We all went to the theatre tonight for Christmas carols. Lots of prep going on for a Christmas bash tomorrow. The latest batch of Kriegie brew distilled from raisins & sugar is pretty strong I hear. I'm not touching the stuff.

Sat. Dec. 25, 1943

      Another Christmas away from home & my first behind barbed wire. Hope it's my last. Slept in. Might as well. Only 1 appell today & that's a gift too. Lot of noisy singing. Snow. My 219th day here.

Dec. 26, 1943

Dec. 26/43

Dear Mom,

      Xmas over for another year. Lets hope we make it this year. I suppose you all had a good time. It was just another day here. The weather has been very cold here for 3 weeks now with no let up. Hope youre putting a full 3 lbs of chocolate in my parcels and still sending stuff. I have just learned how to play chess and pass a lot of time that way. I smoke a pipe now as well as cigarettes. Remember the pipe you were going to send but never did? What little optimism I had has certainly disappeared after recent events. Well say hello to everyone for me. I dont feel like writing any more now so Ill just say bye.

      Lots of love Alb

Heard a bunch of Americans climbed the fence from next door last night to visit & celebrate & a few of our lads did the same. We heard shots fired but apparently no one was hit. Not enough room in the cooler for them all anyway. The goons aren't as forgiving as they used to be. Someone's going to end up getting shot over a prank. Time for the start of a new round of "Home by Christmas" jokes out on the circuit.

Wed. Dec. 29, 1943

Bashed a few circuits with Art & Bruce today. Not as many now that it's cold. We talked about the war as usual & what could happen to us if Germany falls.

Fri. Dec. 31, 1943

Thank God this year is over. Here's hoping this is our last Christmas here & that '44 is a better year. Few of the lads were happy on raisin brew by afternoon appell. A few hooch parties around tonight but I didn't feel like going. All the lads who bet the war would be over by year's end are going to have to make good on their wagers. A lot of chocolate and smokes will change hands.

Prisoner Of War
Stalag Luft III: 1944

Big X decided the new year was time to pour renewed effort into finishing Tunnel Harry. With cold temperatures and snow on the ground making escape "off season", the Germans would be less likely to be looking for tunneling activity; however, the very same reasons would make sand dispersal difficult.

One of the men in the X Organization came up with the idea of storing the sand in the space under the sloping theatre floor. The theatre wasn't raised like the huts so the guards couldn't see under it. Seat 13 in row 12 was adapted so that it hinged back; a trapdoor was cut in the floor beneath it. (This same seat would become the entrance to Tunnel George later in the year.) The 22:00 hours curfew and the cover of night allowed the penguins to speed up the dispersal process by carrying kitbags of sand to the theatre outside of show times. Not to miss any opportunity to disperse sand, a penguin would be directed to attend a theatre production, sit in this special seat, and disperse his sand during the show.

Sat. Jan. 1, 1944

Happy New Year. Hopefully this'll be the year it's all over. Lots of snow today. Not all that cold so it's good packing snow. Great for snowball fights & I've got a pretty mean snowball arm.

Sun. Jan. 2, 1944

Early morning air raid on Berlin. Nothing like an air raid to cheer us up.

Back in 1942, Hitler had ordered the design and construction of a defensive wall along the western coast of Europe to prevent or at least delay an Allied invasion of the continent from Great Britain. The Atlantic Wall, as it was known, consisted of concrete bunkers, minefields and gun batteries, and stretched from Norway to the Spanish border.[1]

Mon. Jan. 3, 1944

Berlin got it again. The German news is full of stories about the invincibility of the Atlantic Wall. Is it all propaganda? We hear about speeches from Roosevelt & Churchill that say the invasion is coming. But when?

Tues. Jan. 4, 1944

Al has an ulcer so he gets up most nights to make himself a cup of warm milk. Food is tight but we're all okay with him having extra if he needs it. The only veg we're getting these days in the goon issue is sauerkraut. Not sure which is worse, the sauerkraut or the swede.

Wed. Jan. 5, 1944

Berlin bombed again. The goons surprised 5 huts with a search. More snow. Must have a foot of it now.

Thurs. Jan. 6, 1944

Art & Bruce & me were talking today out on the circuit about buying a car when we get home. Dad never owned a new car but I'm going to have a new car. Told them about the time I flipped Dad's car at Bolsover. Just slipped off the edge of the old washboard road & then rolled over with Aunt Mary & me in it. Never heard anyone cuss up a blue streak quite like Aunt Mary did except maybe the time I was staying with them for the weekend at their house on Greenwood & Uncle Ed rigged one of her smokes with an exploding cap. It was first thing in the morning & she was still half asleep when that fag blew. I learned some new words from Aunt Mary, God bless her.

Monday Jan. 10, 1944

Watched a hockey game. Life drags on here. I don't know what we'd do without mail, parcels & cards to break the monotony. Argue more I guess. We can argue about anything at all just for something to do. Full moon tonight. No penguin duty.

Jan 8/1944

Got your second parcel the other day. Was okay except for the underwear. How are you all? Okay I expect. Everything is okay here, bad weather lately. Havent had much mail here. When are you going to send some pictures? Well this letter writing is an awful nuisance. Nothing to say. Did you get the picture I sent home? How is my money in the bank piling up? Have you heard from Aileen since I wrote her telling her to break the engagement? So far the weather hasnt been very cold. I hope it stays like that. I suppose you havent sent a blanket or records or good books or things like that. Where is the pipe you were going to send? Say hello to everyone for me. I am very fed up with all this and do nothing but sleep as much as I can. Were just having a small argument here on poker. I hope you get the money I sent you through the bank. Love Albie.

Fri. Jan. 14, 1944

Another freeze your balls off shower this morning. What I'd give for a hot shower. One of the goon orders says "POWs shall have the opportunity of taking a hot shower/bath once weekly."[2] Ha! I haven't had one yet. But I hear that some boys are getting hot showers. I must be chumming with the wrong crowd.

Sun. Jan. 16, 1944

Johnny C. actually made an oven from Klim cans – 98 of them.[3] He's been scrounging them for months. More snow but not too cold.

Wed. Jan. 19, 1944

Some of the lads were building human pyramids on appell today.

Thurs. Jan. 20, 1944

More trees coming down to the west of us. Workers out there going crazy with saws & axes. Another compound? That'll be the end of Dick. Tunnel Harry will be all that's left. Untouchable Berlin bombed again.

The German blockade of Leningrad had been in place since July 8,

1941. One third of Leningrad's population died during the 900-day siege from starvation, disease, exposure, and German air and artillery bombardment.[4]

Thurs. Jan. 27, 1944
Played cards in Slim's room. The cards are wearing out. Big news day. The Ruskies broke through the Leningrad blockade. Leningrad is free after 2½ years but they're saying hundreds of thousands have died.

Fri. Jan. 28, 1944
Berlin hit again.

Sat. Jan. 29, 1944
Berlin bombed again, this time pretty hard. Power cut in the middle of poker. Went on for a long time so we played by lamp light. Just as well to conserve our light bulb because it's near impossible to get a new one. Smokey as hell.

Sun. Jan. 30, 1944
Berlin bombed again tonight. The German newspapers are using Goebbels words & calling us bomber crews TERROR FLIEGERS (Terror Fliers) & LUFT GANGSTERS (Air Gangsters) for what our bombers are doing to their cities & people. What about what they've done to the cities & people of Britain, France & Holland & Poland & Russia? G/C Massey passed the word around from the Kommandant that any escaping prisoners will be shot. No one knows if they would actually do it but I wouldn't press my luck with everything we've heard about the SS & Gestapo.

Wed. Feb. 2, 1944
Some of the boys including Bruce Baker have been purged to another camp not far from here, Belaria. Art & me will sure miss bashing circuits with Bruce. No contact allowed between camps. This is the longest winter of my life. It's so depressing here. I'm not even getting any mail. I don't have the interest or energy to even write a letter home any more & when I do I just bitch anyway. One of the lads insists he's going to write a card home for me to cheer me up. All I have to do is dictate it.

The following Postkarte was written in entirely different handwriting. In it, Dad again asked Grandma to send him gramophone needles. The last time he asked, in early November, it was for "lots" of needles, which was mildly interesting. This time, his request for "a couple of hundred" needles was definitely eyebrow raising. Another request would follow in his November 4, 1944 letter. How could the lads be burning through so many? Although Dad would not have known this, the X Organization was using gramophone needles and records in the manufacture of compasses for escape kits.[5] I wondered if a call had gone out to the Kriegies to request needles from home.

POSTKARTE
Feb. 3rd, 1944
Dear Ma,

All well here. Glad you are okay. Dont bother about looking for a car for me. Send me a couple hundred gramophone needles, 2 sweat shirts. Are you sending any pictures? Did you get my xmas present? Im not getting much mail these days. Why dont you send me more sports & games and book parcels? Bruce Baker has moved to another camp. Well say hello to all for me. Send all candy, gum & chocolate possible. Love Abby

Thurs. Feb. 3, 1944

The west part of the perimeter is off limits now. When we get there we have to turn around & come back. It's confirmed they're building yet another compound.

Sun. Feb. 6, 1944

Jeez it's cold.

Mon. Feb. 7, 1944

Our shared Christmas parcel from Canada finally got distributed today. Our room got an assortment of eating utensils, candy, personal grooming stuff.

Wed. Feb. 9, 1944

Big entertainment tonight was a fire in the vorlager. Apparently a goon hut burned down. Full moon.

Thurs. Feb. 10, 1944

Cold & bleak as can be - the weather & the war news. Hard to not be depressed in this joint. All the work on Dick isn't a lost cause after all. Big X is using it for storage. Good to know our penguin duty wasn't for nothing. Snowstorm - about 6 inches. We heard 14 escaped from east compound during the storm. Can't imagine escaping in any weather let alone a snowstorm.

Fri. Feb. 11, 1944

The cigarettes are flowing in from Loblaws, Toronto Overseas League, Bloor Businessmen's, POW Relatives Association. 300 here, 1000 there. The cigarette companies make it easy for folks back home to send them. The Brits only get 200 at a time. I couldn't smoke all I have if I tried. There are so many around the camp now that their trade value isn't near what it was.

Tues. Feb. 15, 1944

Heard Berlin getting bashed again at 10 tonight. It was heavy & lasted a while. We all talked today about life after the war, what the job situation will be like, what a shock it'll be to go back to a normal life whatever that even means. Still too much for us to get through here without worrying about tomorrow.

Thurs. Feb. 17, 1944

MORE cigarettes. Goon spud issue still reduced.

Fri. Feb. 18, 1944

More boys jumped off a hut roof into the back of one of the trucks carrying pine branches out of the camp. The goons were on to that one a long time ago & were stopping all the trucks & poking pitchforks into the branches. Ouch! What a bunch of dummkopfs as the goons would say. The Allies are pounding German factories.

Sun. Feb. 20, 1944

Heard Leipzig getting it again badly. Early this morning and again this aft.

Thursday Feb. 24, 1944

Last night was bitterly cold. Had to wear extra clothes to bed & use my greatcoat on top of my blanket. Sure could use another blanket. There are rumours going around that anyone

174

considering escaping should think twice because the Gestapo are capable of anything.

Feb 20th 44
Dear Ma,

How are you all? Well the weather has been very cold around here for awhile. Im sure a couple of blankets would have been more appreciated than that bloody long underwear. How about more info in letters, current events. Whats the government going to do for us after the war? Any more boys on our course buy it yet? Got some mail last week. Some of it took 7 months to get here. Wish the warm weather would get here. The winter is very depressing. I dont even think well be out of here by next Xmas now. But hope Im wrong. I received the running shoes and shorts. I get some of those pocketbooks now and then but have no idea who sends them. So thank whoever sent them. Look dont pay so much attention to the Red +. Theyre not God you know. Hope youre sending lots of candy & things in my personal parcels. How are all the aunts & uncles? All well? Did you go to the P.O.W. lecture one of the boys from here who went home gave? Better send another pair of slippers & a sweat shirt (sports parcel). You know there is nothing to say. I can hardly fill this sheet up. Takes a week to write this. Im getting lots of smokes. So thank everyone. Hope you got the picture I sent. Did you get the Xmas present I sent through the bank to you? Bye for now. Lots of love to all, Albie

---

Sun. Feb. 27, 1944

Little sis Betty turns 18 today. Hope she's having a swell day with her friends. I'm glad she's far from this war.

Mon. Feb. 28, 1944

We tried making a cake for tea from biscuits but it was a flop. Flatter than a pancake & hard as a rock. The biscuits are kind of like the soda ones we have back home but round, half inch or so thick & about 4 inches across. Crushed them up fine to make flour & added Klim, sugar, raisins & enough water to make a glop. Baked it & mixed up some condensed milk we traded from a Brit food parcel with goon jam & to put on top. Helped a bit. We ate it anyway, couldn't afford not to. One of the boys said we need baking powder to help it rise. I'll ask Ma to send some in my next parcel.

Tues. Feb. 29, 1944

Thanks to a leap year, an extra day in this joint. Just what I need.

Wed. Mar. 1, 1944

More snow – 6 in or so. Morning appell took a long time. Kept us waiting around while they checked & counted & it was darn cold. Then extra goons showed up with Rubberneck. They moved from group to group calling out names & pulling the lads out. Then marched them all off the parade ground & out of sight. We heard later they've been purged to the camp at Belaria 5 km down the road. 19 or 20 of them. We figure the goons were afraid they were plotting something big. Even if they were this won't stop it.

With room searches heating up, and Tunnel Harry ready to go, Big X was ready to set a break date. He had several criteria in mind: wind to drown out any noise, and decent weather and a moonless night to aid travel. His preliminary shortlist was March 23rd, 24th or 25th. He estimated that 220 men at best could make it out, just over one third of those involved in building the tunnel in one way or another. X and his key men selected 70 names from those who had done the most work, particularly those who spoke German. Another 130 names were drawn randomly from a hat. Big X himself selected the final 20. The order in which they were drawn determined the order in which they would go out.[6]

Thurs. Mar. 2, 1944

Received several letters today. Ma has the idea this joint is like summer camp or a country club or something & we're all frolicking around in swimming pools & eating big & sitting around listening to the radio. If only. Where does she get these ideas? The German propaganda machine is even more powerful than I thought.

Getting the gen

The BBC's V-For-Victory campaign, used successfully by the Belgians in 1941, asked listeners to use the V-sign as a rallying cry for an Allied victory. It was contagious, and Vs were cropping up everywhere across occupied Europe. Prime Minister Winston Churchill made the sign his trademark.[7]

177

Mar 3rd, 1944
Dear Ma,

Received some mail of yours, El, cousin Dorothy, Uncle Al, Dorothy Sproule & Loblaws. Also Aunt Rae. Glad to hear from everyone. Good to hear youre all well and have nothing more than colds. The tank we have here is not a swimming pool. Its a fire tank. Well everything is the same here. The weather is cold, snow, ice & slush. This joint is desolate & grim but shouldn't take over a year to finish off things now. Mar 4th: Got 3 letters today. One from Aileen. Everything is all washed out now. Now one from Aunt Jean, a Xmas card and 1 from Wynne in England. I hear youre writing to her. Well she is a nice gal. I like her. You had better thank Loblaws for the books & games they send. Ma when I ask for something to be sent in my letter send it at once if possible. Dont wait for a few months to do it. Am receiving lots of smokes. Should be playing ball in a month or two. Tell El to thank Nadine for her letters. Theyre interesting. So youve invested my money. Well I hope youre getting at least 3 per cent on it. Heres some stuff to send. Baking powder, onion salt, lots of bulk, hard candies, Xmas candies. Say hello to everyone for me. I cant write everyone. Send some good books, not pocketbooks. Bye for now.
Lots of love, Alb

Fri. Mar. 3, 1944

More letters today including a Xmas card & parcel from Loblaws. It's either nothing at all or all at once. Word has come down that the Germans aren't delivering any mail from home with a V for Victory on it. They consider it propaganda & they oughta know. Looks like Aileen finally got the message. Says she wouldn't marry me now anyway. I'm sorry to hurt her but I didn't know if I was coming or going when I was in Halifax. I'm a different person now. Tells you something when the highlight of my day, week & month is writing to my mother. Watched a USAAF formation fly over today. It's the first Allied bombers we've actually seen in daylight. Probably coming out of a raid.

Monday Mar. 6, 1944

Got called to hut 109 late yesterday for penguin duty again.

It's been awhile. Harry's been back in business & Dick must be full. Wasn't sure what we'd be able to do with the ground still frozen & covered in snow. Then I found out. Was told to load up & go see "Arsenic & Old Lace" at the theatre last night & sit in seat 13 in the back row. Told to light up a smoke too on account of the distinct smell of the sand in a confined space. During the show a trapdoor quietly opened under my feet. I didn't hear it, just suddenly felt my feet dangling. That was my cue to let go of my load. Thank God it was dark so no one could see how nervous I was. Big daylight raid on Berlin today.

Wed. & Thurs. Mar. 8/9, 1944

Berlin bombed heavily again in daylight & we felt the buildings shake. American Forts. We saw the sun glinting off them & we cheered.

Tues. Mar. 14, 1944

Made a pot out of 9 biscuit tins I scrounged.

Sat. Mar. 18, 1944

Haven't seen a fresh vegetable in months not that those Swedes can be called fresh or a vegetable as far as I'm concerned. As for fruit, I've forgotten what it even looks like.

Thurs. Mar. 23, 1944

Getting milder but still 6 in of snow on the ground.

Tunnel Harry was ready to go as far as distance was concerned. All that remained was to dig the short exit shaft. Intense preparations had been going on in the X Organization to manufacture the necessary support for some of the men going out: fake names and background stories, forged identification, clothes and props, maps, compasses, money, food. Others would take their chances "hardarsing" it cross country. Based on the mild weather, and the poor odds of Harry going undiscovered until the next moon-free period, the X men decided the night of March 24th would be it. It was now or never.[8]

Fri. March 24, 1944

This is it. Word went around today like wildfire. Very tense with everyone trying to act normal. The boys who are going out

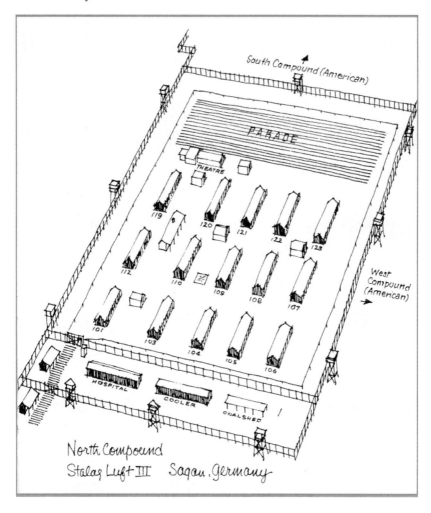

are spending the night in 104. After last appell they very quietly moved in & the ones who live in 104 but are not going bunked in elsewhere. There are supposed to be over 200 going out. At least it's mild out, for now anyways.

Sat. March 25, 1944

Couldn't sleep. A raid on Berlin around midnight scared me good. The goons would have cut the power as usual. Hope that didn't affect the plan. Around 05:00 hours I heard a single rifle shot. I figured the jig must be up & one of the lads must've been shot. We leapt out of bed & took turns pushing open a crack in the shutters to watch as all hell broke loose in the compound. Something had happened. Wasn't long before the goons were all running around frantically & shouting but obviously didn't know which hut was the culprit. But then they must've seen some of the lads jumping out the windows of 104. Took awhile but next thing the Hund Fuhrer was racing to 104 with his dog. Around 06:00 hours what seemed like the whole Wehrmacht poured into the compound all wearing helmets & carrying machine guns. They surrounded 104 with machine guns mounted on tripods & tommys. It was very tense & looked like they were going to mow everyone down as they pulled the lads out of the hut, searched them & stripped them down. It was snowing hard. The Kommandant & Rubberneck & all his men were there with their pistols drawn & cocked. They looked like they were ready to explode. A goon showed up with the ID card trays to find out who was missing by process of elimination. They started with 104 & then went from hut to hut, man by man. It took a LONG time & was deadly serious. No antics today. I was really nervous as they studied the picture on my card & matched it to my face & I didn't even do anything wrong. They finally let us go back to our huts except for the 104 group who had to continue standing out in the cold under armed guard. Everyone knew the cooler wouldn't hold them all & eventually Pieber just dismissed them. I hope the lads who got out had enough time to get a decent head start. I wonder how many? We heard later that Charlie was the only ferret willing to crawl into the tunnel from the exit so they could find the entrance. But then he couldn't get out because the trap was closed & no one but the tunnel & X guys even knew which room the trap was in. We heard later that Red Noble took pity & let him out. Didn't matter by then anyway. Red & Shag Rees lipped off to Rubberneck as usual & almost got shot for their trouble. Rubberneck ordered them stripped. He was just itching for a reason to pull the trigger. Kommandant ordered them to the cooler. There'll be a big price to pay.

Sun. March 26, 1944

It's like doom in the compound now that the Kommandant must know how many are missing. We heard the SS arrested him.

Heard a few more details about last night. The operation slowed down when the lights went out in the air raid. Means Harry's got electric lights! How the hell did they do that? Must have been pretty scary with no lights. Even better, it's outfitted with an air ventilation system made of trusty old Klim cans & an actual railway. Then they had a few cave ins that stopped everything until they could be repaired. But the main problem was that Harry surfaced a good 15 ft SHORT of the woods outside the north wire & within 30 ft of a goon box! The boys must have about had a heart attack when they realized & had to figure out a new plan. Even so that means Harry is over 300 ft long. Incredible. And the Kommandant must also know that Harry runs right under the vorlager too. Talk about rubbing his nose in it. At least we know our bed boards went to an engineering masterpiece.

Word on the circuit is that only 76 are unaccounted for. I'm sure the air raid didn't help. Things obviously didn't go as planned but at least it looks like the 76 are GONE. Johnny C's number was too far down the queue so he didn't make it out. 4 boys were caught at the exit & thrown in the cooler. We heard the SS arrested the Kommandant & he had a heart attack. He'll be court-martialed for sure. He's always acted decently toward us & I actually feel sorry for him.

Mon. March 27, 1944

Very quiet around here. We now have 3 or more appells a day, the theatre is closed, all classes are cancelled, no mail in or out, no intercompound sports, no Red + parcels, no nothing. But could be a lot worse.

In a disastrous attack on Nuremberg, Germany March 30/31, Bomber Command suffered its heaviest losses of the entire war. From the 795 aircraft sent out, 95 failed to return after being heavily attacked by German night-fighters.[9]

Fri. Mar. 31, 1944

Still like a morgue around here. Big search of the whole compound this morning by the Gestapo. Some of the escapers were caught & are now in the cooler. They must have been the last ones out so they didn't get too far. We heard there are others being held by the Gestapo. A lot of worried faces around here. I hope the Luftwaffe is still in charge of this dump – better the devil you know or whatever that expression is. At least that means we're protected by the Geneva Convention. News report of a major raid on Nuremberg & HUGE Bomber Command loss, the biggest yet. Must be hundreds dead. It's all bad news. We heard a new Kommandant arrived - Oberst (colonel) Braune. No one

I know has seen him yet. Apparently the Gestapo searched the other compounds after they left ours.

Sat. Apr. 1, 1944

Heard a good story about the Gestapo search yesterday. Some of them had taken off their overcoats & hats & left them at the door of the hut they were searching. Everything in their pockets was pilfered. I gotta hand it to the boys who were crazy enough to do it.

Sun. Apr. 2, 1944

Still surprisingly quiet around here. No major reprisals against us to speak of. We found out the Gestapo executed the camp electricians who were responsible for all the wire that ended up lighting Harry. Ruthless. We have to be frugal using the light in our room now. After all the light bulbs that went into Harry you can be sure we'll never see another one.

Tues. Apr. 4, 1944

Don Middleton is being repatriated, lucky bugger, tho for the life of me I can't figure out why. It's just not that easy. Must be medical but he's not saying. That's the only way anyone seems to get out of here. He's not even round the bend so far as I can tell anyway but he's been a prisoner for over 3 yrs starting out at Colditz Castle so I guess he's paid his dues. I'd give all the dough in the world to be out of here. Mail is finally moving again. It's about time. Bunch of letters arrived all from December & January. Ma must have told everyone I need cheering up. A parcel from home & another one from Loblaws. Red + parcels back in business too. Some new records at last although we're not really in the music playing mood. We must have listened to Bing croon the same song a thousand times by now. Mom says all my letters & postcards have a Canadian censor's stamp on them & I know the goons censor everything too. It's laughable to me. What on earth I could possibly say in a letter to my mother that would be worth censoring is beyond me. Maybe they think I'm writing in code!

April 4/1944
Dear Ma,

Dear Ma, Received your Dec. clothing parcel. It was very good. Thank you also for the blanket. How about trying to get someone to send some American smokes and food parcels if possible. Now here is something you can send, a medicine parcel. Aspirins, bandages, scissors, iodine, adhesive tape, Mentholatum and other salves. Dont forget some hard candy as well as chocolate in personal parcel. Tell Betty to thank her girlfriend Adele for writing but sorry I cant write her. Not enough forms. That was a good sweater in the parcel. Thank Loblaws. Thank Fran Mitchell, Rolys sister, and Roly, Aunt Rae, D. Sproule for letters. Am writing to everyone I can as my forms last. Well, Im still living and in good health but thats about all. What horrible weather we get here here

Find out the name of the Canadian censor D.B. 405 who censors all my mail. Id like to meet him after the war to take a swing at him. Well, received a lot of mail last month. Say hello to everyone for me. Keep your chins up. Every day brings it one day closer to an end. Thats what I have to put up with in my letters. Bye. Love Alb

Wed. Apr. 5, 1944

The theatre is open again but 104 is still closed & all the lads are still bunked in other huts until further notice. When we opened our latest Red + food parcels we saw the goons had punctured every tin apparently in case we're thinking of storing food for escape rations. Great. Everything will be covered in blue mould in no time. We'll just scrape it off & eat it anyway. We can't afford to waste anything but no one wants to get sick either. It'll be a week of good eating that's for sure. Some of the lads have made a volleyball court. Vballs from the YMCA.

The men of north compound were about to go into shock. The story goes that Hans Pieber entered the compound to invite G/C Massey, the Senior British Officer, to a meeting with the Kommandant. Apparently Pieber would not reveal the reason for his visible upset, saying only that there was terrible news. Following the meeting, word went around quickly that the senior officer from each room was to report to the theatre immediately.

Thurs. April 6, 1944

Unbelievable news came down today from the SBO. The new Kommandant called him to a meeting & read him a statement from the German High Command saying that 41 of the boys who made it out of Harry had been shot for resisting arrest or trying to escape again after being captured. None wounded, ALL DEAD. How likely is that? None of the lads would resist arrest – everyone knows it would be pointless. Why not just come out with it & say they were executed. Murdering bastards. Some of the lads don't believe it & think it's a hoax to stop the escaping & that the escapers are all being held at some special camp. I don't know what to think but it's different here now. Very scary goon attitude. No names yet & a list is supposed to be coming. Does that at least mean the rest of the 76 are safe or just that they're next? Since when was escaping punishable by death? What about the Geneva Convention? A black cloud is hanging over the compound. We are all in mourning for whoever they are although we know who's missing. Apparently none of them wore their ID tags. All the perimeter huts stripped & searched tonight including us. Another mess to clean up.

Friday April 7, 1944

The goons seem just as stunned by the news as we are. They are distancing themselves from it & saying the Luftwaffe had nothing to do with it & that it's a Gestapo matter. To make us feel better they're whispering to us that the escape is creating havoc across Germany. They say that Hitler put out a national security alert. The Germans are searching every train & warning the public on radio that dangerous escapees are at large! I don't care what the goons say. They're all Germans & some of our lads are still dead.

Sat. April 8, 1944

We heard a special gift of billy tins came in from the Cdn Red +. Good thing since my pot making attempts have not been too good & we can at least cook it in its own tin.

Sun. April 9, 1944

Looks like the goons have been told to take a harder line with us now. They're shooting at anyone who breaks the rules. Air raid sirens went off this aft & we saw USAAF bombers flying over. They give us such hope. We all cheered & the goons weren't very happy about it. New orders are that any time we hear the siren we're to return to our barracks immediately, shutter up & stay there until we hear the all clear. Otherwise we risk being shot at by the sentries without warning. There's still no air raid protection for us. They won't even let us dig our own trenches, although in this sand they'd have to be shored up with wood planks & we all know the odds of the goons sanctioning that. Memorial service today for the 50. We're all wearing anything we have that's black to show our respect.

POSTKARTE
April 10th, 1944
Dear Ma,

Well everything bad here. Hope youre all well. One of the boys in our room is being repatriated. He is leaving shortly. His name is Don Middleton, F/Lt. His home is in Brandon, Manitoba. On his way home he should be going through Toronto. Youll see by the newspapers when hes coming. Try & see him or if not, write him. He will give you all the gen on Luft 3.   Lots of love, Alb

---

Mon. April 10, 1944

Another bed board levy. Means there's something new going on. So soon after Harry. My palliasse is already sagging through the empty spaces. Hardly any bed left. Soon I'll be sleeping on the floor. And if I live long enough I'll for sure have a bad back.

Tues. April 11, 1944

The air raid sirens went off again this aft & a huge USAAF formation flew over us. After we got the all clear we came out to see a lot of black smoke rising very high to the west of us. With Harry out of the picture now there's a lot more guys with time on their hands so a lot of baseball practice going on. The season is set to open on schedule this weekend although still no intercompound games allowed. There was an Arts & Crafts show today. Some pretty impressive things. Johnny C. entered one of his clocks.[10]

Wed. April 12, 1944

We heard an American was shot & killed by a guard yesterday in south compound during the air raid because he stood in the hut doorway to watch the raid instead of going inside. Poor bugger. The goons refuse to issue the billy tins from the Canadian Red + because they think we'll use them to store escape rations. What a waste.

Thurs. April 13, 1944

300 cigarettes today from the Canadian Overseas League.

Fri. April 14, 1944

Woke up this morning to hear Berlin being bombed again. Bruce Lowe has taken Don's place in our room. Canadian chap. More of the escapers were brought back to the camp today from Gorlitz prison (Gestapo). They say they were treated very poorly as civilians because they were not in military dress when they were captured. Bad sign. I've heard they make civilians just "disappear". The bed situation is getting dangerous. Guys in the top bunks are crashing regularly now onto the poor bugger sleeping below. Sure hope I don't have a late night drop in visit from Joe.

Sat. April 15, 1944

Baseball season is officially open today! Late this aft one of the goons quietly posted a piece of paper on the notice board. One of our lads realized it was a list of names & word went around quickly for us all to gather. He read out the names & it was somehow more real & horrible for hearing their names. An awful list. Then someone counted & it turned out to be 47 not 41 like they said. More line shooting. Why aren't we hearing anything about this on the BBC? How long can Hitler hide 47 cold blooded murders from the world??? Maybe they're bluffing. I don't feel safe here any more. We're all nervous.

On the subject of punishment of prisoners of war, the 1929 Geneva Convention states:

> Article 50: "Escaped prisoners of war who are re-captured before they have been able to rejoin their own armed forces or to leave the territory occupied by the armed forces which captured them shall be liable only to disciplinary punishment.[11]

> Article 51: "Belligerents [Germany] shall ensure that the competent authorities exercise the greatest leniency in considering the question whether an offence committed by a prisoner of war should be punished by disciplinary or by judicial measures. This provision shall be observed in particular in appraising facts in connexion with escape or attempted escape.[12]

> Article 54: Imprisonment is the most severe disciplinary punishment which may be inflicted on a prisoner of war. The duration of any single punishment shall not exceed thirty days.[13]

Sun. Apr. 16, 1944

Looks like the goons have now inspected Harry every which way. I'm sure they're trying to come up with a way of destroying it without humiliating themselves again after the Tom fiasco last year that we are still laughing about. We watched as they carried a hose from the honey wagon into 104 & turned on the pump. They must be trying to flood the entry shaft in the tunnel room. Then they carried in loads of sand & concrete to seal the top I guess. Later we heard them blow up the exit shaft. And that's the end of Harry. Rubberneck is still around so he must've done some fast talking with the Gestapo to save his own skin.

Mon. Apr. 17, 1944

Pretty bleak around here. G/C Massey was repatriated to England on account of his injured leg. Now at least we know the truth will be told. He's lucky to be getting out of here although I'm glad to have all my original parts. G/C Wilson is now the SBO for the whole camp in addition to north compound.

Tues. Apr. 18, 1944

Hut 104 is open again. Another USAAF daylight raid. The air raid siren went off & the goons ran around chasing us into our huts so we couldn't see the bombers flying over. But they can't close the shutters fast enough to stop us from looking.

> **POSTKARTE**
> *18th April, 44*
> *Dear Ma,*
>   *Nothing doing here anymore than usual. The place is like an abattoir. I've just about worn out that pair of running shoes. Better send a couple more pairs. Size 8. Got a couple of records. Don't know who sent them, but thank them. Also Loblaws for more books. Have had no mail this month. Well this is all for now. Say hello to everyone for me. Bye.*   *Love Abb*

Wed. Apr. 19, 1944

Woke up to Berlin getting it again.

Fri. Apr. 21, 1944

Another early morning raid on Berlin.

Fri. Apr. 28, 1944

Heard from El that another of the lads from my AG training class is gone – Ed Webb. His whole crew killed on an op to Leipzig in Feb.[14]

Sat. April 29, 1944

Went to a concert at the theatre last night. I'm not a symphony kind of fellow but this was a full orchestra conductor & all. Music was good.

Tues. May 2, 1944

Dreamed last night about being home again. I could even smell the bacon & eggs & toast & marmalade for breakfast. And coffee, GOOD coffee. Hard to believe I've been here for almost a year now. The so called second front must be a figment of my imagination or something.

Thurs. May 4, 1944

Windy today. Like a dust bowl around here. Things still tense.

Mon. May 8, 1944

Strange change in the weather today. Really cold. Almost a winter day.

April 25th, 1944
Dear Ma,

After no mail for a month, I received 18 letters this A.M. from 10 different people. If you are speaking to any of them you can thank them. Heres who. El, Betty, Aunt Rae, H. Mowatt, Nadine, D. Sproule, Velma Roberts, 1 from Aileen and some from W. Hands. The latest mail Ive had from Toronto is Mar. 8th. Ive received quite a few smokes from all. I dont play bridge Ma, that's a social climbers game but I may learn yet. I received the blanket, which came late. Its still cold so its very handy. Dont spend your own money on stuff you send. Spend mine. Got books from Loblaws. Thank them also for bonus. Snaps are very good. Glad you got the one I sent. This is to El. I dont know why you always tell me not to worry about marriage and things of that nature. I dont intend to get married for a long time yet. Unquote. When youre sending my personal parcel include lots of dehydrated stuff. Corn, onions, bananas also as well as chocolate, hard candy. Weather is foul here. In a card to Aunt Rae I asked her to tell you to send a couple of items in a parcel. I got 2 records from someone. I dont know who. Thank them if you know who it is sent them. I dont know why you have sent swim trunks. Theres no pool. Youre letting the Red + make a sucker out of you. The gen they push out is mostly baloney. Well Ma lots of love to everyone. Doubt if well be out this year. Bye.

Love Alb

Wed. May 10, 1944

Received 300 smokes today.

Friday May 12, 1944

A year ago tonight we were shot down. Seems like a lifetime ago. I'm not the same man.

Mon. May 15, 1944

I actually saw a woman today out in the vorlager. I thought I was seeing things but when all the wolf whistles started I figured she must be the real McCoy – a censor or secretary. First woman I've seen since leaving England other than the ones in our theatre & they don't count! I bet she never had so many admirers in her life.

Thurs. May 18, 1944

One of the goons posted another list on the notice board today. Just 3 names on it this time – Krol, Long & Tobolski. I didn't know them. That brings the number up to a nice even 50. Don't tell me that's a coincidence. R.I.P boys & may the Nazi bastards that did this rot in hell. Received another cigarette parcel.

On May 18, 1944, the BBC announced "The Polish flag is flying over the ruins of the ancient Italian monastery which has been a symbol of German resistance since the beginning of the year. Polish troops entered the hill-top abbey this morning, six days after the latest attacks began on this strategic stronghold at the western end of the German defensive position known as the Gustav Line. British troops have taken control of the fortified town of Cassino at the foot of the "Monastery Hill". The Allies' hard-fought victory comes four months after their first assault on Monastery Hill failed in January."[15]

Fri. May 19, 1944

At least there was some good news out of Italy yesterday. The Allies took control of Monte Cassino.

Sat. May 20, 1944

Finally the world is finding out what really happened here. It's about time. The BBC reported that Anthony Eden the Minister of Foreign Affairs told the British House of Commons 47 British & Allied Air Force officers have been shot by the Germans after a mass escape from Stalag Luft 3. Apparently the German authorities gave this information to a Swiss inspector during a routine visit to the camp on 17th April.[16] That's a month ago!!!! It said 76 officers had escaped from Stalag Luft 3 on the 25th March. Of the 76, 15 had been recaptured, 14 were still at large and 47 had been shot, some while resisting arrest & some trying to re-escape after being captured." Same story the Kommandant gave G/C Massey. Resisting arrest my arse. They don't even know yet that it's 50 not 47. Probably because an even 50 would be pretty coincidental if not downright unbelievable.

Sun. May 21, 1944

Feeling pretty cheesed off with the world today. Maybe we're not even going to win this war & then who knows what will happen to us. Laid around with a book & wrote to Ma (again). Probably shouldn't write her when I feel like this.

Clearly, the mood at Stalag Luft III was getting the better of Dad. His frustration and loss of optimism came through loud and clear in the tone of the following letter. My poor grandma.

Tues. May 23, 1944

Received another 300 smokes from Mrs. Baird. Bless her heart. Always looking out for me.

Thurs. May 25, 1944

Of the 76 who got out, 50 are dead, 15 have been returned to the compound. Leaves 11 that no one seems to know anything

> *May 21st, 1944*
> *Dear Ma,*
>
> *Nothing new in this hole. Hope youre all well. I am in the best of health. This letter will be inclined to be bitchy on account of several things. The running shoes you sent are worn out after I wore them for 1 month. I have been waiting for sports & games parcels & records of which I am afraid Ill wait in vain cause you dont send anything I ask for. You must think the war is going to end this year. I hope youre putting lots of food, chocolate & hard candy in my personal parcels. If you ever get a chance to send any extra food parcels send them. If any of my dear relations or friends tell you theyd like to do something for me, you tell them okay. Alb says to send sports parcels. This second front or invasion that is supposed to be coming is slower in getting here than the second coming of Christ. You must think by the way I carry on in letters that Im crazy, maybe I am, and very ungrateful*
>
> *Say hello to Dad, Betty & El, give them my love. Dont work too hard. Itll all be over in 5 or 10 years.   Love Alb*

> **Undated, but postmarked May 24, 1944**
> Dear Ma,
>   Youre all in good health I hope. Well I doubt very
> much we will be out of here this year so heres what I want
> for the winter. A good pair of leather mitts with fleece lining
> and some heavy socks, army issue. I wish you would put 2
> packets of tooth powder in my parcel. Also lots of chocolate,
> some hard candy and all the dehydrated foods possible and
> tea coffee & sugar. I suppose you figure that I bitch a lot in
> my letters. But we hear in letters from Canada that the Red
> + tells you what a beautiful place this is and all there is to
> do. Well thats enough to make any of us mad cause its a
> lot of phooey. I told you last summer I gained some weight.
> Well I must have been loony. I havent. I have a lot more
> gray hair now. Things here dont make my temper very good
> so if I let loose at you in a letter dont take it to heart too
> much. Tell Eleanor to try and keep track of most of the boys
> in my course and let me know whats what with them. Well
> Ma say hello to everyone for me, bye for now. Love Alb. Hi
> Dad, Betty & El. More news in your letters please.

about or is saying anyway. We pass a lot of time speculating & wishing home runs for them. Heard today that the ashes of 29 of the lads arrived back at the camp in urns. Very convenient that cremation covers up how they died.

May 26, 1944
It's 1 year ago today I arrived here. Longest year of my life though I guess I shouldn't speak too fast.

Mon. May 29, 1944
Daylight bombing again today. Chased into our huts again but not before we saw 50 or more Forts pass over us. Very tiny they were so high. We keep waiting for an invasion that never comes.

Tues. May 30, 1944
Playing lots of baseball. Still no intercompound games. G/C Wray (Larry) has joined our team. Canadian fellow shot down in March. He's now the senior RCAF officer in the compound. Very friendly, no airs about him. A bat got broken today & Johnny is going to make a mallet out of it. Nothing goes to waste around

May 28th, 1944
Dear Mom,
      This is the 3rd letter I have written you this month. Hope you are all well. I received a sports parcel the other day. It contained 1 softball, a sweatshirt, a pair running shoes, deck of cards, 1 or 2 records. I dont know who sent it. The fellow who picked it up for me thinks it was from you so if you sent it thanks a million. Just got here in time. The other running shoes were worn out. How about writing Aunt May in the States and telling her to send some ciga-rettes here. I like American smokes. I am pretty thorough-ly fed up with this war. I have never seen such miserable weather in my life as what they get here. I had hopes of all of us being out of here by Xmas but have lost them now so keep sending stuff. Dont load my personal parcel up with clothes. Try and make it all food and candy. Say hello to anyone thats interested. I would like a new pr of pajamas. Dont forget socks, heavy socks. I have a little garden here about half as big as our veranda but I dont think anything will grow cause its all sand. Well lots of love. Bye. Alb

here. Heard the goons found clothes & tools & I don't know what all else hidden in the roof rafters in the abort. Not mine but we'll all pay I'm sure. Great place to hide things though – stinks so bad in there the goons haven't gone looking there til now.

Rome was the first of the three Axis (Germany, Japan and Italy) capital cities to be captured, so its liberation was a symbolic win for the Allies. In a radio broadcast in the United States on the evening of June 5, President Franklin D. Roosevelt announced the fall of Rome with the words, "One up, two to go."[17] The next day was D-Day.

Tues. June 6, 1944

      Gray, drizzly day. Goes well with living under guard & be-hind barbed wire. A good day to feel sorry for ourselves & play cards. What else is new? Good news at least on the war front - Rome was liberated yesterday. As Roosevelt said, 1 down & 2 to go.
      Then after lunch a miracle happened! Everyone was shout-

June 3rd, 1944
Dear Mom,
    Hope you are all well at home. I am fine. The other day I ███████████████████████████
██████████████████ *Well I cant see any possible hope of our leaving here this year so send off those leather mitts I asked for and another blanket. I imagine that everything you send me you pay for yourself. I want you to stop paying for it and take it out of my account. And anything you send I dont want nothing but the best. I asked you to send a pipe last year sometime but I never got it. Put several packages of dehydrated onions in my next parcel. It will sure be nice to get out of here and start living again. You better always have lots of food in the cupboard when I get back. I never want to go hungry again. Got some smokes from Mrs. Baird the other day. Thank her for me. If you send any more sweatshirts, dont send white. It gets dirty too easy and I do all my own clothes washing so you see how it is. Well, this is it for now. Bye. Love to all, Alb*

ing & running out to the cookhouse to listen to the German news. THE ALLIED INVASION OF EUROPE FINALLY HAPPENED. We'd all but given up hope for it, or I had anyway. 1 British, 1 Canadian & 2 US armies landed in Normandy France. That's all we know yet. Liberation must be just around the corner. I'll be home for Christmas after all. After 397 days here (but who's counting) I'm almost afraid to be hopeful. A full moon tonight too. The goons are full of doom & gloom. The writing is on the wall for Germany. Tonight we talked well into the night & planned our return home.

Wed. June 7, 1944
    We celebrated the invasion with a raisin pie. Powdered biscuits into flour, added some marg & made it into a pie shell. Not bad but not like Aunt May's of course.

Monday June 12, 1944
    Another breakfast of Reich lead bread & Red + jam & brew.

Bless the Red +. Can't say it enough. I'll never forget them once this is all over. After lunch we played a game of baseball. G/C Wray & me crashed into each other running to catch a fly ball so neither of us caught it. We lost the game too. Elimination trials all week for the big sports meet next week.

Back at 419 squadron base in Middleton St. George, Canadian P/O Andrew Mynarski, mid upper gunner, would be heading out with his crew in a Lancaster bomber to attack the rail yards at Cambrai, France. They were attacked by a German night fighter resulting in two engine failures, multiple fires and ultimately an order to abandon the aircraft. As Mynarski made his way toward the rear escape hatch to bail out, he saw that the rear gunner, F/O Pat Brophy, was trapped in his turret. Mynarski made his way through the flames and, with an axe, tried to free Brophy. The story goes that Brophy, once realizing the effort was in vain, gestured to Mynarski to save himself. His clothing and parachute on fire, Mynarski went to the hatch, turned to face his crewmate and friend, stood at attention and saluted before he jumped. He was found by French people on the ground, but later died from his severe burns. F/O Brophy miraculously survived the crash of the aircraft. P/O Mynarski was posthumously awarded the Victoria Cross, the highest decoration for military bravery and 6 Group's only Victoria Cross of the war. Brophy passed away in 1991.[18] The axe Mynarski used is on display at 419 squadron in Cold Lake, Alberta.

Tuesday June 13, 1944

The German news is full of bragging about how one of their new secret weapons - the V-1 "Flying Bomb" - actually hit London today & killed civilians. So now Britain has a taste of its own medicine they said. Too bad the barrage balloons didn't stop it. I don't know if there's an A/C that can even shoot it down. It's got me worried. Maybe we won't be out of here by Christmas after all. I can't even imagine another winter here. Everyone's betting again.

Mon. June 19, 1944

Big camp field meet today. Lots of events going on. Art came first in the hop, skip & jump, 2nd in discus, 2nd in cricket ball throw & 3rd in broad jump! Camp Champ! Great Britain team won overall, Canada came 2nd, then New Zealand, South Africa & Australia. BBC report says there's a big memorial service for our 50 boys tomorrow in London.

When I asked, Dad had no recollection of the special gift for his mom that he referred to in the below letter.

> *June 21st/44*
> *Dear Mom,*
>   *Got a letter of yours this morning. Mar 26. You say you havent received any mail from me this year. Thats peculiar cause Ive written plenty. Glad youve sent a kit bag but hope you have put lots of food in as well. Glad the car is okay. Hope you have an easy time when you have your tonsils out. Ive thought of a nice present to give you when I get home but wont tell you now. Im sure you will like it. I received a letter from Aileen yesterday & 1 from D. Sproule today. Well looks like my second birthday coming in a couple of months. Its nothing to look forward to* ████ ████ *Will write Uncle Al and D. Sproule a card as soon as I finish this although I have written them both lately. You know Id give $50 for an apple, orange or banana. I havent tasted a piece of fruit since I left Canada. Love to all, Dad, Betty & Eleanor. Love Alb.*

Wed. June 21, 1944
      Big daylight raid again. Suspended our ball game against Earl Clare's team until it was over. Earl is Canadian, a navigator, shot down in a Lanc on a Berlin raid in January. Got blown out of his A/C – lucky he survived at all. He's from Brechin close to Beaverton like Art. Small world it is. Came all the way to Germany (the hard way) to meet up with guys practically from my own backyard.

Thurs. June 22, 1944
      Heard today that 2 of the lads who made it out of Harry - Norwegians – Rockland & Muller - travelled together & actually made it to England through Sweden. Home runs to freedom! Apparently they had arranged with their roommates to send letters to the camp under fake names if they were successful. Imagine the stories they have to tell. That leaves 9 unaccounted for by my count.

Sat. June 24, 1944

Our news says Anthony Eden told the British House of Commons that the German authorities have now "officially" advised that 50 officers were shot & not 47 as they previously reported. The full truth is finally coming out. The Germans claimed there were so many escapes from all camps in March & so many prisoners at large that "public safety was at risk" requiring them to take "severe action" - or some such rot. But G/C Massey has saved the day. His repatriation has allowed him to tell the world the REAL story. Eden said when the war is over that every one of the German murderers involved will be tracked down wherever they are & brought to justice.[19] We're counting on it.

Thurs. June 29, 1944

Whole compound searched today. Took all day.

Now that Tom, Dick & Harry were all kaput, the new X Organization began building Tunnel George from the theatre in case the day came when the men would need a secret way out of the camp.

Fri. June 30, 1944

Everyone is optimistic that this'll be the summer we finish Germany off. Hard to even comprehend that I could be home for Christmas.

Tues. July 4, 1944

Big exhibition baseball game today – the Challenge Cup match between the American & Canadian All Star teams. The Americans challenged the Canadians to the match. A few of the lads from Earl Clare's team made the Canadian All Star team - Art in the outfield, Earl on 3rd base, Gee Rainville shortstop & Smitty as catcher. G/C Wray was the ump. Bill Paton was the pitcher & you don't mess around with him. He pitched in the Beaches League back home in Toronto. He just knocked those American lads off one after another with his magnificent pitches. The game was over half over before they even got a hit. Huge crowd watched, even the Kommandant. Canadians won!

Thurs. July 6, 1944

New guy in our room - Stuart Hunt. He's a tail gunner from 425 squadron, shot down in April on a Karlsruhe raid. Canadian lad.

> **July 9th**
> *Dear Mom,*
>
> *Got 2 of your letters today. Very glad to receive them. Also got mail from Aunt Rae, D. Sproule, Eleanor, Aunt Jean, Loblaws, Audrey Fry (cant remember her) and Nadine Anderson. Glad to hear from everyone. Have just written Aunt Rae & D. Sproule a card apiece. Yes I have received all the personal boxes so far except for the March one. Hope for it shortly. They have all arrived in good shape. Yes we have a garden outside. Its about as big as the floor space of the bathroom at home. Thanks for sending the 9 records and cigars. I shall wait patiently for them. Thank Aunt Jean for having that sport box from the Sports League sent. I imagine it will be a swell box of equipment. Well Ive really nothing new to say.* ████████████
> ████████ *Say hello to Dad, Betty and Eleanor. Thats all I've got to say this time. Bye.*   *Love Alb*

Sun. July 9, 1944

Huge storm today – lightning & dust all whipped up. Something to see. I'm easily entertained these days.

Mon. July 10, 1944

Poured rain today. Our sorry little garden got drowned.

Thurs. July 13, 1944

Ma's birthday today. She's 52. Hope the family is doing something nice for her. She deserves it. Happy Birthday Mom!

Friday July 14, 1944

Lots of mail in the last few days. It's either a lot all at once or none at all for a while. Received another 300 smokes. Ma's all worried that I've got myself mixed up with fast girls who just want to marry an officer. Either that or I'm a cad. I must've been round the bend to give Aileen & Wynne her address. Who knows what they're writing.

POSTKARTE
July 14th, 1944
Dear Ma,

Got letters from yourself, Aunt Rae, El and Mrs. Steele this A.M. Good to hear from all. How about a total figure of all the dough I got? Dont worry Mom. I dont intend to get married to anyone. Get that? No one. Dont write too many letters to that girl in Eng. She may get ideas. Ill be a lone wolf when I get home. Expect a parcel on Sat., thats tomorrow.   *Love Alb*

Tues. July 18, 1944

The Gestapo were in the compound again today searching everything & everyone. It was obvious even the guards were afraid of them. Just plain clothes, no uniforms. They weren't brutal, just scary types.

Wed. July 19, 1944

Rehashed the Gestapo search today while we bashed 10 or so circuits. Heard they searched the guards quarters looking for contraband. They don't even trust their own people. Get caught with anything & I hear it's off to the Russian front for you. Might as well just kill yourself & get it over with.

Thursday July 20, 1944

Letter from Ma today. She's giving me grief again for not "improving myself" while I'm here. I suppose I could but I haven't the energy or the drive. I'd rather read.

Fri. July 21, 1944

The big news is that an inside German plot to assassinate Hitler with a bomb failed. Too bad but good news for us that his own people are trying to kill him. The goons are a bit tense. They don't want their loyalty under scrutiny.

Sat. July 22, 1944

More speculation on the circuit today about what might happen to us if Germany falls & I don't think there's much doubt any more that Germany is going to fall. It's only a question of time. One rumour has it that we could all end up like the 50. Americans who have come here from Buchenwald say that pris-

G/C Wray & G/C Wilson judging at the camp meet last month

Art at Sports Day – 3rd in broad jump

oners are shot there every day. Mail is taking longer than ever to
get here.

Thurs. July 27, 1944

Good news is that American forces in Normandy broke
through the German line at Avranches. Good moods all round.

July 23rd 44
Dear Mom,
> Received the March personal parcel the other day.
> Cant say as I was exactly too pleased though with the small
> amount of chocolate. Nevertheless thanks very much. Glad
> you have sent the cigars & H. James records. I got 1000
> smokes from the Bloor Businessmen's the other day. Would
> you please thank them. Also some from Aunt Jean. Re-
> ceived a letter from Mrs. Steele, Aunt Rae and Roly a few
> days ago. Glad theyre all well. Look Mom ninety percent
> of the guys in this camp do nothing but sit on their butt
> the same as me. I dont know where you get the idea that
> this is an educational tour for me because I dont intend to
> study or do anything. The only thing I study is the war and
> how much longer we stay in ▐▐▐▐▐▐▐▐▐ However, you
> never know. Bye for now. Love, Alb

More good news about another escaper from Harry – a Dutch
lad named Van Der Stok made it to freedom too through France
& Spain! That's 3 home runs that we know of out of 76 but better
than none given the fate of the 50. Still leaves 8.

In the final tally of the 76 men who escaped through tunnel Harry, 17
were returned to Sagan, 50 were murdered by the Gestapo, 4 were
sent to Sachsenhausen concentration camp, 2 were sent to Colditz
Castle prison camp, also known as the "Bad Boys Camp", and 3 made
it home safely: Rocky Rockland, Jens Muller and Bob Van Der Stok.[20]

Fri. July 28, 1944
Big lightning storm today.

Mon. July 31, 1944
Saw more of the stuff that Johnny has made. Clocks that
actually work. He built up the stove in their room & it's so good
they don't need to use the block kitchen at all any more. It took
120 Klim cans.[21] Pots & pans. Coffee percolator. I don't think
there's hardly anything he can't make. A supreme scrounger
AND craftsman.

On August 1, 1944, the BBC reported that the Polish Home Army had begun a battle to liberate Warsaw, which had been the first European capital to fall to the Germans almost five years earlier. When the Germans began their counter-offensive on August 5, they ordered that civilians be round up and shot. Women were used as human shields for the German tanks. By the time the battle ended 63 days later with a German victory, 200,000 Polish civilians would be dead.[22]

Wed. Aug. 2, 1944

Inoculated for Typhoid today – the whole camp. Heard that my friend Keith Fleming from AG training got the chop back in May. His whole crew too. They were on a daylight anti-sub patrol. He was with 422 squadron. Only 20.[23] Keith was a good guy. We had some fun. Can't be many of our class left.

Sat. Aug. 5, 1944

Baseball game today had to be postponed. Few of us not feeling up to it after our Typhoid shots.

Wed. Aug 9, 1944

Appell earlier than usual today. The goons checked each of us to our ID photo. Took forever considering that most of us (all of us?) sure look a lot worse now than we did when our photos were taken – thinner, more hair, less hair, whiter hair, facial hair, definitely a scruffier lot.

Thurs. Aug. 10, 1944

Received a Dear John letter from Wynne. She's met someone else & is getting married.

POSTKARTE
Aug 2nd 1944
Dear Mom,
Received March personal parcel a few days ago. Today got a sports parcel from you as well. Thanks very much. Have had some mail lately. Glad everyone is well. Things sure look good at this time. I give it about a month or six weeks to end. Got a letter from Audrey Fry. Cant place her at all. Got a letter from Aunt May with picture. She looks good. Bye. Love Alb

Aug 21st 44
Dear Mom,
    Nothing much new here. Things just the same except the ████████████████ *8 in a room* ████ ████████████████████████ *Hope youre all well at home. Im fine. Weather is very hot here. Our team had a ball game this morning and we lost but thats the first one in 4 played that we lost. Sure hope I get the H. James records and the cigars. Cigar with music a pretty good combination. Glad to hear youre socking my dough in bonds. They pay better interest than the bank. Well, how is the garden at Bolsover? Good crop this year? I hope Ill be able to help you plant the one next year. Im sure looking forward to a good feed of bacon, eggs, coffee, toast & marmalade when I get home, so have lots in the icebox. Love to all. Bye for now.*
                            Alb

Tues. Aug. 15, 1944

More boys are pouring in here all the time & we're running out of space. There are now 8 of us in the room – 7 Canadians & 1 American - & it's crowded. Carpenters came in & built more bunks. Triples now. We had to move our lockers out into the hall to make room. Jim Crider is from Tennessee. Dave Stubbs is from Barrie. He flew in the same crew as Stu but was off sick the night Stu & crew were shot down. Just a matter of time.

Wed. Aug. 16, 1944

Saw "Palina Panic" at the theatre. Pretty good. Ball game today. We won.

Mon. Aug. 22, 1944

Our new American roommates told us stories about landing their Forts in Russia to refuel. They said the Germans have this mine called a Bouncing Betty. Small spring-loaded affair that fires shrapnel when it's triggered. Designed to inflict serious damage. They said the Russians were kicking them around the airfield for fun just to watch them explode. Meantime our guys took cover in the slit trenches! Crazy. Then they said the Germans flew over the next day & bombed all the A/C they'd flown in on. Who knows if it's true or not. Lot of line shooting around

POSTKARTE
21st Aug 1944
Dear Ma,
No letters for some time now. We now have ▬▬▬▬
▬▬▬▬▬▬▬▬▬▬▬▬▬▬▬▬▬ *The weather*
has been very good but hellishly hot. The 2 new fellows in
our room are Americans. 1 is from Wisconsin and the oth-
er is a jerk & no good at all. Hope you get this.   Love Alb

here & I think these guys are full of it.

Friday Aug. 25, 1944

News: Paris is liberated after 4 years!

Sat. Aug. 26, 1944

Earl Clare's baseball team won the major league champi-
onship. Pieber was taking team pictures. The goons love these
pictures so Hitler can flash them around & show the world this
place is like summer camp. Ha! Pieber at least is okay for a goon.

Tues. Aug. 29, 1944

It was a soup day today so one of the boys went up at lunch
to fetch it. Bruce was out playing soccer & the rest of us were

22nd Aug 44
Dear Sis, you old Phonus Balonus. How goes it? I am quite
well. Hope you are too. Have had no mail for a month & a
half but guess the war has buggered up the transportation.
Well how long do you say now? I say a few months. I think I
have about all the pictures you have sent and theyre pretty
good. Nadine and you look very much alike. Not much new
here. The days are getting shorter ▬▬▬▬▬▬ *Can you*
imagine what its like ▬▬▬▬▬▬▬▬▬▬
not so good but I guess the Lord sent us here to try us. Dont
worry. Im not going religious on you. Hows Lloyd? Still a
L.A.C. or is he up to that yet? El this is all for now. Bye. Lots
of love. Your bruzzer Abe

EARL CLARE'S CARDINALS – 1944 Major League champs
Back row: "Gee" Rainville (shortstop from Quebec), Smitty (catcher from Kingston),
Joe Loree (pitcher from Guelph), Stevens (outfielder from Ontario),
Jim Egner (2nd base from South Africa), Jim Lang (outfielder from England),
Bill Ransom (outfielder from Alberta)
Front row: Art Hawtin (1st base & outfielder from Beaverton),
Earl Clare (3rd base & captain from Brechin), Tom Jackson (outfielder from B.C.),
Glenn Gardiner (1st base from Toronto), Ernie Soulier (pitcher from Roseland, Ontario)

OUR TEAM
Back row: Taylor, Osborn (Winnipeg), Scott, Coste (Calgary),
Acheson (Winnipeg), me, G/C Wray
Front row: Pozer (Duck Lake, Saskatchewan), Beaupre,
Soulier (Roseland, Ontario), Tiger McKim (Delhi, Ontario)

hungry so we started eating without him. That's what happens when you're late. As we were slugging it down I felt something in my mouth. I spit it out & next thing the other boys were picking things out of their soup too. Maggots & well-boiled ones at that. That's enough to put you off your lunch. So we decided to play a trick on Bruce. We all poured our soup back in the jug & put it back on the stove. Bruce roared into the room after winning his match & asked what's for lunch. He looked in the jug & couldn't believe how much soup was left for him. None of us said a word. Can't believe he didn't smell a rat. He filled up his bowl & gobbled that soup down without noticing a thing. Even went back for more. We all had to leave the room. Fast.

Sun. Sept. 3, 1944

Our news is that British Second Army liberated Brussels & Antwerp, Belgium after 4 years of German occupation.

Tues. Sept. 5, 1944

We're cut to half Red + parcels. I'm hungry already just thinking about it.

Thurs. Sept. 7, 1944

The goons have put up propaganda posters warning us that THE ESCAPE FROM PRISON CAMPS IS NO LONGER A SPORT! It accuses England of illegal warfare, gangster commandos & other malarkey. Says Germany has created "death zones in which all unauthorized trespassers will be immediately shot on sight." But the best part is where it says "Germany has only punished recaptured prisoners of war with minor disciplinary punishment." All lies. But I don't know why anyone is still trying to escape anyway. It's useless. The war is going our way & it's only a matter of time before it's all over & we're on our way home. Just survive until then.

Fri. Sept. 8, 1944

Our news is that the Germans launched some kind of missile weapon on London.

This was the first V2 rocket launched against Britain. It was launched from The Hague and landed in Chiswick, killing three and wounding 17.[24]

Sat. Sept. 9, 1944

Happy Birthday to me. 24 today & feeling pretty old. Never thought I'd see a second birthday in this joint. Very little mail these days.

Mon. Sept. 11, 1944

Another daylight raid today.

Tues. Sept. 12, 1944

Saw several formations of American Forts flying over again today.

Wed. Sept. 13, 1944

American First Army troops invaded Germany from the west!

The Battle of Arnhem was a massive joint land-airborne operation that marked the beginning of the airborne invasion of Holland. The total amount of men in the initial drop was more than 16,500 paratroops along with 3,500 troops in gliders.[25]

Sun. Sept. 17, 1944

Our news is of a huge Allied air invasion in Holland today. Lancs & Forts cleared the way for paratroopers. They said the sky was filled with thousands of parachutes. Let's hope this is the beginning of the end.

Tues. Sept. 19, 1944

Dreaming again about my first day back home. Breakfast will be bacon & eggs, soft white bread toasted, marmalade & plenty of real coffee. And a banana.

Fri. Sept. 22, 1944

You know that something very unnatural has happened in your life when you're only 24 & you think & talk about food more than girls. That's all we did on the circuit today. A form of self torture under the circumstances.

Tues. Sept. 26, 1944

The German news today said most of the British near Arnhem withdrew or were captured. So much for the end being in sight.

Sept 26, 1944
Dear Mom
Well, nothing much new here. Weather is cold. We are on half Red + parcels so food is not too plentiful. Glad you liked your trip to Montreal. I guess you were pretty scared when the guy started going over 50 on the takeoff. Well Ive only had 4 letters in over 3 months now. 1 from Nadine, Aileen, Helen Campbell and yourself. So news to me is pretty scarce. Hope youre sending all the chocolate possible in my personal parcel. 3 lbs to be exact. Sorry to hear about Aunt Mary. Hope she gets well soon. How is Betty, Dad, El and all the other relations? All well I hope. We have 2 American boys in our room. Canadians as well ▓▓▓▓▓
Well, this is it for now. Bye. Love to all, Alb

Sat. Sept. 30, 1944

It's gotten bloody cold & some nights it's hard to stay warm. Have to wear my greatcoat indoors sometimes. There's never enough coal for the stove. One of our boys has figured out how to get into the coal room in the cookhouse through the window. Making a plan to liberate some coal. Still on half Red + parcels.

Mon. Oct. 2, 1944

Last night after dark we waited until the Hund Fuhrer & his dog had gone by. We all got our kit bags & sneaked out the window & up to the cookhouse. Had to dodge the searchlights & be quick about it because it was a full moon too. One of the boys opened the window & climbed in. We handed him our kit bags & he filled them with coal & passed them back. We made it back to our room safely & hid some of it in Red + parcel boxes under our bunks. We stacked the rest in behind. All brickettes. Piles beautifully. Must have been crazy.

Tues. Oct. 3, 1944

Joe & Al have finally talked me into learning bridge. It's not my game but I might as well learn…nothing but time to put in since none of us are escape types, not even old-timers like them. Stu plays too. The news is that the Polish Home Army surrendered & the rebellion in Warsaw is over. So much for the Red

Army liberating them. They were out of food, water & ammo. At least they went down fighting.

Wed. Oct. 4, 1944

It was cold again last night & what a fire we had in the stove! The boys coming to visit came in shivering wearing their great-coats & toques & there we were sitting around with our shirt sleeves rolled up warm as bugs in a rug. Of course everyone wants to know our secret so we told them it's on account of the new stove pipe we made from Klim cans & they bought it. Even if we get caught & have to spend time in the cooler it'll be worth it. Some of us in our room aren't getting along too good though but our newcomers have a chance to move to an all American room so they're leaving us shortly. Can't say I'll miss them.

Postkarte
Oct 5th 1944
Dear Sis,

Well have received some letters from you today 2 in fact. Good to get some letters for a change. How was Haliburton and Atherley? I guess you had a good time. We have had a little trouble in our room. One of our new Americans is the dirtiest creature youve ever met. Washes about once a week. But theyre moving this afternoon. Bye for now.
Love Alb

Fri. Oct. 6, 1944

Still on half parcels & I'd even eat brussels sprouts at this point. Never thought I'd say that. Received a parcel from Ma with 50 cigars. 50! They're like pure gold here. I'm going to savour every one.

Sat. Oct. 7, 1944

Received another 300 smokes. The number of cigarettes in this compound boggles the mind. We made another coal run – 6 kit bags full. That should keep us going for a while.

POSTKARTE
Oct 5th 1944
Dear Mom,
I have received the 50 cigars. They are really swell.
Thanks. Have got some mail lately. Hope your throat is
all better now. So you have a new refrigerator. What kind
is it? Glad to hear Swanie is still around. I am anxiously
awaiting the records. Hope theyre not all broken. Eatons &
Simpsons are very bad packers. Well love to all, Alb

The T. Eaton Company Limited, known to most Canadians as simply "Eatons", was a major retail department store founded by Timothy Eaton in Toronto in 1869.[26] Simpsons Limited (Simpsons) was another major Toronto-based retailer founded in 1872 by Robert Simpson.[27]

Tues. Oct. 10, 1944

I think stuff is going missing from my personal parcels. I've thought it for a while now. Ma says she sends it but it doesn't arrive & some of the parcels are definitely lighter than 10 lb. Maybe the X org is helping themselves for escape rations again. Disappointing when there's so little to look forward to as it is. It's a miracle the cigars made it at all. Heard the St. Louis Cardinals beat out the St. Louis Browns in the World Series 4 games to 2.[28]

Wed. Oct. 11, 1944

Looks like our ex-roommates blabbed our coal secret. So the cookhouse coal room is under double attack now. Won't be long before the goons notice the coal level going down faster than usual. I just don't want to get caught & have to do time in the cooler because of them.

Thurs. Oct. 19, 1944

My June personal parcel finally arrived today.

Fri. Oct. 20, 1944

Well the extra coal was nice while it lasted. We went last night for a new supply & found the window padlocked. We're just lucky the goons weren't waiting for us.

> **Oct 13th 1944**
> Dear Mom,
>
> It looks very certain well be here this winter. Thats bad, but anyway I have had about 12 letters in the last few days. I received the cigars a week ago. Theyre really swell. Thanks very much. I havent received the June personal parcel yet but maybe soon. I hope there are a couple of lbs of chocolate in it as well as the hard candy. Glad to hear you have the well in now. That will make things nice. Id like you to put as much chocolate & candy in the parcel as you can. Glad to hear Tommy & Doug O. are still going. Sorry to hear about Frans husband. Oct 19th. Got the personal parcel today. The sunglasses, onion salt, B powder and pipe were not in it. In fact the whole parcel weighed about 7 lbs and I believe you are allowed to send 10lbs or more and all you sent was 1 bar of chocolate. Ma if you send me any more personal parcels please put 3 lbs of chocolate, some hard candy and 2 large tins of tooth powder in it. I dont care what else you put in. Bye.   Love Alb.
>
> The wedge cap fits very nice. Thanks a million.

Mon. Oct. 23, 1944

Aachen has fallen – the first major German city to be captured. Jolly good show.

Wed. Oct. 25, 1944

Another 300 smokes from the Toronto Hamper Fund.

The Caterpillar Club was created in the early 1920s by Mr. Leslie Irvin, after whom the Irving Air Chute Company was named. The club recognized those who had saved their lives with an Irving parachute. The club's name was inspired by the parachute's silk canopy and rigging with a nod to the lowly caterpillar or silk worm that lets itself to the ground by spinning a silk thread. The Caterpillar Club still exists today, and its membership, greatly expanded by the war, spans the globe. Dad received his club membership card and gold caterpillar lapel pin with ruby eyes, engraved with his name and date of jump, following the war.[29] Dad doesn't go anywhere without that pin on his lapel.

Sun. Oct. 29, 1944

Some of the lads are receiving their Caterpillar Club membership cards here. The Irving company runs the club for anyone who has had to make an emergency parachute jump to save their life. That sure includes lots of us here.

Oct 1944

Dear Mom,

Hope you all are well at home. Im fine. Had a couple of letters from El and from Roly also 1 from Loblaws. I just received a sports parcel, 2 records and 1000 cigarettes from Loblaws. You had better phone them up and thank them. I hear you see Alfred & Vince a lot when you are in the country. Has he started bootlegging again? As you can see by the top of the letter I dont know what date it is. I dont bother to keep track any more. About all I know is which month it is. Dont bother trying to look Don Middleton up. He has been home since July. This guy El mentioned, George Coleman, a P.O.W. who used to work for Swifts, sleeps in the same barrack. Doesnt live in the same room though. Well so long for now. *Love to all. Bye. Alb*

P.S. I dont know whether Ill bother to write much this winter, so if you dont hear anything just relax.

Wed. Nov. 1, 1944

G/C Larry Wray is our new SBO.

Wed. Nov. 8, 1944

Went to a show last night. Female impersonators could've fooled me if I wasn't on to them.

Thurs. Nov. 9, 1944

Another 4 year term for President Roosevelt.

Friday Nov. 10, 1944

I'm running out of steam. Winter is coming again. We don't have enough to eat. There's lots of betting on when it's all going to be over. Some think it's soon but I'm not optimistic. Maybe even this time next year.

> *Nov. 4th, 1944*
> *Dear Mom,*
>   *The cold weather has come. Rain, mud and what have you. I received a parcel the other day containing 6 records, 4 books, 1 game, but I dont know who sent it. So when you find out thank them very much especially for the records. Well its a cinch now were here for the winter, spring and next summer probably. We will be lucky if were out of here next year at this same time. Dont stop sending stuff. Keep it coming but please use my money in the bank and buy the best. Send more running shoes, playing cards, sweat shirts, shorts, records, gramophone needles and some books, but not pocket books. Good books, book of the year. Well, glad youre all better after getting your tonsils out. We have been on half parcels for 2 months now* ▮▮▮▮▮▮▮▮▮▮ *I have started playing a little bridge now. Passes time. There are 7 Canucks & 1 American in our room now.* ▮▮▮▮▮▮▮ ▮ *Can you imagine 8 men sleeping, eating and living in a room* ▮▮▮▮▮▮ *Well try to. Lots of love to all. Alb*

Sat. Nov. 11, 1944

   Another Remembrance Day in this joint. Rained the whole day & cold. Lot of the fellows passed the day gambling. I've got better things to do with my dough when I get home, if I get home. I mended some socks & read. Even tho our food is low we voted for a treat of Klim & goon jam spread on biscuits. 2 each.

Sunday Nov. 12, 1944

   Another long winter coming. Heavy frost this morning. Being hungry is bringing out the worst in some of the lads. Mind over matter I say tho it helps that I'm not a big guy to begin with & I'm sure my stomach has shrunk some. Main thing is I have to stay healthy & fit for who knows what's coming next.

After several attacks, the German Navy's battleship Tirpitz, sister ship to the famous Bismarck, was fatally attacked once and for all on November 12, 1944.[30] This was great news for the Kriegies.

Tues. Nov. 14, 1944

A Lanc raid sunk the German's last battleship Tirpitz. Take that Germany! Ma drives me crazy sometimes. She still writes me to ask if I'm thanking people for the stuff they've sent me. Geez.

POSTKARTE
Nov. 16 1944
Dear Mom,

We had our first snow, sleet & slush. Today I received the records you sent in May. Havent got them yet. There still being censored. Hope everyone is well. Im fine. Food is getting scarce here. Better have lots of good food around when I get home. I now play a little bridge to pass time away. Well, this is it. Merry Xmas.   *Love Alb*

Sat. Nov. 18, 1944

The goons are starting to issue our rations one day at a time. They don't want us stockpiling anything. Would be no great loss except that we're still on half Red + parcels too. Another winter & (another) Christmas coming. Pretty depressing.

Sunday Nov. 19, 1944

Our news is that a major Allied offensive has started. Thank God. Still on half parcels. A new batch of records arrived from Ma & Dad. 9 of them! The lads'll be happy. Bing Crosby, Judy Garland, Harry James, Andrews Sisters, Frank Sinatra, Vera Lynn. SWELL!

Tues. Nov. 21, 1944

Locked out all morning. Another search on another miserable day. The goons ordered us to eat any extra rations we have on hand. Something's up.

Fri. Nov. 24, 1944

Berlin bombed again.

> *Nov 19th 1944*
> *Dear Mother,*
> *I got 3 letters the other day, 1 from El, Betty and your-self. Glad to hear youre all well. Sorry about Aunt Mary. That will be swell to have Joe & Mary at the Bolsover store. Yes, Ive sent Loblaws a card for everything. Well everything looks as though well have a swell Xmas here. Our Red Cross food supply runs out in a month. Betty is working for a trust co. now. Guess she likes that. Glad youre fixing Bolsover place up. It should be nice now. I sent you some flowers for Xmas. Hope you get them. Things are just as dull here. I received the 9 records you sent. Thanks very much. Nov. 25th. Thought I'd better finish this before the months out. Well Mom, I cant think of anything more to say. So see you sometime next fall. Love to everyone.*
> *Bye for now. Alb*

Sat. Nov. 25, 1944

Allied drive is going well. Heard Berlin getting hit again. The map room has become a popular place to gather. We all cheer every time the troop line advance is updated.

Mon. Nov. 27, 1944

Berlin hit again.

Wed. Nov. 29, 1944

Sunny today. Frost. Nothing but time on my hands & too much time to think. Read some more. The list of books I've read since I've been here is now quite long – more than I ever read at home. Cold at night with full moon.

Sunday Dec. 3, 1944

Today is El's 26th birthday. Happy Birthday sis. Hope you're having a better day than I am.

Monday Dec. 4, 1944

Funeral service today for the 50 murdered men but it was outside the camp at the cemetery memorial that some of the lads designed & built on the okay of the Kommandant. Only a few senior officers were allowed to go. Was apparently quite the service.

Tues. Dec. 5, 1944

Received 300 smokes today from the POW Relatives Assoc.

Prison camp, with all its time to think, was making Dad quite philosophical about life. He couldn't recall who Alex Mollison was, nor could I find any record of him as a casualty or a prisoner of war.

> *Dec 6th 1944*
>
> *Dear Mom,*
>
> *Dec. is here again. Pretty soon be Xmas. This will be the 3rd Xmas away from home and not one of them has been worth a pinch of you know what. You know Mom in this life we dont live in the present. Here we merely exist. All we live for is the future. I hope Alex Mollison is all right. They sure have had some tough fighting there. Money doesnt mean a thing around here not having had any money since we were shot down. You know that you can sell chocolate (if you have the chocolate to sell) for 30 dollars and up a pound. You wont believe me but its quite true. For a brand new officers uniform you can get about 200 dollars. Naturally liking chocolate as I do I eat all I can get. Tooth powder is a very scarce item. Why dont you put a couple of tins in my parcel. I am thinking of a few improvements for the house at Bolsover which Ill go to work on when I get back. Mom, why dont you give up the house on St. Clarens, get a smaller one and quit work. I dont think you should work at all. Bye for now. Love Alb*

Fri. Dec. 8, 1944

Each of us received a Christmas card from the Prime Minister just like last year. A small personal gift is coming & some books for the compound to share. The best wishes they could possibly send us is that the war is over.

The following letter would be the last that Grandma would receive from Dad until he was liberated on May 2, 1945. It's just as well that

GEPRÜFT
85

Canadians everywhere join me in sending to you heartiest Christmas greetings and the best of good wishes for the New Year.

W.L. Mackenzie King

1944

Prime Minister

she didn't know anything about the conditions the men would have to endure during the two forced marches that would begin the following month.

Thurs. Dec. 14, 1944
　　Snowed today.

Hitler, realizing the war was all but lost, launched a highly secret, last-ditch major offensive into the Ardennes region of Belgium on the western front in an attempt to split the Allied front and recapture Antwerp, a critical port for Allied supplies. The counter-offensive would become known as the Battle of the Bulge in a nod to the shape of the Allied front line on the press report maps. The Allies were caught ill-prepared; however, in the end, "more than a million men fought in the battle, including some 600,000 Germans, 500,000 Americans, and 55,000 British. Churchill called it the greatest American battle of the war which would be regarded "as an ever famous American victory"."[31]

218

Dec 9th 44

Dear Ma,

Thought Id write another letter off as probably all the German censors will be on vacation soon for Xmas. The weather is pretty fair here, cold but clear however well get all the bad weather in Jan & Feb. Well I hope you havent stopped sending stuff cause the war is not over by a long shot. I see everyone had a big optimistic jag in Canada in Aug. & Sept. I was sucked in myself, however never again. I got the pictures of Aunt Mary & you also & Fred. Theyre very nice. Say Ma, Ill have to visit Aunt Dell in New York. Thats not very far. Hope youre sending lots of chocolate and candy ████████████████████████████████

██

████████████████████████████ *I still have a butt of one of the cigars you sent me. Ill smoke it on Xmas day. That will be my Xmas present for this year. Well, give my love to the gals & Dad. Bye for now.   Love Alb*

Sunday Dec. 17, 1944

Huge German counter-offensive in the Ardennes forest to turn back the Allies in the west. Not a good day for us.

Mon. Dec. 18, 1944

Thousands of Americans have been taken prisoner in the Ardennes. The boys flooded the skating rink. Shouldn't take long to freeze at these temperatures. There are skates here from the YMCA. Still on half Red + parcels. Christmas dinner is going to be slim pickings this year. Even brussels sprouts are starting to sound good to me & that says a lot.

Wed. Dec. 20, 1944

Very cold & miserable. Some of the lads went skating on the new rink. Still not a skater myself. Even this boredom can't compel me to risk breaking my neck on skates.

Fri. Dec. 22, 1944

We can hear the sound of Russian artillery getting closer all the time from the east. A Christmas carol to our ears. It's got us all obsessed about what's going to happen next. Will the Germans move us west or move themselves & leave us behind? Or use us as hostages? Would they actually shoot us all? Let's face it, Hitler's already shown the world what he's capable of in that department. Will the Russians liberate us or take over the camp or just leave us here? Will they see us as with or against them? Doesn't look good either way.

Sat. Dec. 23, 1944

Heard talk out on the circuit today that the Russians look on POWs as cowards. Doesn't bode well for us. Each of us received a SMALL amount of Canadian chocolate today from the Prime Minister's Christmas gift. I'm so ungrateful. Ma would say it's the thought that counts...

Sun. Dec. 24, 1944

Watched the first hockey game. We are living for the BBC updates. Morale is very low. After all, it's Christmas again. The sky is quiet at the moment.

Sat. Dec. 25, 1944

Merry Christmas. Like everyone I'm homesick for family, good food, laughs & warmth. The family here is all we have. Shaved specially for the occasion & smoked my last cigar butt. Oh the sweet smell of a good cigar even if it's only a nub. I'll have to hang on to that memory. Like everyone else I'm making a plan. I'm sewing a backpack from an extra goon blanket. I want to be ready when the time comes. Thank goodness I have a pair of spare boots that are in decent shape. Xmas dinner a pretty low key & sorry affair. Not even worth writing about. We passed the time talking about better Christmases gone by & how we'll celebrate next Christmas at home again.

A report written in 1945 by Group Captain D.E.L. Wilson, Senior British Officer, Stalag Luft III, stated:

> "Since June 1944, communication on the Continent of Europe had been so interrupted that for the last four months of that year all prisoners at Sagan had received only half a Red Cross Parcel per week instead of the prescribed whole. Their diet, as

analysed by a reputable nutrition expert, was 1,000 calories per day per head below normal requirements and well below a healthy standard. This included German rations."[32]

Thurs. Dec. 28, 1944

Word around the compound is that the goons are offering us an "opportunity" to join up with them to fight the Russians. Not likely.

Fri. Dec 29, 1944

Full moon tonight.

Sun. Dec. 31, 1944

My 585th day here but I think the end is getting close. It's clear & really cold & there's been snow on the ground for weeks. I'm sleeping in my clothes these nights covered with my great-coat – partly for warmth & partly to be ready to go at a moment's notice. I'm worried about surviving if we have to evacuate. Went to sleep to the sound of guns in the distance. The Russians I hope. May better days lie ahead in 1945.

The First Forced March
January 27 - February 5, 1945

Tues. Jan. 2, 1945

There's a crowd every day at the cookhouse to hear the German news. The news is bad for them but of course they make it sound in their favour. Nothing we don't already know. But their news is already old by the time we hear it & the Russians & Allies are moving fast.

Sat. Jan. 6, 1945

Russians destroyed or damaged over 60 German tanks in Budapest.

Wed. Jan. 10, 1945

They're still street fighting in Budapest. The Russians are getting close to Vienna.

Fri. Jan. 12, 1945

Major Soviet advance happening. Received my personal parcel from September. Leather mitts & warm socks just in time. Chocolate always welcome.

Sun. Jan. 14, 1945

Soviet offensive is getting bigger & closer. Trying not to worry.

Tues. Jan. 16, 1945

Soviets captured Radom. Thank God we can get the real gen from the BBC.

Fri. Jan. 19, 1945

Red Army has liberated Warsaw. They're within striking distance of Breslau & Posen. Our map shows we're only 75 miles from Breslau. Something has to happen here soon but the goons aren't saying a word. We're told the SBO has asked the Kommandant about moving us but the Kommandant says the German High Command is confident of holding the Russians on the River Oder. They may be the only ones sure about that. It's looking more & more likely that we'll be evacuated & most of us are making preparations. Food supply is still skimpy. Fried some old potatoes & the peels for dinner tonight.

Mon. Jan. 22, 1945

Seems the Kommandant's confidence is slipping. We now have permission to make a rucksack & that makes it sound like we'll be out of here VERY soon. Mine's ready to go. Still the compound is like a sewing bee & an anxious one. The talk is of how much we can carry, how long we'll be able to march, where we'll go, what kind of weather we might have to deal with. The Russians have taken Posen. They're closer than 100 miles. Washed some clothes.

Tues. Jan. 23, 1945

Finally back on full Red + parcels thank God. Big cheer! We can have a decent dinner again tonight. The goons cut our bread ration to 2 slices a day.

Wed. Jan. 24, 1945

The Russians are shelling Breslau. It's all but certain we'll be marching out of here but no official word yet. It's at least 20 below zero & we were locked out on the parade ground all morning while the goons searched our rooms yet again. I mended some clothes. I've come this far. Let's hope my luck holds out.

Thurs. Jan. 25, 1945

Our news: German forces in East Prussia are cut off & the Germans are evacuating military & civilians. We hear guns & explosions all the time now in the east so we know Stalin's army is getting close. SBO is advising us about the food & clothing we should pack in case we're ordered to march. He suggests our packs weigh no more than 40 lb. Added a sling to mine that I can pull over my forehead to lighten the load on my back. We'll have to leave behind most of our belongings. Some of the boys are re-soling their boots. The circuit is crowded with men toughening up their legs & feet for marching but it's too late for that. The rumours are rampant – we're good at that. I'm glad I've walked 10-20 circuits most days since I've been here but even so I didn't do it with a pack on my back. The cold & all the snow are going to be a problem too not to mention that we haven't had enough to eat for months now.

Fri. Jan. 26, 1945

The guns are rumbling day & night. There seems little doubt now. We're preparing to march. Where is the West Front? Russian armies are making them look pretty bad even to us eternal optimists.

On January 27, 1945, the Red Army liberated Auschwitz, the biggest and reputed to be the most notorious Nazi concentration camp. Few details of the horrors of the camp were revealed by the British news and many were not known until much later. The Auschwitz Museum later estimated the death toll at between 1 and 1.5 million, almost a million of whom were Jews.[1] It would take the four-year-long Nuremberg trials, which began in November 1945, to show the world the horrors the Nazi committed in occupied Europe.

At the same time, the lads at Stalag Luft III's north compound (and all the compounds, for that matter) were anxiously preparing to march and waiting for orders. This forced march and those from other camps that took place in the final months of the war are amongst the lesser known horror stories of the war. Although little has been written about these marches, Group Captain D.E.L Wilson (RAAF), Senior British Officer, initially of north compound and later of all six Stalag Luft III compounds (including Belaria), wrote a comprehensive report about the north compound march called "Report on the Forced Evacuation of Allied Officer and Other Rank Prisoners of War from Stalag Luft III, Sagan, Germany – January/February 1945." His report, preserved as AIR 40/269 in the National Archives in the U.K., is prefaced with the following:

> "The Geneva Convention lays down certain conditions for the treatment of Prisoners of War and it will be seen from this Report that no regard was paid by the Germans to the provisions of the Convention in carrying out the move from Sagan or in the reception at Marlag-Milag Nord [the next camp]. The pur-

pose of this Report is to give a true history of the evacuation and later reception of the Camp of destination and to comment on the infringement by the Germans of certain Articles of the Convention."[2]

G/C Wilson's report cites several factors which, already being in place before the evacuation even began, further contributed to the harshness of the marches:

- Age of some of the prisoners. Stalag Luft III included some of the oldest prisoners of war in Germany, many interned for three or more years and a few in their sixth year
- Physical health of the prisoners. Below standard, supported by an unhealthy diet, particularly since September 1944 when Red Cross parcels were cut in half
- Compromised mental health of the prisoners. Events surrounding the escape of 76 prisoners in March 1944 (50 officers shot and ensuing reprisals) had taken their toll on morale[3]

Sat. Jan. 27, 1945

We hear the Ruskies are only 20 miles east of us & getting closer all the time. This place is buzzing. Still no orders to evacuate. Kommandant denied us permission to make sleds to carry extra food & clothing & the goons are confiscating some the boys already made.

It's getting dark & we're all sitting around on pins & needles waiting for something to happen. We're as ready as we'll ever be. Might as well play cards. It's bloody cold outside & there must be 6 inches of snow.

20:30 hours. Finally – one of the boys came running down the corridor yelling that goon orders were that we're to be ready to leave camp in ONE hour. We were stunned & all hell broke loose in the hut. Leaving at such short notice, on foot, in the middle of winter taking only what we can carry… how can they get away with this?

I changed into as many warm clothes as I could wear under my battledress. Snacked the whole time. Barley oatmeal & meat issue from the kitchen. Finished stuffing my pack with everything I was taking – extra shirts, trousers, a blanket, socks & underwear, shaving kit, extra shoelaces, toothbrushes & powder, as much of my chocolate as possible, my dishes, couple of cooking pans, pictures from home, first aid stuff. As many smokes as I can manage to use & trade. No choice but to leave everything else.

Too bad to lose the gramophone. Heard that someone has the radio. We divided up our most easily carried food between us. Some of the boys from other rooms were in no condition to leave & others pretended because sick cases are ordered to stay behind. They know they won't make it going cross country in these conditions & they can only hope the Russians will liberate them.

Still no official permission from the Kommandant to build sleds but the goons said it would be OK as long as they don't slow the march down. A lot of last minute sleds were constructed mostly by Canadian boys. The South African fellows don't know winter like we do so they scrambled to learn. Red + parcel crates, chairs, stools & whatever boards left in our bunks were turned into sleds. Some of them were 1 man affairs & some were enormous & quite impractical. Panic is trumping reason.

Rumours flew everywhere. We put on our packs ready to go & then heard our departure was delayed so we ate again & repacked. Pack was too heavy so I took some stuff out.

21:30 hours. Another delay. Heard a rumour that the Germans had asked for a truce.

22:30 hours. Still waiting. Rumour of a truce denied.

In addition to Dad's recollections and Group Captain Wilson's official report, I relied on a number of ex-Luft III POW sources to construct Dad's logbook entries for the period of the two forced marches: F/L John Colwell's A Wartime Log, F/L Robert Buckham's Forced March to Freedom and Stuart Hunt's Twice Surreal. I summarized the estimated mileage the men covered in Appendix 6.

Sun. Jan. 28, 1945

00:30 hours. Still waiting. The goons finally lined us up block by block ready to go. Other than that we weren't getting any direction or help from them. They were searching the huts & making sure no one was trying to hide & stay behind. Sticking together in their own groups. It was clearly every man for himself. They were as nervous as us. South & west compounds left first. Our room planned to travel together so we could help each other out – Al, Joe, Stu, Dave, Bruce, Doug & me. We're like family more than ever now.

After 01:00 hours. Order came down from the CO that we are not to try escaping on the march or risk being shot. We finally passed through the main gate into the vorlager. I was ecstatic. I hadn't walked through that gate since I arrived on May 26 1943. So long ago. We filed past the Red + storehouse & were offered another parcel if we wanted it but my pack was already heavy enough. I wasn't about to add another 10 lb. We don't know where we're going & it seems neither do the guards other than to tell us we're to cover 75km in 3 days & go at least as far as Schlossberg with our first halt at Halbau in 17km. Heading west to get away from the advancing Russian army. That's all we know.

Little information about route or destination would become the norm, contravening Article 26 of the Geneva Convention: "In the event of transfer, prisoners of War shall be officially informed of their new destination, and they shall be authorized to take with them their personal effects." Additionally, Article 7 states: "Evacuation on foot shall be made in stages, not normally exceeding 20 kms per day."[4]

Cold & clear night. Our room stuck together & as close to the front of the column as we could. The column was miles long. What a sight. There must have been close to 2,000 of us in the north compound column alone. As scary & unknown as it was, part of me was happy just to see trees & something other than barbed wire for a change. I was actually walking outside the wire. Didn't even feel real. The end of the war was finally in sight & we were full of Kriegie optimism. How bad could it be? For the first time I got a good look at just how big the camp really is.

In the first few kilometers, some of the sleds were already breaking down and fellows were ditching food and clothing, especially those last minute Red Cross food parcels they'd picked up. German civilians lined the road and were quick to pick up all the discarded food. Salmon, biscuits, powdered milk, cheese – stuff they (and the guards) probably hadn't seen in years. "The absence of any agreed system of halts caused trouble in the rear [of the column], where at least four officers, in difficulty with their packs or sledges, were forced at the point of the gun to abandon their kits. In the case of three of them, civilians were standing around and began to collect the food even before the officers left."[5]

We stopped for a brief rest after an hour or so. I didn't know how long we'd be stopped so I didn't take my pack off as much as my back would have liked a break. Besides it was actually keeping my back dry & warm. After that it got colder & windier & started snowing. At least the guys ahead of us had tramped down the snow so it was easier to walk. Ice underneath made it slippery. Better to keep on moving than to stop for a rest.

We heard south compound had planned to stage the play "You Can't Take it With You" last night. Might as well laugh. Or maybe it was a bad joke.

Marched all night under a full moon. Our column stretched out as far as I could see & we were a pretty ragged looking lot. The villages we marched through were all neat & clean. We reached the town of Halbau in the morning & the town was still asleep. We were allowed to sit down for 1 hr. Just getting light. **17km** someone said we'd come. No food or water from the goons. The food & bread we carried was frozen. G/C Wray came by & suggested we carry any food we want to eat right away next to our body. Same for drying out wet socks. Civilians are friendly enough & most even helped with hot water.

G/C Wilson reported that although some of the guards tried to prevent civilians from giving the men water, they, in general, did not interfere. Often, German women refused to take anything in exchange at all, but were always pleased with a present of soap."[6]

We talked about all the stuff we left behind at the camp to pass time – what a gold mine. The goons will be millionaires if they sell it all.

"At least 23,000 Red Cross Food Parcels were left behind intact... Clothes, also the property of the Red Cross and worth more than £3,000 were left in the State Rooms of the German Compound. A very large number of books variously estimated as being between 100 and 200 thousand were left behind. Although these included many cheap editions, many thousands were valuable works of reference and a high proportion on loan from the Y.M.C.A. and other educational institutions (refers to all compounds). At least 200,000 cigarettes were left in the North and East Compounds alone. Many valuable musical instruments, some on loan from the Y.M.C.A., had to be abandoned."[7]

Sun. Jan. 28, 1945

Pulled out around 08:00 hours & it was good to get moving again to warm up. The goons told us our next stop where we would billet for the night would be at a town called Freiwalden. **11km** from here. The road was very exposed & the wind really cold. Lots of the guards were already in worse shape than us. At least we're young – in our 20's & 30's. Most of the goons are old. Some of our lads offered to haul their packs on their sleds. I even saw 1 of our lads carrying a goon's rifle for him! We arrived at the town square around noon. Told we would billet there but there were only 2 buildings & it turned out there wasn't enough room for us all. Everything is so disorganized & vague. Old ladies & children offered us hot water & coffee even though some German army soldiers objected. They have lost control. Some of our German speaking boys tried to make their own overnight arrangements with the locals. Amazing what you can trade for coffee & a couple of smokes or a scrap of soap. Waited around the town square tired & cold & then after an hour told we weren't staying after all. The goons counted us several times until they seemed happy they got it right & then we were on the road again around 15:00 hours. Couldn't believe how tired I was. My pack felt like it was getting heavier. The sling helped. Just outside town we passed a big crowd of Americans on a halt who said they were from west compound. I would've chain smoked if only I wasn't worried I'd run out of fags. Need to make them last & hang on to some for trading. What a bedraggled lot we were. Like refugees. I could barely tell the prisoners from the guards. Only our air force greatcoats distinguished us. It was so disorganized our room kept getting split up. I don't know what happened to Joe & Al.

Went another **6km** to Leippa. 17:00 hours & I was exhausted. Cold but luckily no frostbite - yet anyway. Thank goodness for my heavy socks & boots. We'd been marching for 16 hr without a meal break. Nothing is organized at all. There was 1 big stone barn for us to stay in for the night but it wouldn't even begin to hold us all. We had to line up.

We packed in as many as possible - maybe 700 but some of the men had to wait outside until more barns were found. Our room got separated again. The goons issued bread & marg but it was so crowded & dark that everyone didn't get some. Some had to spend the whole night outside. Very cold night too. My boots were soaked but I couldn't take them off for very long or they'd freeze & I wouldn't be able to get them back on. Already learned that lesson. Heavy snow. We were packed into the barn like sardines but at least body heat helped keep us warm. Stone floor with a small amount of straw for us to lie on. Rats running around. Doug & me huddled together for warmth & used both our greatcoats & blankets. We were in the middle of the barn so we couldn't get out to go to the bathroom without trampling guys in the dark. As tired as I was, I was afraid to go to sleep in case I didn't wake up. Some of the lads were smoking & I was terrified of burning to death in a fire. Freezing or burning…some choice. Finally I dozed off listening to some lad vomiting & crying close by. If I die here no one at home will ever know.

G/C Wilson noted that this and other accommodations on the marches contravened Article 10 of the Geneva Convention: "Prisoners of War will be lodged in buildings or huts which afford all possible safeguards as regards hygiene and salubrity. All premises shall be entirely free from damp, and adequately heated and lighted."[8]

Mon. Jan. 29, 1945

Still snowing this morning. Up at 07:00 hours. Ate some prunes & a piece of bread for breakfast. Some of the men who had to spend the night outside are frostbitten. No medical help from the goons. They are more interested in looking after themselves than patrolling the column & watching us. They couldn't even count us so we organized a count for them. It would be so easy to escape but the odds of surviving aren't good.

08:00 hours. Started marching. Still freezing cold. 1 fellow I saw was too sick to go on. We saw so many civilians fleeing the Russians just as we are. Horse & ox drawn carts & wheelbarrows carrying everything they own. Old people, women, children. They all looked like terrified beggars & I felt sorry for them. They don't pay much attention to us. They have their own survival to worry about.

11:30 hours. Reached a town called Priebus & stopped for lunch – our own food of course. **12km.** Piece of dry bread & a bit of cheese. No rations or water from the Germans. Some friendly civilians offered us hot water for coffee. The stragglers, the lame & sick are falling to the back of the column. We're helping each other as best we can. G/C Wray is walking the length of the column & at least encourages everyone. He's good for morale. Thank God for the leather mitts & hat Ma sent me but I'm still cold. I just kept my head down to keep the wind out of my face & walked in the foot prints of the guy in front of me. I was starting to think it might not be so bad to just freeze to death. They say you just go to sleep.

After 17:00 hours. We reached a placed called Muskau & the goons told us we'd be stopping for 24 hr. **16km.** It was a little more organized this time & there were a few billets for us – a theatre, a glass factory, a stable, a riding school, a laundry & a pottery.

Spoke too soon. There wasn't enough room for all of us so Doug & me & the rest of us at the front of the column had to keep marching another **5km** to a French POW camp. Our room got split up again. Stu & Dave stayed in Muskau. The goons were so disorganized.

When we arrived at the camp, the French POWs were happy to see us & offered their bunks when they saw how exhausted we were. We ate some bread & cheese & collapsed. My feet were numb & my boots soaked. There was at least a medical officer for those who needed help.

Tues. Jan. 30, 1945

Spent most of the day resting. Thank God because I have no energy. Some of the fellows boots are falling apart already. Mine are starting to dry out.

Wed. Jan. 31, 1945

Another day of rest. Received some goon bread ration & partial Red + food parcel issue. The weather is getting milder & everything is starting to thaw. The sleds won't work much longer. Lots of trading of smokes & food for wheels.

Thurs. Feb. 1, 1945

Another disorganized day. Ready to go at 07:00 hours but at 11:00 told we'd be staying. Didn't receive orders again until 16:00 hours. We had time to eat a big meal & it was almost 23:00 hours before we finally left in the middle of an air raid. A group of POWs from east compound joined us & some of our north compound lads left to march with Americans from west compound. Couple of thousand of us in the column. Sleds were breaking down before we'd even left town. The number of fellows too sick to march is growing. Several boys are dead of exposure. We marched all night. Very hilly going. It was the worst yet. Even the guards were complaining. It got very quiet. We were each in our own private hell & even Doug & me stopped talking to each other. Just one foot in front of the other & all the willpower I could muster up. The boys with sleds were becoming exhausted pulling them through the slush. The snow is all but gone. Our column stretched out as far as I could see. The road is lined on both sides with ditched kits. The boys at the back of the column can pick up anything they need. By dawn practically no sleds left. Good for firewood. Some of the lads have traded for anything on wheels.

G/C Wilson reported: "more than one Officer had frostbite too badly to wear boots and finished the march in socks... Only the hardiest had any spring in their stride by the time the night was through."[9]

Fri. Feb. 2, 1945

06:00 hours. Arrived at the town of Graustein, **18km.** Still a ways from Spremberg our destination. Halt until 11:00 hours gave us time to rest in a barn. Heavenly dry & warm with lots of straw to lie on. Just not enough time. Farmer provided hot water. Washed & had a shave. Felt good to clean up a bit. Heard that some of the boys who stayed in Muskau got billeted in the stable of a castle & a select few actually had a bath tub & hot water!! What luck. I would have given a lot for that. Haven't had a hot bath in years. Joined up with some of the lads who stayed in Muskau. One of them had a baby pram carrying his pack. He traded 100 smokes & ½ tin of marg for it.[10]

11:30 hours. On the road again to Spremberg.

G/C Wilson wrote: "On the outskirts of Spremberg, an Officer walking on the footpath to avoid water in the road, was shouted at by a guard, and when he stopped to try and understand what was being said, was struck with the butt end of a rifle. On several occasions, civilians were prevented from giving the prisoners water. At one place where a young woman was giving the prisoners hot coffee, a guard told her to keep it for civilian refugees. The woman burst into tears and replied that her husband had been captured and was a prisoner in British hands. He was being well-treated and she wished to do something in return."[11]

Arrived at Spremberg sometime after 14:00 hours at some army barracks. **10km.** Hot water & barley soup issued & it's the first hot food we've had since we left Sagan. Boy did it taste good. Never thought I'd say that about German rations.

The hot meal provided at Spremberg would be the only one of the march, contravening Article 2 of the Geneva Convention, which states: "Prisoners are to be humanely treated at all times."[12] G/C Wilson would later conclude: "The supply of German rations on the march was pitifully inadequate and hopelessly administered."[13]

16:30 hours. Started marching again for the train station only it's more like shuffling now. Left more sick fellows behind. Stu & Dave caught up with us but Stu looked terrible. They & others got sick in Muskau where they were billeted in a riding school, probably dysentery. Stu wouldn't stay behind & I don't blame him. After about **3 or 4km** we reached a rail siding where they counted us off into groups & herded us into wooden cattle cars – over 40 of us per car that's meant to hold 8 cattle or horses. The boxcar was dirty with shit & dark except for the slivers of light coming through the cracks of the siding. Not even any straw on the floor. It was so crammed that we could only sit leaning against the siding or lie on our side. Rivets sticking out of the floor so it was impossible to get comfortable. We hung as much gear as we could on the walls to create some space. Impossible to move. Issued some lead bread & part of a Red + food parcel. No water. Then that awful sound of a bolt sliding & we knew we were locked in from the outside. Finally they told us where we were going – a Royal Navy prison camp called Marlag und Milag Nord near Tarmstedt & it will take 2 days & 2 nights to get there. Can't even think about being in here that long. I'm told we've marched almost 100km since we left the camp a few days ago.

22:30 hours. Train is pulling out. No room to even lie down. They're not giving us any water. Only a can in the corner for a toilet & some of the boys are sick with it coming out both ends. I've been lucky so far. I'm pretending in my mind that I'm back home maybe out at the farm fishing with Uncle Sid. Anywhere but here. This train has to be such a target from the sky. It'll be a miracle if we're not shot up by our own A/C. At least it's dark.

Sat. Feb. 3, 1945

A bad night but we survived. Being packed in has 1 benefit only - body heat. I now know that thirst & hunger are terrible things. I don't even care where we're going anymore just so long as we get there. Couldn't be any worse than the hell we're already in.

13:00 hours. The train stopped & we could at least get out & stretch. What a relief. Civilians were staring at us from behind a fence like we were monkeys in the zoo. We were supposed to get water here but there was none. All day again in the boxcar. It doesn't take a doctor to know that some of the men will not survive this trip. The only good thing about no water is I don't have to step over a bunch of guys to go pee.

Sun. Feb. 4, 1945

Another long night. The car was silent except for the sounds of groaning & vomiting - Stu & Dave included. The bucket in the corner was full & overflowing. We all just quietly willed ourselves to get through this nightmare. Our minds & bodies are numb. A few of the lads just didn't wake up this morning. I wondered if this is what it feels like to be dead. The Germans would probably treat dogs better. We're men just like them but then I remembered all the stories I'd heard at Luft 3 about how they treated the Russian & Polish prisoners – like they were sub human.

07:30 hours. The train stopped finally & we were allowed to get water from houses close by. First water since we left Spremberg a day & a half ago. We are filthy. I have a cold, I ache all over & I'm hungry but lucky nothing worse. Stu is in bad shape. All this time we've been dreaming about being free but first we have to survive long enough.

G/C Wilson wrote: "That thirst was serious is shown by the fact that a Canadian Red Cross Padre, who had carried a 70lb pack containing in part his devotional objects throughout the march, saw fit to distribute his "holy" water in relief. On two occasions, guards fired at prisoners who were fetching water, and though no one was hit, one Officer only saved himself by diving under the train."[14] The lack of water also violated Article 11 of the Geneva Convention whch states: "Sufficient drinking water shall be supplied."[15]

16:30 hours. Arrived at Tarmstedt where we could finally get off the train & stretch & move around. My legs were numb. Marching to the camp in the rain was a huge relief. Stuck out my tongue to catch some drops. We were at the front of the column again except for Stu. In exchange for some smokes the goons let Stu lie down on the back of their supply wagon. He wouldn't have made it otherwise. It was getting dark by the time we neared the camp. Even prison camp life sounded good to us.

17:30 hours. Arrived at Marlag und Milag Nord. **3km or 4km** walk. Stu was already there sitting on the ground in the rain waiting for the column to arrive. They wouldn't let him in. We couldn't see much of the camp in the dark. It looked pretty deserted but the guards stopped the column at the gate & wouldn't let us in. They lined us up by hut. Word went around that they insisted on searching every one of us for contraband! We waited & waited in the rain. I was so fed up. We had nothing to hide. Boys who passed out got in first. Stu was one of them but I wouldn't have traded to be in his condition. We were close to the front of the line anyway. The camp is surrounded by the same double barbed wire fence as Sagan. Who could ever have guessed that we'd be wishing to get INTO a prison camp. It's been 100kms or so of pure hell.

19:00 hours. They let our hut through the gates & vorlager & through a barbed wire fence to a building where they took forever to search each of us & our few pathetic belongings for 20 minutes. Had a stage – looked like a theatre. No heat. Finally we crossed the compound to a barracks where we spent a cold night on the floor. Camp is pretty bare. Our room is together again except for Stuart. It's a miracle we all made it. Another uncomfortable night. I'm so tired of this.

G/C Wilson reported: "Apart from exhaustion after the march and train journey, many were suffering from frostbite, dysentery and vomiting. Several collapsed and had to be taken to hospital. Indeed, for the majority, this wait after eight days of movement under the conditions described, proved the breaking point, and more than 70% of the camp suffered from gastritis, dysentery, colds, influenza and other illnesses during the first week."[16]

Mon. Feb. 5, 1945

Heard the last men got into the camp around 02:00 hours. Stu's in the hospital. Most of us are sick to some degree. Appell this morning & then we were assigned quarters. Our room is a bit larger than what we had at Sagan but we expect they'll pack more of us into it. To say the rooms are bare is an understatement. There are only bits & pieces of broken furniture. A few

Route Map
Sagan to Tarmstedt
Jan.27 to Feb.5, 1945

rooms are lucky enough to have triple bunks & palliases. Others have none at all. We're in luck on the bunks in our room but not on the palliases. They're all damp & alive with bed bugs that bite like a son of a gun. I took a lower bunk again. We have a stove but many rooms don't & there's no kitchen in the hut. Since there's no firewood it looks like the best we'll do for fuel is wet wood chips until we start taking the building itself down. We set up a cooking schedule again & it's back to our old prison camp life. We're worn down but still resourceful as ever. At least we can have the odd hot meal as long as our food supply lasts or we get more Red + parcels. Back to 2 appells a day & the same kind of routine we had at Luft 3 but it's a helluva lot better than the cattle car. Washed my clothes although I don't know how anything will ever dry. Security isn't as strict here. I went to see Stu in the hospital & tell him the bunk over Doug is waiting for him. He looked terrible all skin & bones with bad colour but says he feels a bit better. Told me he bribed a goon to wash his clothes in return for 10 packs of smokes so I know he's feeling better. Asked me to help him make good on the payment. The hospital is overflowing with sick men. Lots of sunken eyes & cheeks. Most are lying on the floor. Stu is lucky to have a cot.

On February 2, 1945, the Norwegian newspaper, Aftenposten, published an article in German-occupied Oslo with the headline (translated into English): "BRITISH AIRCREWS PREFER TO REMAIN GERMAN PRISONERS RATHER THAN BE RELEASED BY THE RUSSIANS". It also said that 30 officers and a large number of other ranks volunteered to fight with the Germans against Bolshevism. The Kriegies protested this article strongly. G/C Wilson responded: "It can be stated categorically that each of these statements – typical products of the German Ministry of Propaganda – is wholly unfounded...the exact reverse of the truth."[17]

Tues. Feb. 6, 1945

Extra long appell this morning, in the rain of course. No wonder I can't shake this cold. Stalag Luft 3 was a holiday resort compared to this dump. 15 of us in our room. We heard the naval prisoners who were here before us wrecked the place before they left because they thought the Germans were going to use it themselves. There are 2 compounds & we're all housed in 1 of

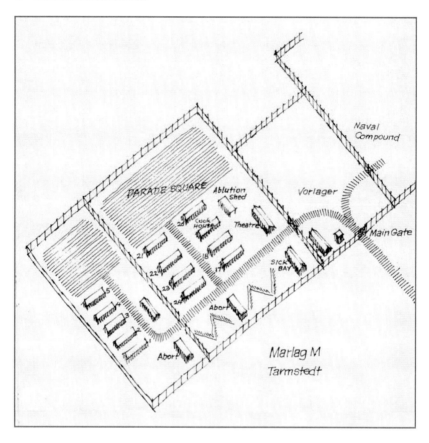

them called Lager Luft. Our compound is divided in 2 sections by a barbed wire fence (no gate) & our part has 7 wooden barrack blocks, a cookhouse, a washhouse, an abort & the theatre building where we were searched the other night. Not much of a theatre. The other part has another cookhouse, an abort, a parade square & 5 barracks. Both sections have slit trenches dug in the sand inside the north wire & parade squares inside the south wire. There are naval fellows in the other compound with a vorlager in between us. The SBO is in a rage because the living conditions are so bad. We number over 1,900. Went scrounging for tin cans to make a few supplies. Thank God I brought my soldering torch & lead supply. Everyone doesn't have a mug & plate so we share until we can make some. Flattened a few Klim cans today to make plates.

Wed. Feb. 7, 1945

Another 2½ hr appell this morning in the cold & rain. Even then the goons still weren't happy with their count of us. Then they searched all the huts & checked each of us against the picture on our ID card. Issued 1 wet stump to each hut for firewood. Each room got rationed a few chips off it. Afternoon appell canceled on account of the never ending rain. No spud issue yet & bread ration is 2 slices each day per man. We can get a jug of hot water at the cookhouse twice a day at 08:00 & 15:00 hours.

Thurs. Feb. 8, 1945

We heard there's a conference going on between Churchill, Roosevelt & Stalin.

According to the BBC, the three Allied leaders - Prime Minister Winston Churchill, US President Franklin D. Roosevelt and Marshal Joseph Stalin – were meeting in a secret location to plan joint military operations to end the war against Germany. "The leaders announced their determination to stamp out Nazism and to disarm and disband all German armed forces and bring all war criminals to justice."[18] The foundation was thus laid for the Nuremberg trials what would begin postwar in November.

Fri. Feb. 9, 1945

Morning appell cancelled. Rumours galore about the conference & the end of the war. We heard that a shipment of Red + food parcels arrived from Lubeck & that we can expect a half parcel issue within days. Thank God. We haven't had enough to eat since our parcels were cut in half last Sept. Feels like a lifetime ago. Afternoon appell 2½ hours in the pouring rain. I may never be dry again.

Sat. Feb. 10, 1945

Only 1 shower in the washhouse that's mostly open to this foul weather. The freezing cold water is shocking as hell but a quick in & out is worth it to wash off some of the grime. I actually shaved. Hardly recognize myself. There is NO firewood & certainly no coal. Will it ever stop raining? The whole place leaks. Another long afternoon appell on the parade square in drizzle & then a few smokes & circuits of the perimeter with Doug.

Monday Feb. 12, 1945

Stu came out of the hospital. Good news but he's very weak.

We're all full of lice & bed bug bites. A bit of sun in the afternoon before it started to snow.

Tues. Feb. 13, 1945

The snow turned to rain this morning. Library opened in the theatre building. Not much of a theatre, just a stage really. The books are courtesy of the Navy types next door. Nice to be able to read a book again. Not as if I don't have the time. The sun came out briefly this afternoon. The goons authorized a log issue for firewood per block but it's nothing more than another wet stump. The damp chips we got out of it barely cooked a meal. Filled the room with smoke. We are starting to burn wood from the hut itself – wall planks & floor boards. The warmer weather better come soon.

Wed. Feb. 14, 1945

On a delousing trip today Stu traded some smokes for beets. We cooked them for dinner & they were terrible. I'm adding beets to brussels sprouts on my NEVER EAT AGAIN AS LONG AS I LIVE list. We heard RAF bombers firebombed the heck out of Dresden last night & American B-17 Forts joined in today. I don't know why the Germans don't just give up. Bets tonight on when it'll all end except no one has much left they're willing to lose in a bet.

Fri. Feb. 16, 1945

The goons are upset about the condition of Dresden. They say the destruction & civilian losses are enormous.

British and US forces dropped over 2,600 tons of bombs and incendiaries on the city of Dresden that night. The city was so full of refugees fleeing the Soviet forces advancing from the east that the BBC could only broadly estimate the number of deaths from fire and suffocation at between 25,000 and 100,000. Debate about the morality of the Dresden bombing and the entire strategic bombing campaign against Germany, which continues today, began quickly and publicly with Winston Churchill distancing himself from it.[19] In 2007, Canadian Bomber Command veterans protested the wording on a Second World War exhibit at the Canadian War Museum in Ottawa. Although the text used in the exhibit was factual as far as events were concerned, the veterans felt it portrayed them as war criminals when they were just doing their job against the odds, and losing friends in the process. The veterans were ultimately successful in their lobby to have the wording changed.

Sunday Feb. 18, 1945

According to our map we are 25km or so NE of Bremen. The higher ups have confirmed that 6,000 Red + parcels are here from Lubeck but we have yet to see any sign. In anticipation we dipped into our stores & treated ourselves. Doug & me are staying fit walking the perimeter. It's not over yet. Rumour has it the goons are running bets on the day a peace treaty will be signed – in 4 to 6 weeks.

Tues. Feb. 20, 1945

Johnny C. is busy as a Canadian beaver tinbashing again. Not at all put off by the state of this dump. He's made all kinds of things since we arrived – beds, pots, plates, pails, a table, stools, wash basins, dhobi buckets you name it. He turned 4 beds into 9.[20] I think it keeps him sane. Even a stove & oven. I made another margarine lamp but it smokes so much it's not good for much. Heard that 1 of our boys got shot by a goon while trying to trade with another goon for some food. He had stepped across the warning wire to collect his payment. Doesn't sound good for him.[21] Still no sign of a Red + parcel issue.

G/C Wilson later reported that Flight Lieutenant C.K. Bryson, RAF, died from his injury.[21]

Sat. Feb. 24, 1945

US marines raised the American flag in Iwo Jima yesterday. The Japanese aren't giving up easily but it won't be long now.

Although the men were primarily interested in what was going on in "their own war" in Europe, they would, of course, hear news of events taking place in the Pacific theatre. Iwo Jima was an extinct volcanic island held by the Japanese. After four days of intense air and naval attacks, US Marines landed on the island on February 19, 1945. The BBC News reported: "The Japanese army and naval troops under Lt-General Kuribayashi Tadamichi fought to the death but the US Marines finally secured the whole island on March 26 in one of the bloodiest battles of the war. Out of the 74,000 Marines that landed, more than a third were killed or wounded. The US then used the island to launch bombing raids on Japan. The photograph of the US Marines raising the flag over Mount Suribachi is one of the most famous images of the war, winning the Pulitzer Prize in 1945."[22]

Mon. Feb. 26, 1945

The goons are refusing another log ration. Our clothes & shoes are still damp from the march & they won't dry. Some classes have started up again but not much. We have no classroom or books or anything really to help. Sure wish I had the gramophone & even 1 good record. Starting today Reich food ration per man cut by over 20% & we are never actually issued everything we're supposed to get anyway. That hasn't changed.

Tues. Feb. 27, 1945

Fuel is a problem for heat & cooking. No coal. The goons are letting us organize groups to gather brush outside the camp & dig up stumps to burn but it's not enough. Broken windows are at least being fixed. I bet we can thank G/C Wray. Heavy daylight attack on Berlin today. Full moon tonight.

Wed. Feb. 28, 1945

Went on a brush gathering party today. The news is that the Russians are only 40 miles from Berlin. I wrote a letter to Mum even tho there's no way to mail it. Something to do. Rumour is the German rations will be cut again March 5. Raining & snowing.

Fri. Mar. 2, 1945

Snow & rain for days & now it's all freezing. Red + trucks finally pulled into camp this morning from Lubeck & unloaded American food parcels. Good thing since our food & smoke supply is very low & the American parcels include cigarettes. We're told there are enough parcels for a full issue starting next week. I try not to think about all the smokes I left behind in my locker at Luft 3. Foodacco cigarette prices for chocolate are up of course. 101 smokes for a D bar compared to 65 a couple of days ago.[23] Big RAF raid on Cologne today.

Sat. Mar. 3, 1945

The promise of new supplies has us obsessing about food again – what we'd like to eat, our favourite meal back home & whatnot. Self-torture.

Mon. Mar. 5, 1945

We have lights only every other night now on account of the local power plant being bombed. Have to make do with a smelly & smoky marg lamp or just sit & talk in the dark. New ration cuts take effect today. Bread issue is down to 1 loaf per day shared amongst 7 of us. Marg & sausage cut too.

Tues. Mar. 6, 1945

Daylight raid flew right over us – hundreds of American B-17 Fort & B-24 Liberator bombers all in formation. What a beautiful sight. Our news is that American troops captured Cologne. Cologne was my very first air op. Over 2 long years ago.

Thurs. Mar. 8, 1945

Another big raid on Hamburg last night. We had the best seats in the house for watching the air battles with the night fighters. We could hear the cannons & the .303s firing back. Watched several A/C come down – 8 or 9, some of them ours – Hallies & Lancs - but not always easy to tell. It took each of us back to our own nightmare of being shot down only some of these guys weren't so lucky. Felt helpless watching the A/C catch fire & plunge to earth. In the light of the fire saw the odd parachute coming out. It was horrible to watch knowing that some of the lads were still in the A/C. Made us realize again how "lucky" we are to be prisoners.

The sun finally came out today good & proper! We packed into any sheltered spot to feel a little bit of it on our faces. Full parcels again so it's been a good week. We were pretty low on smokes. There are rumblings about another march. I patched up my backpack just in case. One of the fellows has made a stove & oven from 150 Klim cans. Way beyond me. We watched another raid tonight for a while. Very close, must be Hamburg again.

Sun. Mar. 11, 1945

Our news is of a big raid on Essen. We're waiting to hear that the Allies have crossed the Rhine because that'll be it for Germany.

243

Thurs. Mar. 15, 1945

We hear the Lanc is now carrying a bomb called the Grand Slam – 22,000 lb! One was dropped on a viaduct yesterday.[24]

Sat. Mar. 17, 1945

Lead bread & spud issue cut again. Our bodies are missing the bulk. As long as our Red + parcels continue we'll be OK. New bets on when armistice will happen. I say April 5.

Mon. Mar. 19, 1945

Kommandant has ordered all Red + food tins opened & the contents emptied into new containers before they'll issue any more parcels. It's so the goons can have all the tins. They need a hell of a lot more than a bunch of tin cans to win the war at this point. G/C Wilson met with the Kommandant to protest on the grounds that we can't afford to have our food go bad. We also don't have anywhere to put the food & any empty tins we have we are using ourselves to make stuff. G/C Wilson refused to accept any open parcels which means no parcels at all.

Tues. Mar. 20, 1945

The Kommandant & SBO met again over the parcel business & now they're having a stand off. All we're getting to eat is the goon rations such as they are. So G/C Wray is stepping into the conflict to mediate. We hope his common sense, good nature & diplomacy put a quick end to this nonsense. Another daylight raid on Hamburg – Forts & Liberators.

G/C Wilson's report indicated that his repeated attempts to advocate for the prisoners and improve their living conditions "ultimately led to a state of tension which resulted in my dismissal from my post and transfer to another camp."[25]

Wed. Mar. 21, 1945

Goon food issue today is 4 slices of bread each, swede soup for lunch & hot water for brew. Ripped down more of our walls for firewood. Good thing it's getting milder. Another raid on Hamburg tonight. Lot of smoke – oil refinery.

Thurs. Mar. 22, 1945

The German food issue is meager at best & about to get worse tomorrow now that they cancelled the swede soup at lunch on account of there being no firewood for the kitchen. Some of the boys are keeling over from hunger.

Fri. Mar. 23, 1945

The sound & sight of Lanc's flying overhead on a bombing run got our attention today. We were all counting them – lost count after 120 or so. Looked like they were headed in the direction of Bremen. Put us all in a better mood. Our Red + parcels have resumed but we gained nothing. All the canned food is being emptied into whatever containers we can drum up & the goons are taking the tins. We're at least getting our food again & we need it badly. We just have to use it more strategically now. As if we weren't already. Sunny all day today.

Sat. Mar. 24, 1945

Hard to believe the big escape from Luft 3 was a whole year ago. Big news is that the Allies have crossed the Rhine. It's the beginning of the end for the war. Have I said that before? We're less sure about ourselves & what happens next. More talk of another march.

Sun. Mar. 25, 1945

The Kommandant allowed a memorial service today for our 50 lads who were executed. The goons wisely stayed clear.

Tues. Mar. 27, 1945

News from the front is good. I go to bed every night wondering if tomorrow's the day. We heard that the Germans have freely admitted they can't possibly feed all the prisoners in camps across Germany & that we will have to rely on Red + food parcels. We also heard that living conditions at most other camps are terrible. We are to consider ourselves lucky.

Wed. Mar. 28, 1945

More rumours of another march. Rumours too of surrender. Full moon tonight.

Thurs. Mar. 29, 1945

The G/C is denying the march rumours. Seems pointless to

me but these are desperate times for the goons. My pack is ready to go. Someone is playing a harmonica as I write.

Sat. Mar. 31, 1945

Hamburg hit again. There can't be much of Hamburg left.

Sun. Apr. 1, 1945

Clocks moved ahead 1 hr for daylight savings. My watch is long gone & so are the D Bars I got for it.

Mon. Apr. 2, 1945

More of the lads are preparing for a march just in case. Backpacks & homemade carts. Still only a rumour of course. Montgomery is advancing quickly.

Thurs. Apr. 5, 1945

We've been here for 2 months. Last night we heard a long rumble then saw a big flash & a tail of fire in the sky that came from somewhere northwest of us. A rocket. Later we saw flares & there were rumours of paratroopers landing. Near midnight we saw glowing & smoke over the direction of Hamburg for close to an hour. It was something to see. Today bombs are falling close by & everyone is on edge. Word went around quickly that one of the goons has a suitcase with him at his post by the wire. Seems he's ready to run at a moment's notice. The goons are done with it all. There was actually mail today from Canada that caught up with us from Luft 3, the first since we arrived here. 30 letters dating back to December but nothing for me. Won't be much longer now.

Sat. Apr. 7, 1945

Last night we heard a fighter strafing close by. No light in the camp. Had to cook while there was still daylight. The marg lamp throws more smoke than light. Bets are on that we'll be freed in the next few days. Hard to believe. We sat in the dark & talked about our plans for when we get back to England & finally home.

Sun. Apr. 8, 1945

Another rocket fired last night. Lot of activity out on the road today – tanks, cannons, ambulances, staff cars all camouflaged with leafy tree branches. This must be it. The Germans are retreating. Freedom is so close. We watched a Mossie fly over & strafe a truck on the road. You never heard such cheering! Still no power in the camp & water is available only 3 times a day for 20 minutes at a time. We've been told to fill every container we can find because there may not be any more water come 18:00 hours.[26]

Mon. Apr. 9, 1945

Appell at 15:30 hours & the goons told us to be ready to leave at 18:30 hours. Goon order says "Failure to comply will result in the use of force."[27] G/C told us NOT to prepare.

16:30 hours. Another appell. More details. Issued 2 food parcels each. We ate & packed. This pack is much heavier than my last one & I hope my weakened back can take it. I'll be on the lookout for a wagon to hitch off. Some of the lads broke into the kitchen & pilfered soap powder. Used it to spell a huge message in the parade ground sand to our fighters overhead "RAF P.O.W. MOVING" with a big arrow pointing in the direction we're sure to go.[28] Anything to hasten our liberation. Too, we're so afraid of being shot up by our own fighters after having come this far. It's chaos. We were so preoccupied we barely noticed another air raid not far from here. Hamburg may have got it again. The sun is shining through all the empty spaces in the walls of our room.

20:00 hours. Hut 17 left just as heavy fog started rolling in. G/C Wray was still trying to delay our exit hoping we run into the British on our retreat. Timing could be critical for us. I dread another march but at least it's not January this time.

23:00 hours. Half the camp has left & we're still waiting our turn. The fog is getting thicker & thicker. Another air raid.

23:15 hours. So much for leaving tonight. The fellows who had already left were turned back because of the fog & bombs dropping close by. It's another night here after all in what's left of our room. Looks like a hurricane or 2 went through it.

The Second Forced March
April 10 - May 2, 1945

Tues. Apr. 10, 1945

We're finally leaving Marlag M. this morning. Good riddance. At least it's sunny again. Maybe today's the day Allied tanks will intercept us. We're all praying for it. Our room is planning to march together again, or try to anyway. There's a horse drawn wagon carrying the sick & wounded. The Naval types from the other compound are forming a second column behind us. Much different than our departure from Luft 3.

G/C Wray ordered us not to escape. During the day he countermanded the Kommandant's orders a few times to slow down the pace so no one would be left behind. Also in hopes that our tanks near Bremen would intercept our retreat & release us. I hope he doesn't end up in the hands of the Gestapo for his trouble but I doubt it. The Germans have lost control. Many of the carts broke down early on.

Twice during the day we hit the ditches in panic. The second time, we were marching on a country road when we saw 6 A/C in the distance. They were Allied fighters & what a sight they were for our tired eyes. They flew across the road in front of us & then the lead fighter winged over & started flying toward us. The rest followed him in fighter pursuit & next thing we knew their wings were winking as they started firing on us. We're such a straggled lot they couldn't tell whose side we're on. It was like slow motion. We ran like hell to get off the road & I flattened myself in the ditch & prayed. Some guys ran for the fields. They hit the wagons & I could hear screaming as some of our lads got hit – lads who were already sick & wounded for God's sake.

248

Stopped for a short rest at Zeven around 19:00 hours. After dark we halted in a big field near Heeslingen where we spent the night. Wide open, no protection & very damp. **16km** today. Starry night. 2 lads ventured out to gather some hay to sleep on & got shot in the leg for it. G/C Wray complained loudly until an ambulance arrived & took them to hospital. Lot of noisy trucks & troop movement on the road made for lousy sleep.

Wed. Apr. 11, 1945

Foggy again this morning. The goons made a laughable attempt to count us at appell. We left the camp under new army guards. Very loose with their guns.

11:00 hours. Strafed again. Every time it happened we ran for cover. Some of the boys made a run for it in the bush. These new guards don't seem to care.

17:00 hours. Halted & made camp in a field for the night. **12km.** Weather OK still. Issued some goon rations – a loaf of lead bread each & some canned stew. Have to make it last through Friday. Washed in a creek.

Thurs. April 12, 1945

Woke to a sunny morning. On the road by 09:00 hours. Bad news. We heard 2 of the Naval prisoners marching behind us were killed & 7 were wounded when we were strafed the other day. To be killed in any way so close to the end let alone like that sickens me & makes me wonder at the same time. Only a few minutes different & it could have been us. Is it just luck to have made it this far? Good news is that Magdeburg has fallen. Strafed again on the road.

We halted early around 15:00 hours which greatly improved our mood especially on such a nice day. We set up camp in a field outside Harsefelt. **10km.** Went quite a distance foraging for firewood. Stole some potatoes & then relaxed in the sun. No water for us. It was an easy day until 2 British Tempests shot up something in the field & scared the hell out of us. We hit the ditches & at least no one bit it this time. Rumour has it we're staying here 1 more day.

Fri. Apr. 13, 1945

Here for another day thanks to G/C Wray so we can relax. Allowed to use a farmer's pump down the road for water. Loafed around camp all day. Windy & cloudy. Used up the last of our goon rations at dinner & issued 3 more days worth – a loaf of bread & a can of meat each. Heard a goon shot at a few of the boys who were scrounging for firewood. No one hurt. We all made blanket tents in case of rain. Looked like a refugee camp. I guess that's what we are. We are in good spirits.

Sat. April 14, 1945

Didn't rain last night after all & we had a good sleep. On the road again around 09:30 hours. The sunny day put everyone in a good mood even the guards. When the guard wasn't looking, many of us went scrounging for whatever food we could find. Stu traded some smokes for eggs. Got some spuds from a generous Russian POW. The guards care less & less each day. Set up camp around 15:30 hours in an orchard outside Neucloster. **6km.** Borrowed some apples from the farmer. We were shocked to hear tonight that President Roosevelt is dead. We'd put the flag at half mast if we had one. Germany's war is lost anyway. Mosquito raid on the town during the night was a little too close for comfort. Hamburg got it too.

Sun. April 15, 1945

Cold & dull this morning. There's a cloud of smoke hanging over Hamburg. Headed out some time after 09:00 hours after a hot brew.

Stopped for lunch near the town of Jork in a fruit district. Lots of orchards. Traded smokes for apples with some civilians who were happy to do business. Some of the lads traded whatever they had for anything on wheels to carry their packs – chocolate, coffee, smokes, soap. One lad pushing a baby pram piled high with his belongings gave us a few good laughs & lots of jokes.

Marched along the top of a dyke on the Elbe River & arrived at the town of Cranz at the end of the day. Pitched camp on the bank between the dyke & the river & lit a fire. **15km** today. We cross the Elbe tomorrow to a village called Blankenese. River looks to be about a mile wide. I'm afraid we could be sitting ducks on the trip across. I can swim all right but the water will be bloody cold. We gathered leaves to sleep on. Doug & me slept together again for warmth. Cold & damp night. We can see Hamburg in the distance up the river. Seems to be fewer guards around & the ones still around look to have all but given up.

Mon. April 16, 1945

Waited around most of the day for our turn to cross. Received ½ a Canadian Red + parcel. Our group finally left some time after 15:00 hours. Crossed in under 30 minutes. Pleasant enough other than all eyes anxiously watching the sky. No strafing thank God. We climbed up a steep hill from the waterfront & marched at an easy pace on cobblestone streets through the town while we waited for the rest of the ferry loads to catch up. The town seemed a good size with hotels & hospital. Stu was able to trade coffee for bread & some of the boys scrounged beer for smokes at an inn – 1 smoke per glass of beer! We marched on to a village called Sulldorf where we camped in a field. **4km.** Cold shower from a farmer's pump felt good once I got over the shock. Slept on pine boughs. It's warming up.

Tues. Apr. 17, 1945

Left this morning around 10:00 hours & marched all day. It was actually hot & sticky & we just wished it would rain & get it over with. Cleaned up in a brook. Finally it stormed around 18:00 hours making for a wet field to camp in. Stu ate some rhubarb he scrounged this morning & is sick again. We're camped near a village called Ellerbek. **18km.** There are fewer & fewer guards around so we can wander more freely. We explored the field & came up with some boughs & leaves to sleep on in our blanket tent.

Wed. Apr. 18, 1945

A rest day. Loafed around & washed some clothes. A lot of us walked into town & the guards didn't even care. The town was practically overflowing with Kriegies. Later we were hungry & needed food so I went scrounging for whatever I could get in exchange for some coffee, smokes or soap. About a half hour away from camp I knocked on the door of a farmhouse & when a woman answered I asked her in my best German if she had any potatoes. I think she would have given me some until I saw her looking past me. When I turned around a goon was right behind me out of nowhere pointing his pistol at me & telling me to go back to the camp. I pretended not to understand.

Finally, a Canadian Red + food parcel each & a goon issue of bread & meat.

Thurs. Apr. 19, 1945

We moved out around 09:30 hours & spent the day marching on back roads & through bush. We marched near the front of the column again where we had better luck bartering - a bar of soap for 4 eggs. Camped in a field. **14km.** We are pretty beaten down. Poured rain in the night. Our blanket tent was sodden & drooping but at least hanging on.

Fri. April 20, 1945

Left camp around 09:00 hours & marched all day. Set up camp near a town called Elmenhorst just before the rain came down. **15km.** Once again we heard a report that the Allies are very close but we've already had more than enough false hope of being intercepted. Slept with some snorting pigs. Their smelly home was at least out of the wind & the rain that poured down all night. The town got shot up in the night by some Mossies. The cannon fire was close. Morale is low but we are dry.

Sat. Apr. 21, 1945

G/C Wray ordered a 24 hour halt this morning & told us we could pack up & find better billets if we want. Lubeck is still about 28km away. We pushed on to the next village - Neritz & found a shed. **7km.** Later we heard that SS officers were searching for the prisoners who had gone ahead of the column so we laid low. More Mossies in the night close by. We heard tonight there is street fighting in Berlin & Soviet flags are flying. This could finally be it for Hitler & his untouchable Berlin.

Sun. Apr. 22, 1945

We moved off around 11:00 hours. Met up with the others. Heard that some had close calls yesterday with local SS troops. We got pelted with rain & even hail throughout the day. G/C Wray again countermanded the goon orders & slowed down our pace. We're told we're to reach a camp in Lubeck in the next day or so. Halted around 15:00 hours & billeted in a barn near Kleinborintz for the night. We have a roof over our heads again tonight. **17km.**

Mon. Apr. 23, 1945

Cannon fire, bombs & more Mossies woke us last night. Very uneasy sleep. We pushed off after 10:00 hours & marched until about 13:30 hours to a large farm near Hamburg. **8km.**

There are several huge barns & some cow sheds for us to sleep in. We're allowed to sleep in the stables but not in the hayloft. I can see the outskirts of Lubeck up the road. We heard the camp conditions at Lubeck are lousy. G/C Wray, the Kommandant & a Red + officer went ahead to inspect it. We're to stay put until our billets are decided. I'm very tired.

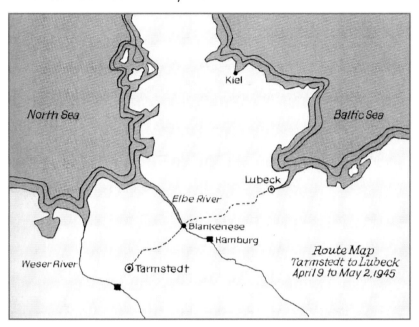

Tues. April 24, 1945

Spent the day here in the barnyard. The soles of my boots are starting to come off so I scrounged some wire & wrapped them. They won't last much longer. Red + parcels arrived from Lubeck so at least we have some rations - 1 American food parcel each, 1/3 loaf of lead bread & some smelly goon blood sausage. The guards would starve if we didn't share our food with them. There's a pond here so I took a bath & washed some clothes. That at least felt good. Air raids during the day.

Wed. Apr. 25, 1945

Nearby cannon fire last night. Frosty night but today is sunny so we spent it lying around. Most of our guards are nowhere to be seen. I'd be gone too if I were them. More air raids. G/C Wray & the Red + inspector arrived back from Lubeck & word is the billets there are very poor – no bunks, no palliases, cramped (as in 1800 of us to go into a space meant for only 500), 1 abort per 1000 men. Makes Marlag M sound like paradise. The Red + inspector declared them medically unfit & G/C Wray ordered us to stay put here or at other farms nearby for the rest of the war. He's a brave man to again stand up for us. Heavy frost again tonight.

G/C Wray was later made an Officer of the Order of the British Empire cited "For outstanding gallantry and distinguished services rendered whilst a prisoner of war of the Germans. As Senior Administrative Officer in Stalag Luft III he continually, with utter disregard for his own safety, countermanded the orders of the German Commandant on behalf of the hundreds of prisoners of war who were incarcerated at the time, and as a result of the outstanding devotion to duty which he displayed, he was largely responsible in obtaining better conditions for prisoners of war."[1]

Thurs. Apr. 26, 1945
Spent the day resting in the sun & swimming in the river.

Fri. Apr. 27, 1945
Heavy rain today. Dull. We played cards. Cards are more worn out than us. The German news said that Russian & American troops have united at the Elbe splitting the German army in half. This is it. Full moon tonight. Seems to me there was a full moon the day I enlisted so I've come full circle. Such a long time ago.

Sat. Apr. 28, 1945
We've apparently worn out our welcome with the farmer. We were moved out at 09:00 hours & marched about **11km.** We arrived at Wulmenau, a large farm just after 12:30 hours. Billeted in cow barns. The price for a roof over our heads was that we first had to clean out the barns. What a mess. Received a loaf of goon bread to share amongst us & some marg. The rest of the lads are billeted at another estate farm at Trenthorst. Our news is that Mussolini was murdered by the resistance today in Italy.[2]

Sun. Apr. 29, 1945
Rained all day again.

Mon. Apr. 30, 1945

More rain. Another Red + parcel issue. One of the boys found a swell German Schmeisser machine pistol in his wanderings & gave it to me knowing how much I like guns. It's a classy outfit too – an automatic pistol that I figured out can be attached to its carry case to turn it into a sub machine gun. Keeping it well hidden although not sure what I'll do with it.

At 22:30 local time on May 1, Hamburg radio announced that Hitler had "fallen at his command post in the Reich Chancery fighting to the last breath against Bolshevism and for Germany". With church bells pealing in the background, the BBC followed up with this:

> "We are interrupting our programmes to bring you a news flash. This is London calling. The German radio has just announced that Hitler is dead. I'll repeat that. The German radio has just announced that Hitler is dead."

Details were sketchy and it would take until June 20 for the world to hear that Hitler had married his long-time companion, Eva Braun, on April 29 and committed suicide with her the next day. Hitler's Third Reich, which he had boasted would last one thousand years, had lasted twelve years.[3]

Tues. May 1, 1945

More rain. The fighting is all around us now. We're hearing the British army guns boom day & night. Tonight we were stunned to hear that according to German radio Hitler is dead. No details but it happened at his command post in Berlin "fighting for Germany until the end". Is it a hoax?

Free At Last
Wednesday, May 2, 1945

Wed. May 2, 1945

Last night the goons announced the British had taken Bad Oldesloe (between Hamburg & Lubeck). This morning they're deserting. It's every man for himself now & they couldn't care less about us. We can hear artillery very close.

Noon – A British army Churchill tank with another behind it pulled into the farm yard. The hatch opened and up popped a Tommy who smiled & waved at us. Second British Army. He yelled out THE GERMANS HAVE SURRENDERED. Music to our ears!! When it sunk in the cheer we sent up was more like a roar & it went on for a while. We laughed & cried & hugged each other all at the same time. Some of the lads were shocked speechless & some got down on their knees & prayed. Some of the remaining goons took off in a hurry to get rid of their uniforms I'm sure. What an incredible feeling – I AM FREE. I just can't believe it. I'm numb. No more guards. V signs for Victory everywhere.

22:00 hours. What a day it's been. The Brits rounded up the goons who were still here & marched them off. Someone lifted a radio from the goon quarters & we all sat glued to the BBC news. Then we found a station with dance music & had a huge party. We're all madly writing letters home although no one's sure about mail service. Doesn't matter.

Thurs. May 3, 1945

Best sleep in over 2 years! We still aren't allowed to wander outside the camp for our own safety. They told us we'll be here for a few more days before they transport us to an airbase & fly us back to England. Seems like forever. Some of the boys can't wait & have taken off on foot to find their own way. Stu & Dave hopped a ride into Lubeck in search of beer. I'm not going far. There's no way I'm missing my ride out of here.

One of the lads commandeered a motorbike from who knows where & roared up to me this aft shouting WALLY, WANT TO GO FOR A RIDE? Foolishly I said yes. He drove it like a mad man & scared me half to death.

Red + trucks arrived this morning with a load of parcels. At least we'll be able to celebrate properly.

A Canadian liaison officer visited the camp today & is arranging for our mail to be picked up & sent home.

Another of the lads has been hiding a flag for just this moment. Others produced homemade jobs. We raised them with tremendous fanfare & sang our various national anthems at the top of our lungs.

It's been 722 days since I was shot down, 2 years of my life that I'll never forget as long as I live. Bacon & eggs, coffee, a banana, a hot shower, clean clothes & a decent bed will make me the happiest man on earth. I'll even eat a brussels sprout. Just one. If necessary.

May 2nd

Dear Mom

Well liberated at last. Have been on the road for 3 weeks. Lots to eat. Am feeling good in fact never better. Dont know when we will move back from here but hope soon. I just finished peeling a pot of spuds for supper. Hope to see you in a month or two. Love to Betty, El & Dad and everyone. Tell Dad to have the car all ready. Im a comin. Bye now.   *Love Alb*

Liberated Canadians

The names of the following personnel are included in a further list of liberated prisoners announced by the Department of National Defence for Air.

The total of RCAF prisoners of war officially announced as liberated (all lists to date) now stands at 1,746.

The latest list with Ontario names follows:

AIKENS, Stanley John, PO. Barrie.
AMES, Walter Ernest, FO. 69 Marion St., Toronto.
ARMSTRONG, John Archibald, WO. Kirkland Lake.
ASHDOWN, Evans Farrell, Flt. Lt. Alfont Hotel, New Toronto.
ASHLEIGH, David Douglas, Flt. Lt. 3097 St. Clarens Ave., Toronto.
BAMFORD, Jack, DFC, FO. Hamilton.
BARNES, Stanley, WO. 99 Edwin Ave., Toronto.
BAZINET, Joseph Omer, PO. Timmins.
BELL, Elmer Warrenner, Flt. Lt. Hanover.
BESTEL, Emmanuel George Robert, WO. Hamilton.
BOEHMER, George Arthur, FO., Kitchener.
BONDETT, Howard John, WO. North Bay.
BROWN, Henry Donald, Flt. Lt. Copper Cliff.
BRUCE, Gerald Joseph, Flt. Lt. 901 Manning Ave., Toronto.
BUCKLES, Robert James, FO. Whitevale.
CANTIN, Joseph George Albert Benoit, PO. Moonbeam.
CHARLES, John Frederick, PO. 229 Heath St. E., Toronto.
CLARK, Donald Albert, Flt. Lt. Windsor.
COEDY, Herbert John Wellington, WO. Galt.
COOPER, Kenneth Ellis, Flt. Lt. Sheffield.
COWTAN, Thomas Henry, FO. Westboro.
CUFFE, George Leonard, PO. Cobourg.
DALSEG, Paul Ivar, WO. Morson.
DANES, Arthur Ernest, WO. 131 Summerhill Ave., Toronto.
DAVID, Bruce Arnold, FO. Hamilton.
DECHAMBEAU, Maynard Oliver, WO. Welland.
DIEBEL, Harold Melvyn, PO. Copper Cliff.
DOBIE, James Robert, WO. Clifford.
DONALDSON, Kenneth James, WO. Timmins.
EVERARD, Hedley Joseph, DFC, SL. Timmins.
FOSTER, William Wells, Flt. Lt. Kingston.
FRAIR, Harold Kenneth, FO. North Bay.
FRAUTS, David John, Flt. Lt. Trenton.
FRIDAY, John William, PO. Port Arthur.
FROATS, Thomas J., WO. Prescott.
GALLAGHER, William James, Flt. Lt. Port McNicoll.
GORMAN, John Richard, FO. 2074 Queen St. E., Toronto.
HARRIS, Percy Harold, FO. Forest.
HEWITT, Isaac, WO. Port Dover.
HEWSON, Geale William, Flt. Lt. Niagara-on-the-Lake.
SCHMEHL, William Rudolph, Flt. Lt. Elmira.
SHEA, John Thomas, FO. 457 Jane St., Toronto.
SHEILER, Lorne Melvin, FO. Napanee.
SOVRAN, Americo, FO. Windsor.
SPARKS, George, FO. 68 Frankdale Ave., Toronto.
SPEARS, James Elgar, WO. 337 Hillsdale Ave., Toronto.
STALEY, Austin Lynch, FO. 473 Broadview Ave., Toronto.
STANLEY, Lloyd Oliver, Flt. Lt. 66 Strathcona Ave., Toronto.
STEPHENSON, William Harry, Flt. Lt. Belleville.
STEWART, Duncan Thompson, FO. Stratford.
STRINGER, Richard James, Flt. Sgt. 603 Lansdowne Ave., Toronto.
SULLIVAN, Harold Erwin, Flt. Lt. Englehart.
SWEANOR, George Joseph, Flt. Lt. Port Hope.
TIERNEY, Francis Otterson, WO. Brockville.
TOPPLIN, Mack, Flt. Lt. 9 Major St., Toronto.
TURNER, Ronald Alfred, FO. Woodstock.
WALKER, Frank William, F. Sgt. St. Catharines.
WALKOM, William James, FO. 264 Strathmore Blvd., Toronto.
WALLACE, Albert Randall, Flt. Lt. 270 St. Clarens Ave., Toronto.
WATSON, Earl Carruthers, FO. 320 Lauder Ave., Toronto.
WEEPERS, David James, FO. Galt.
WELWOOD, Norman Joseph, WO. Whitechurch.
WHITE, Joseph Gordon, Flt. Lt. Ridgetown.
WHITE, Thompson Stewart, WO. Orillia.

WILLIS, James Ralph, FO. Calabogie.
WILSON, Maxwell Clare, Flt. Lt. Petrolia.
WILSON, Russell Scott, FO. Oshawa.
WINKLER, Eric Alfred, WO. Hanover.
WOODS, Ronald Charles, F. Sgt. 451 Markham St., Toronto.
WRIGHT, Gordon Grange, WO. Bracebridge.
WRIGHT, William Arnold, Flt. Ltd. Carleton Place.
WYNVEEN, William Richard, WO. Leamington.
ARMSTRONG, Donaldson Scott, Flt. Lt. 464 Oriole Parkway, Toronto.
AUSTEN, Roy William, FO. 112 Langley Ave., Toronto.
BARNES, Wilfred Henry, FO. Sundridge.
BEDARD, Jacques Robert Andre, North Bay.
BOWLEY, Theodore Lionel, WO. Waterford.
BOWMAN, Allan Murray, WO. Goderich.
BRUNO, Dennison, WO. 351 Victoria Park Ave., Toronto.
CAPREOL, Edward Louis, WO. Ottawa.
CARTIER, Joseph Lionel Louis, FO. Cornwall.
CLINTON, Edwin Omar, WO. Thessalon.
COLEMAN, Lionel Udolphus, FO. 23 31st St., Long Branch.
CONLON, William Charles, WO. London, Windsor.
COUSINEAU, Joseph Thomas, WO. Windsor.
CRATE, Gerald Watson, Flt. Lt. Smiths Falls.
DAVIES, David Myrddin, PO. Windsor.
DAVIES, Donald Stewart, FO. Ottawa.
DELUCA, John Martin, FO. Port Arthur.
DENISON, William Young, WO. Ottawa.
DUFF, Thomas Alexander Stuart, WO. Corinth.
DUGDALE, Kenneth James, FO. Russell.
DUNN, Edward Maitland, FO. 163 Hope Ave., Toronto.
FARRELL, James Thomas, FO. Ottawa.
FAULKNER, Emmet Justin J. Sgt. Sudbury.
FERGUSON, John Ambrose, FO. Port Arthur.
FINDLAY, James Bruce, Flt. Lt. Ottawa.
GORDON, John Sinclair, DFC, Flt. Lt. 59 Maxwell St., Toronto.
GRANT, Thomas Henry, FO. 238 Hanleigh Ave., Toronto.
GRAHAM, Harold Joseph, PO. Stratford.
GRAVES, Fred Thompson, FO. Ottawa.
GRIFFIN, William Frederick, FO. Hamilton.
GUERTIN, William Norman, WO. Wallaceburg.
HALL, Richard Manning, WO. 420 Coxwell Ave., Toronto.
HALVERSON, George Patrick, WO. Coniston.
HARE, Harry Edmonstone, FO. St. Catharines.
HARRISON, Stanley Armitage, FO. Camlachie.
HAYES, Harold Bernard, PO. Ottawa.
HOGAN, John Kenneth, WO. Collins Bay.
HUGHES, George Douglas, Flt. Lt. 514 Riverside Dr., Toronto.
HUMPHRIES, Michael, FO. Richmond Hill.

The Globe and Mail,
May 25, 1945

Epilogue

GERMANY SURRENDERS, screamed the four inch headline in the Toronto Daily Star on Monday May 7, 1945. The paper reported that at 2:11 a.m. (French time), a school house in Reims, France bore witness to Germany's unconditional surrender to the western Allies and Russia. It had been five years, eight months and six days of bloodshed and destruction in Europe. The price posted on the newspaper was 3 cents per copy.

Army supply trucks soon transported Dad and the other men, technically liberated but not yet free, to an airfield where Dad remembers the thorough delousing, the first hot shower in two years, the smell and feel of new clothes and boots, and, of course, the food, especially the soft, white bread. No more lead bread. They were warned to resist the temptation to overeat, but their shrunken stomachs wouldn't let them anyway.

The flight back to England was Dad's first and last in an Avro Lancaster bomber. Back in Bournemouth, where it had all begun two and a half years earlier, Dad was officially questioned about the details of the night they were shot down (see Appendix 4 for all the surviving crew interview transcripts), medically examined, and declared fit for leave and repatriation to Canada. A few days into his leave, a telegram tracked him down in London and instructed him to proceed to Southhampton immediately to catch his trans-Atlantic passage to Halifax booked on the SS Louis Pasteur steamship.

Grandma, Grandpa and the family were waiting for him at Union Station in Toronto when he finally arrived by train to much fanfare. Dad recalls the first thing he asked for at home was a banana. Following a grand homecoming, he continued his leave with a trip to Dearborn,

Michigan to meet up with fellow Luft III ex-POW roommate Stuart Hunt and his family. An extra unauthorized week of leave resulted in an AWOL charge (Absent Without Leave). There's more to that story, I'm sure.

Dad and Stuart Hunt
in Michigan, 1945

Dad and Stuart Hunt
in San Diego, 2011

Loblaws, who had generously supported its enlisted employees during the war, had a job waiting for Dad, and it's a good thing he took it, because it's where, in 1946, he met my mom, Mary Juniper, while she shopped at the store where he worked on Oakwood Avenue in Toronto. They were married in 1947 and together raised my sisters and me: Patricia, Anne, Barbara and Susan, plus two dogs (Sandy and Sasha), and a plethora of fish, turtles, canaries and budgies. Dad went on to enjoy a 34 year career with Loblaws, rising to the rank of vice president. Sadly, Mom passed away in 2009.

Ever grateful for the support he received while a prisoner of war, Dad took any opportunity to give back to the Red Cross. First, he became a blood donor since, at that time, Canada's blood donation system was administered by the Red Cross. He donated regularly throughout his life until his age precluded his eligibility. Much later, he joined the Red Cross volunteers helping less able veterans living in the veterans' wings at Sunnybrook Health Sciences Centre in Toronto. His commitment to helping fellow veterans would be acknowledged in 2003 with the Governor General's Caring Canadian Award, in 2006 with a Minister of Veterans Affairs Commendation, and in 2010 with an Ontario Volunteer Service Award.

It would be forty years before life, family and career would give Dad the time and distance to reconnect with his wartime experiences and comrades, including the four surviving members of his crew. He attended his first RCAF ex-POW reunion in Calgary in 1985. The motto for all the communications leading up to the reunion reflected the ex-POWs' continuing sense of humour and resilience: "Stay alive 'til '85". The occasion was commemorated with a reprint of the May 9, 1945 special victory issue of the Canadian Forces weekly newspaper, The Maple Leaf; its succinct 12-inch high headline read KAPUT. Many more reunions would follow in England, Vancouver, Ottawa and Halifax. Dad became actively involved with the Toronto branch of the RCAF ex-POW Association, serving as chairman from 1992-2002. He's currently a member of the Toronto Aircrew Association, the 408/437 (Toronto-York) Wing Air Force Association of Canada, and of the Armour Heights Officers' Mess in Toronto. In 2001, Dad joined the Memory Project Speakers' Bureau to share his wartime experiences with students and community groups.

Dad attends weekly lunches as well as regular social functions with a circle of local ex-POWs - several of them from Stalag Luft III and all of them in their nineties - their wives, and in some cases, their widows. I join them often, because I enjoy their company, and have such respect and admiration for their experience, survival, positive outlook and humour. There's no doubt in my mind that their POW experience helped shape who they are. Dad remains good friends with Luft III ex-pats Stuart Hunt and his wife Bridget, and Art Hawtin and his wife Noreen. Dad is now the only surviving member of his 419 squadron seven-man aircrew.

On June 28, 2012, the 125,000 airmen of Bomber Command were finally honoured as Her Majesty Queen Elizabeth II unveiled and dedicated a memorial in Green Park, London to their bravery and sacrifice, especially the 55,573 who lost their lives, over 10,000 of them Canadian. The Bomber Command casualty rate, including those wounded or taken prisoner of war, was a shocking 60%. Average aircrew age was only 22. All controversy aside - debate as to the effectiveness and the morality of bombing heavily-populated areas in war will never end - the memorial is an impressive nine-foot high bronze sculpture depicting seven Bomber Command aircrew. The roof of the memorial is made from aluminum recovered from RCAF 426 "Thunderbird" squadron Halifax bomber LW682 that was shot down and crashed into a swamp in Belgium in May 1944. The eight crew – seven Canadians and one Brit - were killed. In 1997, the bodies of three of the Canadian crew – entombed in the bomber all these years - were recovered and given a full military funeral in Geraardsbergen, Belgium.[1] Dad was one of the 42 Canadian Bomber Command veterans who were privileged to attend the event as guests of Veterans Affairs Canada. Dad was awarded the Queen Elizabeth II Diamond Jubilee in 2012 to honour his contribution, and later, the Bomber Command Bar.

Bomber Command Memorial,
Green Park, London

As Dad himself said in a 2011 video made by radX, "Being a prisoner of war was unfortunate, but I was a survivor. Would I do it again? Why sure I would, yeah, if I was 21, yeah, sure I would."[2]

Oh, and to clear up a few loose ends about Dad's wartime experiences, I can tell you the personal cheque that fellow Stalag Luft III POW Skinner gave to Dad in payment for his beloved Gruen watch, resoundly bounced when cashed after the war. Dad eventually developed a love for Brussels sprouts. And bacon and eggs is still one of his favourite meals.

Appendix 1: RCAF Ranks

Air Vice Marshal	A.V.M.
Air Commodore	A.C.
Group Captain	G/C
Wing Commander	W/C
Squadron Leader	S/L
Flight Lieutenant	F/L
Flying Officer	F/O
Pilot Officer	P/O
Warrant Officer Second Class	WOII
Warrant Officer First Class	WO1
Flight Sergeant	FS
Sergeant	Sgt.
Corporal	Cpl.
Leading Aircraftman	LAC
Aircraftman Class 1	AC.1
Aircraftman Class II	AC.2

Appendix 2: 15 ½ Operations –
Official 419 Squadron Aircrew Lists (excerpts)

1. Aircrew List DT 798 – Feb. 14/15, 1943

Cologne

14th-15th Feb.	HALIFAX II DT.798	P/O J.D. Snider	Captain
		Sgt. Pope, E.B.	Navigator
		Sgt. Bruce, A.W.A.	Bomb Aimer
		F/Sgt. Pretty, H.C.	W/Op A.G.
		Sgt. Johnson, T.B.	F/Engineer
		P/O A.R. Wallace	M-U. Gunner
		F/Sgt. Goodridge, W.H.	Rear Gunner

2. Aircrew List DT 798 – Feb. 16/17, 1943

Lorient

16th-17th Feb.	HALIFAX II DT.798	P/O J.D. Snider	Captain
		Sgt. Pope, E.B.	Navigator
		Sgt. Bruce, A.W.A.	Bomb Aimer
		F/Sgt. Pretty, H.C.	W/Op. A.G.
		Sgt. Johnson, T.B.	F/Engineer
		P/O A.R. Wallace	M.U. Gunner
		F/Sgt. Goodridge, W.H.	Rear Gunner

3. Aircrew List DT 548 – Feb. 18/19, 1943

Gardening

18th Feb.	HALIFAX II DT.548	W/O McMillen, G.A.	Captain
		Sgt. Klein, W.J.	Navigator
		P/O H. Enever	Bomb Aimer
		Sgt. Alison, W.H.D.	W/Op. A.G.
		Sgt. Howell, W.J.	F/Engineer
		P/O A.R. Wallace	M-U. Gunner
		Sgt. Boss, H.G.	Rear Gunner

4. Aircrew List W 7869 – Feb. 19/20, 1943

Wilhelmshaven

19th-20th Feb.	HALIFAX II W.7869	W/O McMillen, G.A.	Captain
		Sgt. Klein, W.J.	Navigator
		P/O H. Enever	Bomb Aimer
		Sgt. Alison, W.H.D.	W/Op. A.G.
		Sgt. Howell, W.J.	Flight Eng.
		P/O A.R. Wallace	M-U Gunner
		Sgt. Boss, H.G.	Rear Gunner

5. Aircrew List DT 641 – Feb. 28/Mar. 1, 1943

St. Nazaire

28th Feb.-1st Mar.	HALIFAX II DT.641	W/O McMillen, G.A.	Captain
		Sgt. Klein, W.J.	Navigator
		P/O H. Enever	Bomb Aimer
		Sgt. Coburn, C.S.	W/Op. A.G.
		Sgt. Howell, W.J.	F/Engineer
		P/O A.R. Wallace	M.U. Gunner
		Sgt. Boss, H.G.	Rear Gunner

6. Aircrew List DT 672 – Mar. 1/2, 1943

Berlin

1st/2nd March	HALIFAX II DT.672	Sgt. Jackson, T.K.	Captain	18.49
		F/Sgt. Carlton, J.M.	Navigator	
		F/Sgt. Fry, J.R.	Bomb Aimer	
		Sgt. Crandell, T.M.	W/Op. A.G.	
		Sgt. Sebastian, O.J.	Flight Eng.	
		Sgt. Jury, E.	M-U Gunner	
		P/O A. R. Wallace	Rear Gunner	
		P/O W. J. Boyce	2nd Pilot	

7. Aircrew List DT 548 – Mar. 3/4 1943
Hamburg (incomplete)

3rd March	HALIFAX II DT.548	W/O McMillan, G.A.	Captain
		Sgt. Klein, W.J.	Navigator
		P/O H. Enever	Bomb Aimer
		Sgt. Alison, W.H.D.	W/Op.A.G.
		Sgt. Howell, W.J.	Flight Eng.
		P/O A. R. Wallace	M-U Gunner
		Sgt. Bees, H.G.	Rear Gunner

8. Aircrew List DT 689 – Mar. 29/30, 1943
Berlin (incomplete)

29th/30th March	HALIFAX II DT.689	Sgt. Morris, J.A.	Captain
		Sgt. Godbold, K.H.	Navigator
		P/O A. R. Hickey	Bomb Aimer
		Sgt. Amos, R.J.	W/Op.A.G.
		Sgt. Turner, L.E.	Flight Eng.
		P/O A. R. Wallace	M-U Gunner
		Sgt. Way, D.C.	Rear Gunner

9. Aircrew List BB 323 – April 10/11, 1943
Frankfurt

10th/11th April	HALIFAX II BB.323	W/O McMillan, G.A.	Captain	23.47
		Sgt. Klein, W.J.	Navigator	
		P/O H. Enever	Bomb Aimer	
		Sgt. Alison, W.H.D.	W/Op.A.G.	
		Sgt. Howell, W.J.	Flight Eng.	
		P/O A.R.Wallace	2nd Gunner	
		Sgt. Bees, H.G.	Rear Gunner	

10. Aircrew List DT 689 – Apr. 14/15, 1943
Stuttgart

14th/15th April	HALIFAX II DT.689	W/O McMillan, G.A.	Captain
		P/O R.W.Lowry	Navigator
		P/O H. Enever	Bomb Aimer
		Sgt. Alison, W.H.D.	W/Op.A.G.
		Sgt. Howell, W.J.	Flight Eng.
		P/O A.R.Wallace	2nd Gunner
		Sgt. Bees H.G.	Rear Gunner

11. Aircrew List JB 923 – Apr. 16/17, 1943
Pilsen*

16th/17th April	HALIFAX II JB.932	W/O McMillan, G.A.	Captain
		P/O R.W.Lowry	Navigator
		P/O H. Enever	Bomb Aimer
		Sgt. Alison, W.H.D.	W/Op.A.G.
		Sgt. Howell, W.J.	Flight Eng.
		P/O A.R.Wallace	2nd Gunner
		Sgt. Bees, H.G.	Rear Gunner

*The reference to JB 932 is a typo. It should have read JB 923.

12. Aircrew List JB 923 – Apr. 26/27, 1943
Duisburg

26th/27th April	HALIFAX II JB.923	W/O McMillan, G.A.	Captain
		Sgt. Pope, E.B.	Navigator
		P/O H.Enever	Bomb Aimer
		Sgt. Alison, W.H.D.	W/Op.A.G.
		Sgt. Howell, W.J.	Flight Eng.
		P/O A.R.Wallace	2nd Gunner
		Sgt. Bees, H.G.	Rear Gunner
		Sgt. Adams, C.	2nd Pilot

13. Aircrew List JB 923 – Apr. 27/28, 1943
Gardening*

27th/28th April	HALIFAX II JB.929	W/O McMillan, G.A.	Captain
		Sgt. Simpson, A.	Navigator
		P/O H.Enever	Bombx Aimer
		Sgt. Alison, W.H.D.	W/Op.A.G.
		Sgt. Howell, W.J.	Flight Eng.
		P/O A.R.Wallace	2nd Gunner
		Sgt. Bees, H.G.	Rear Gunner

14. Aircrew List JB 791 - April 30/May 1, 1943
Essen

30th Apr/ 1st May	HALIFAX II JB.791	W/O McMillan, G.A.	Captain
		P/O W.S.Hendry	Navigator
		P/O H.Enever	Bomb Aimer
		Sgt. Alison, W.H.D.	W/Op.A.G.
		Sgt. Howell, W.J.	Flight Eng.
		P/O A.R.Wallace	2nd Gunner
		Sgt. Bees, H.G.	Rear Gunner

15. Aircrew List JB 791 – May 4/5, 1943
Dortmund

4th/5th May	HALIFAX II JB.791	W/O McMillan, G.A.	Captain
		Sgt. Klein, W.J.	Navigator
		P/O H.Enever	Bomb Aimer
		Sgt. Alison, W.H.D.	W/Op.A.G.
		Sgt. Howell, W.J.	Flight Eng.
		P/O A.R.Wallace	2nd Gunner
		Sgt. Bees, H.G.	Rear Gunner

16. Aircrew List JB 791 – May 12/13, 1943
Duisburg

12th/13th May	HALIFAX II JB.791	W/O McMillan, G.A.	Captain	23.18	-	Target DUISBERG with bomb load as above. Nothing further was heard from this aircraft after take-off, and its failure to return to base is presumed to be due to enemy action.
		Sgt. Klein, W.J.	Navigator			
		P/O H.Enever	Bomb Aimer			
		Sgt. Alison, W.H.D.	W/Op.A.G.			
		Sgt. Howell, W.J.	Flight Eng.			
		P/O A.R.Wallace	2nd Gunner			
		Sgt. Bees, H.G.	Rear Gunner			

Last entry in Dad's Flying Log

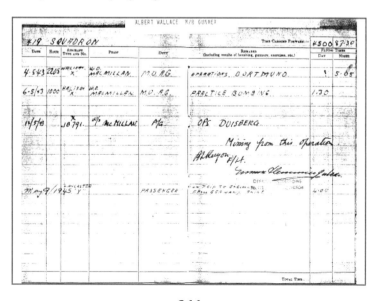

266

Appendix 3: 6 Group Bomber Command RCAF,
Daily Operations Report - May 12/13, 1943

19 Halifaxes from 408 and 419 Squadrons were joined by 51 Wellingtons from 426, 428, 429, and 431 Squadrons on an attack at Duisburg. The crews were over the target at between 13,000 and 20,000 feet, releasing 70,000 lbs of high explosives and 153,000 lbs of incendiaries. According to reports, the weather was clear and severe damage was caused to the port area and industrial sector, including the Thyssen steel works.

Sgt D. Brooke from 408 Squadron returned early as the compasses were u/s.

S/Ldr W. Newson returned early as the oxygen system was u/s.

--- --- --- --- --- --- --- --- ---

Sgt J. McIntosh from 419 Squadron returned early as they were unable to climb through the severe icing.

Sgt P. Johnson returned early as all the windows frosted over.

F/O W. Keddie and crew, flying Halifax II BB-376 coded VR-G, were attacked by an unidentified aircraft, there was no claim or damage.

Sgt R. Harrison and crew flying Halifax II JB-929 coded VR-J were attacked by an unidentified twin engine aircraft, the rear turret was damaged and Sgt E. Morgans RCAF, the rear gunner, were injured.

WO1 G. McMillan RCAF ✿ and crew, flying Halifax II JB-791 coded VR-X, failed to return from this operation.
Sgt W. Howell RCAF–POW
Sgt W. Klein RCAF–POW

P/O H. Enever RAF–POW
Sgt W. Alison RAF ✿
P/O A. Wallace RCAF–POW
Sgt H. Bees RCAF–POW
5 POWs and 2 killed after they were shot down by flak

WOII J. Palmer RCAF✿ and crew, flying Halifax II JB-861 coded VR-C, failed to return from this operation.
F/Sgt W. Simonett RCAF ✿
Sgt H. Walsh RAF ✿
P/O T. Brown RAF ✿
F/Sgt R. Weedy RCAF ✿
F/Sgt R. Ratelle RCAF ✿
Sgt A. Gearing RAF ✿
All were killed when they were shot down by a Nightfighter.

--- --- --- --- --- --- --- --- --- --- --- ---

Sgt M. Summers from 426 Squadron returned early as the oxygen system was u/s.

Sgt F. Stuart and crew flying Wellington X HE-904 coded OW-C were attacked by an unidentified enemy aircraft, there was no claim or damage.

WOII K. Fighter RCAF ✿ and crew, flying Wellington X HE-157 coded OW-N, failed to return from this operation.

F/O G. McMillan RCAF
F/Sgt D. Maxwell RCAF
Sgt E. Betts RAF
F/O H. Drake RCAF
All were killed.

Sgt I. Runciman RCAF–POW
  and crew, flying Wellington X
  HE-905 coded OW-V, failed to
  return from this operation.
F/O D. Fraser RCAF
F/O G. Miller RCAF–POW
P/O D. Laskey RCAF–POW
Sgt D. Pennock RAF–POW
F/Sgt D. Forland RCAF–Evader
4 crew were POWs, one killed,
  and one evaded capture after
  being shot down by flak.

WO1 A. Harrison from 428
  Squadron returned early as the
  pilot's escape hatch blew off.
P/O A. Reilander was attacked by
  an ME-109, there was no claim
  or damage.
P/O G. Fanson landed at East
  Moor on return.
F/Sgt A. Hatch RCAF and crew,
  flying Wellington X HE-321
  coded NA-Z, failed to return
  from this operation.
F/O R Baumgarten RCAF
F/Sgt D. Horwood RCAF
Sgt W. Leven RAF
F/Sgt C. Hildreth RCAF*
All were killed when shot down
  by a Nightfighter.

F/Sgt W. Mann RCAF and
  crew, flying Wellington X
  HE-656 coded NA-A, failed to
  return from this operation.

F/O W. O'Brien RCAF
F/O L. Dingley RCAF
P/O P. Kelly RCAF
Sgt E. Lundy RCAF
This crew gave a position off the
French coast. All were killed.

Sgt J. Pendleton from 429 Squad-
  ron was hit by flak, not
  serious.
P/O B. Geale RAF and crew,
  flying Wellington X HE-423
  coded AL-O, failed to return
  from this operation.
P/O H. Tennis RCAF
WOII J. Vose RCAF
Sgt J. Piggott RAF
WOII R. Crimmins RCAF
All were killed after being shot
  down by a Nightfighter.
Sgt A. Halstead RAF and
  crew, flying Wellington X
  HE-913 coded AL-L, failed to
  return from this operation.
P/O P.Dunger RAF
P/O S. Willoughby RAF
Sgt C. Taylor RAF
Sgt D. Broughton RCAF
All were killed after being shot
  down by a Nightfighter.

Sgt J. Reynoldson and F/Sgt P.
  Davis from 431 Squadron
  returned early due to severe
  icing.
Sgt J. Esdale returned early as the
  navigation aids were u/s.
F/O H. Wilkinson returned early
  as the rear gunner, Sgt R.
  Jenkins RAF, was sick.
Sgt K. Smith landed at Finning-
  ley on return.

Sgt G. Wood RAF 🌺 and crew,
   flying Wellington X HE-440
   coded SE-Y, failed to return
   from this operation.
Sgt E. Gummer RAF 🌺
Sgt I. Mobley RAF 🌺
Sgt A. Cresswell RAF 🌺
Sgt T. Smith RAF 🌺
All were killed. 🌺

---

* F/Sgt C. Hildreth RCAF graduated
from the same Air Gunner training class
as Dad in September 1942 at #1 Bombing
& Gunnery School in Jarvis, Ontario

Appendix 4: Loss of Bomber Aircraft Questionnaires of Returned Aircrew 1945

Squadron: 419

Aircraft Letter: VR-X

Type of Aircraft: Halifax II

Date of Loss: May 12/13, 1943

Target: Duisburg

NUMBER: R-112596	RANK: WO1	NAME: Howell, W.J.
HOW MANY OPS HAD YOU DONE: 12	DUTY IN AIRCRAFT: Engineer	DATE OF INTERROGATION: May 11, 1945

"Took off May 12th about 11:00 P.M. Climbed for an hour over base to 16,000 ft. and set course. Arrived at target 5 mins. early and did circuits outside target until P.F.F. flares were dropped. Made run in and then pilot had difficulty in opening bomb doors. I stepped forward and managed to get them open. Bombs were released and photo flash red light came on. I asked bomb aimer on intercom for permission to close doors and heard him say O.K. Closed doors and then bomb aimer called up to say bombs had not all gone. Re-opened doors and pilot was still flying straight and level. Bombs all gone - doors closed - and just as we commenced evasive action we were hit by heavy flak in stbd. wing and stbd. side of A/C. Perspex blown in front of second dickey seat. Pilot asked for goggles to protect eyes against wind. After we were hit I called all members of crew up on intercom and all reported O.K. Check of instruments revealed leaks in stbd. wing tanks and then fire was sighted behind number 5 & 6 tanks. All tank cocks closed immediately by mid upper gunner in waist and as fire appeared in front of stbd. outer it was feathered and button pressed. Fire then broke out in front of No. 1 tank and pilot feathered port inner by mistake for stbd. inner. He still managed to fly straight and level while I came forward and unfeathered port inner and feathered stbd. inner. Pilot refused to dive A/C in attempt to put flames out and as fire spread and our attempt to make Zuider Zee and ditch became impossible and pilot gave order to bale out. Navigator had difficulty opening front hatch and as I had gone down to waist to close hot air intake and check cocks pilot ordered me out back hatch to relieve congestion forward."

NUMBER: R-114160	**RANK:** F/S	**NAME:** Klein, W.J.
HOW MANY OPS HAD YOU DONE: 8	**DUTY IN AIRCRAFT:** Navigator	**DATE OF INTERROGATION:** May 11, 1945

"We took off around 23:30 hours climbing to 10,000 feet over the drome and climbed to 15,000 feet immediately to get over a nasty front which was stretched across the North Sea 50 miles from the coast. We were soon above the front where the weather was quite favourable and navigating by instrument was quite satisfactory. We crossed the Dutch coast on time where we encountered some flak but nothing serious. We encountered nothing until we reached the target where flak was coming up plenty hot. Pilot run up on target and bomber dropped his bombs - bomb doors were closed only to find incendiaries were still in aircraft. Pilot had to hold aircraft steady and re-open bomb doors to release incendiaries. It was at this moment that we were hit by flak - the only apparent damage being the pilots perspex which was smashed so badly he had to put on goggles. I gave pilot course for home and we carried on for about 5 - 10 minutes before fire broke out in starboard engine. After feathering and attempting to put fire out with extinguisher we prepared to bale out as fire seemed to be getting worse. I set detonator on G box and destroyed my chart. When pilot gave order to bale out bomb aimer jumped out just in front of me. Wireless operator was ready with his chute on to follow me out. Shortly after I baled out I heard an explosion which I believe to be our aircraft and later as I came floating down I could see a solitary aircraft burning on the ground. I landed in a clearing in a bush uninjured."

NUMBER: 126872	**RANK:** P/O	**NAME:** Enever, H.
HOW MANY OPS HAD YOU DONE: 13	**DUTY IN AIRCRAFT:** Bomb aimer	**DATE OF INTERROGATION:** May 8, 1945

"We took off from Middleton St. George at approx. 23:30 hours in not too good weather and met with little opposition before reaching the target area. We arrived 5 minutes early and circled north of Duisburg as instructed until bombing time. On making our bombing run we were coned by searchlights but lost the cone by taking violent evasive action which put us east of the target, therefore bombing run was made from E. to W instead of N-S as instructed. As the bombs were released over Duisburg we were hit by flak, the main damage being sustained in the starboard wing. The outer engine caught fire and the inner had to be feathered for some reason with which I am not familiar. Attempts were made to put out the fire but were unsuccessful. On being hit the pilot gave the order to prepare to abandon A/C. The A/C was behaving well so we decided to stay with it in case it was possible to make base or ditch in the channel. Eventually the engineer decided this was impossible as fires were out of control and the wing was in danger of breaking off. Order was given to abandon. Rear gunner left from turret, engineer and mid upper gunner from rear hatch. Meantime front hatch would not jettison and had to be taken inside A/C causing only momentary delay. Navigator and myself left from front hatch. W/Op and pilot unaccountably stayed with aircraft and were killed. Germans reported us shot down by fighter."

NUMBER: J-14982	RANK: P/O	NAME: Wallace, A.R.
HOW MANY OPS HAD YOU DONE: 15	DUTY IN AIRCRAFT: Mid upper gunner	DATE OF INTERROGATION: May 12, 1945

"We took off from Middleton St. George around 23:00 hours and climbed to altitude over the drome. Set course for our target. We arrived at target early and made a couple of circuits till Pathfinders dropped flares, then went in to bomb. We dropped our bombs but bomb doors were closed before all our load was dropped. Doors were opened again to drop rest when we were hit apparently by a flak shell in our Stbd. outer. No one was injured and aircraft seemed all right. A few minutes later Stbd. outer was on fire. Fire seemed behind motor in wing. Fire extinguishers were used but fire would not go out. Motor was feathered a few minutes later. Stbd. inner had to be feathered as well. Pilot gave orders to abandon aircraft. 5 members of the crew baled out at 12,000 feet. We were a long way off course, flying north. 2 members of the crew were in aircraft when it crashed and were killed."

NUMBER: R-124488   RANK: WO1   NAME: Bees, H.G.
HOW MANY OPS HAD   DUTY IN AIRCRAFT: DATE OF
YOU DONE: 14   Rear gunner   INTERROGATION: November 30, 1945

Please Note:
No photo
of
WO1 Bees
available

"We proceeded on a normal operation to Duisburg. While bombing the target we were unfortunate in being hit directly by heavy flak, explosions very shortly after bombs were released. Fire broke out immediately and engineer feathered the engines as they lost power. Owing to steady loss of height and fire, the pilot ordered me to bale out first. I went out the rear turret and noticed sparks and fire breaking out from the stbd wing. I baled out approximately 50 miles from Duisburg West. Right foot was injured on landing, still occasionally painful after two years. Both boots came off in the air, no straps round ankles."

Appendix 5: The Great Escape – "The Fifty"

CANADIAN (RCAF)
F/L "Hank" Birkland
F/L Gordon Kidder
F/L Patrick Langford
F/L George McGill
F/L James Wernham
F/L George Wiley

AUSTRALIAN (RAAF)
S/L James Catanach
F/L Albert Hake
F/L "Rusty" Kierath
S/L "Willy" Williams (RAF)

NEW ZEALANDER (RNZAF)
F/L Arnold Christiensen
F/O "Johnny" Pohé

NORWEGIAN (RAF)
F/O Hallada Espelid
F/O Nils Fuglesang

SOUTH AFRICAN (SAAF)
Lt. Johannes Gouws
Lt. Clement McGarr
Lt. Rupert Stevens

LITHUANIAN (RAF)
F/L Romas Marcinkus

BELGIAN (RAF)
F/L Henri Picard

GREEK (RAF)
P/O Nick Skanzikas

BRITISH (RAF)
F/L Gordon Brettell
F/L Johnny Bull
S/L Roger Bushell
F/L Mike Casey
F/O Dennis Cochran
S/L Ian Cross
F/L Brian Evans
F/L William Grisman
F/L Alastair Gunn
F/L Charles Hall
F/L Anthony Hayter
F/L Edgar Humphreys
S/L Thomas Kirby-Green
F/L Thomas Leigh
F/L "Cookie" Long
F/L Harold Milford
F/O Robert Stewart
F/L John Stower
F/L Denys Street
F/L Cyril Swain
F/L "Tim" Walenn
F/L John Williams

POLISH (RAF)
F/L Antoni Kiewnarski
F/O Wlodzimierz Kolanowski
F/O "Danny" Krol
F/O Jerzy Mondschein
F/O Kazimierz Pawluk
F/O "Peter" Tobolski

FRENCH
Lt. Bernard Scheidhauer

CZECH (RAF)
F/L "Wally" Valenta

Appendix 6: The Two Forced Marches 1945
Estimated Mileage

Date	From	Destination	Kilometers (estimated)	Total Distance
First March, January 28-February 4, 1945				
Jan. 28 *	Stalag Luft III	Halbau	17	17
	Halbau	Freiwalden	11	28
	Freiwalden	Leippa	6	34
Jan. 29 *	Leippa	Priebus	12	46
	Priebus	Muskau	16	62
	Muskau	French POW camp	4	66
Jan. 30-31	No marching			
Feb. 1-2 *	French POW camp	A barn near Graustein	18	84
	Graustein	Spremburg	10	94
	Spremburg	Railway siding/ Train to Tarmstedt	4	98
Feb. 3-4	On the train	Tarmstedt		
Feb. 5	Tarmstedt	Marlag und Milag Nord (a naval POW camp)	3	101
Second March, April 10-28, 1945				
April 10	Marlag und Milag Nord	A field near Heeslingen	16	117
April 11	A field near Heeslingen	A field	12	129
April 12	A field	A field near Harsefeld	10	139
April 13	No marching			
April 14	A field near Harsefeld	An orchard near Neucloster	6	145
April 15	An orchard near. Neucloster	Elbe riverbank near Cranz	15	160
April 16	Elbe riverbank near Cranz	A field near Blankenese	4	164
April 17	A field near Blankenese	Near Ellerbek	18	182
April 18	No marching			
April 19	Near Ellerbek	A field	14	196
April 20	A field	A field near Elmenhorst	15	211

April 21	A field near Elmenhorst	Neritz	7	218
April 22	Neritz	A barn near Kleinborintz	17	235
April 23	A barn near Kleinborintz	A barn in Hamburg	8	243
April 24-27	No marching			
April 28	A barn in Hamburg	A barn in Wulmenau	11	**254**
April 29-May 1	No marching			
May 2	Liberated			

* G/C Wilson reported that travel on these days showed a ruthless disregard for the prisoners' welfare and violated Article 7 of the Geneva Convention: Evacuation on foot shall be made in stages, not normally exceeding 20 kms per day.[1]

Notes

1   "There are no words": Sir Arthur Harris, Air Marshall of the Royal Air Force, www.bombercommandmuseum.ca

PROLOGUE
1   "They took me out into an office": We Were Freedom: Canadian Stories of the Second World War. Key Porter Books, 2011 (An excerpt of Albert's story as told to Shayla Howell, Research and Collections Officer, The Memory Project, Historica Canada)

CHAPTER 1: EARLY DAYS
1   "131,553 aircrew had graduated:" Sights on Jarvis, Robert Schweyer, Heronwood Enterprises, 2003, p. 7

2   "The Blitz": BBC: On This Day – September 7, 1940. http://news.bbc.co.uk/onthisday/hi/dates/stories/september/7/newsid_3515000/3515708.stm

3   "bloodthirsty guttersnipe": BBC: On This Day – June 22, 1941. http://news.bbc.co.uk/onthisday/hi/dates/stories/june/22/newsid_3526000/3526691.stm

4   "training accidents": Canadian Military Journal, Spring 2002, p. 66; Schweyer, pg. 7

5   "A,B, C, or D": Schweyer, p. 65

6   "the worst disaster and largest capitulation": BBC: On This Day – February 15, 1942. http://news.bbc.co.uk/onthisday/hi/dates/stories/february/15/newsid_3529000/3529447.stm

7   "Air Marshall Sir Arthur Harris": Royal Air Force.

    www.raf.mod.uk/history/bombercommandthethousandbomberraids3031may.cfm

8   "The Silver Cross": Veterans Affairs Canada.

    http://www.veterans.gc.ca/eng/remembrance/medals-decorations/memorial-cross

9   "Dieppe": The National Archives of Canada

CHAPTER 2: OVERSEAS
1   "over the course of the war": www.wintonforum.co.uk/qp/charminsterswar.html

2   "26 Focke Wulf 190 fighters": www.rafcommands.com/forum/showthread.php?3668-Attack-on-the-Hotel-Metropole-23-May-1943

3 419 Squadron: RAF History. www.raf.mod.uk/bombercommand/ h419.html

4 Halifax vs. Lancaster: For more detailed analysis, see Harris, Stephen J. (2006) "The Halifax and Lancaster in Canadian Service", Canadian Military History: Vol. 15: Iss. 3, Article 2. Available at: http://scholars.wlu.ca/cmh/vol15/iss3/2

5 "the BBC news reported": BBC: On This Day – February 2, 1943. http://news.bbc.co.uk/onthisday/hi/dates/stories/february/2/ newsid_3573000/3573003.stm

6 W/C John "Moose" Fulton: www.419squadronbewarethemoose. com/fulton.html

7 "Lord Nuffield": The Nuffield Trust: For the forces of the crown, www.nuffieldtrust.org/fifty.htm

8 "P/O Harling was indeed a lucky man": http://airforce.ca/uploads/ airforce/2009/07/ALPHA-HA.02.html

9 "According to 419 Squadron History": The Moose Squadron 1941-45, The War Years of 419 Squadron. Canadian Forces Training Material Production Centre (CFTMPC) Winnipeg, June 1977. Acknowledgement reads: "The Manuscript used for this Book is held in the Directorate of History, National Defence Headquarters, Ottawa, under Accession Number 73/331." p. 84

CHAPTER 3: SHOT DOWN

1 "Nothing further was heard from this aircraft": 419 Squadron: RCAF 1941 to 1945, www.419squadronbewarethemoose.com/ crews/May-5-43.jpg

2 "A third double loss of aircraft": The Moose Squadron 1941-45, The War Years of 419 Squadron, p. 90

3 "the Red Cross organization": Canadian Red Cross Society pamphlet: Prisoners: Wounded, Missing, Sick, December 1942

4 "the 1929 Geneva Convention": International Committee of the Red Cross, Convention relative to the Treatment of Prisoners of War. Geneva, 27 July 1929, www.icrc.org/ihl.nsf/full/305?open-document

5 "According to 419 Squadron History": The Moose Squadron 1941-45, The War Years of 419 Squadron, p. 89

CHAPTER 4: PRISONER OF WAR – STALAG LUFT III, 1943

1 "one of the most popular men": excerpt from a letter to Mrs. K. Wallace from Mervyn Fleming, Commanding Officer 419 Squadron a letter dated May 26, 1943

2 "They're [the three tunnels] are all to be known by their names": Brickhill, p. 37

3 Red Cross Canadian parcel contents: A Wartime Log, John Colwell, p. 19. Original resides in the Comox Air Force Museum, Canadian Forces Base, Comox, B.C. Reproduced with permission of Captain John Low, 19 Wing Heritage Officer

4 "Hildreth and Richmond": They Shall Grow Not Old: A Book of Remembrance. Les Allison and Harry Hayward. Commonwealth Air Training Plan Museum Inc., Brandon, Manitoba, p. 322 and 642

5 "Foodstuffs issued to POWs": Colwell, p. 76

6 "German radio": BBC: On This Day – July 10, 1943. http://news.bbc.co.uk/onthisday/hi/dates/stories/july/10/news-id_3587000/3587283.stm

7 "Mussolini has quit": BBC: On This Day – July 25, 1943. http://news.bbc.co.uk/onthisday/hi/dates/stories/july/25/news-id_3600000/3600649.stm

8 "Norm Notley": Allison and Hayward, p. 564

9 "The dress and bearing of the POWs": Colwell, p. 75

10 "Don Kelly": Allison and Hayward, p. 380

11 "The more resourceful Kriegies": Colwell, p. 105, 122, 123

12 "Turn Back the Clock": Colwell, p. 64

13 "Italy surrendered": BBC: On This Day – September 8, 1943. http://news.bbc.co.uk/onthisday/hi/dates/stories/september/8/newsid_3612000/3612037.stm

14 "Don Morrison": http://www.acesofww2.com/Canada/aces/morrison.htm

15 "Heard 3 Americans escaped": Colwell, p. 65

16 "George and Margaret": Colwell, p. 65

17 "New York Yankees": www.baseball-reference.com/postseason/1943_WS.shtml

18 "Shall We Dance": Colwell, p. 65

19 "There's a goon rule that says": Colwell, p. 77

20 "Heije Schaper": Ben van Drogenbroek

21 "My old pal Huck from Jarvis": Allison and Hayward, p. 341

22 "Doug Storey and his whole crew": Allison and Hayward, p. 733

CHAPTER 5: PRISONER OF WAR – STALAG LUFT III, 1944

1   "Back in 1942": www.historylearningsite.co.uk/atlantic_wall.htm

2   "One of the goon orders": Colwell, p. 76

3   "Johnny C. actually made an oven": Colwell, p. 68

4   "The German blockade of Leningrad": BBC: On This Day – January 27, 1944, http://news.bbc.co.uk/onthisday/hi/dates/stories/january/27/newsid_3498000/3498330.stm

5   "gramophone needles": Brickhill, p. 119

6   "With room searches heating up": Ibid., p. 152-154

7   "The BBC's V-For-Victory campaign": www.bbc.co.uk/historyofthebbc/resources/bbcatwar/overseas.shtml

8   "Tunnel Harry was ready to go:" Brickhill, p. 160

9   "disastrous attack on Nuremberg": www.raf.mod.uk/history/raf-historytimeline1944.cfm

10 "Arts & Crafts show": Colwell, p. 70

11 "Escaped prisoners of war": The Geneva Convention. www.icrc.org/applic/ihl/ihl.nsf/ART/305-430051?OpenDocument

12 "Belligerents shall ensure": International Committee of the Red Cross, Convention relative to the Treatment of Prisoners of War, Part III, Article 52: www.icrc.org/applic/ihl/ihl.nsf/ART/305-430053?OpenDocument

13 "Imprisonment is the most severe": Ibid., Part III, Article 54

14 "Ed Webb": Allison and Hayward, p. 801

15 "On May 18, 1944": BBC: On This Day – May 18, 1944, http://news.bbc.co.uk/onthisday/hi/dates/stories/may/18/newsid_3544000/3544047.stm

16 "the world is finding out": Anthony Eden, House of Commons, Hansard, May 19, 1944, http://hansard.millbanksystems.com/commons/1944/may/19/officer-prisoners-of-war-germany-shooting#S5CV0400P0_19440519_HOC_8

17 "Rome was the first": BBC: On This Day – June 5, 1944, http://news.bbc.co.uk/onthisday/hi/dates/stories/june/5/newsid_3547000/3547329.stm

18 "Back at 419 squadron base": National Defence and the Canadian Forces. www.cmp-cpm.forces.gc.ca/dhh-dhp/gal/vcg-gcv/bio/mynarski-ac-eng.asp

19 "Anthony Eden": House of Commons, Hansard June 23, 1944, http://hansard.millbanksystems.com/commons/1944/jun/23/officer-prisoners-of-war-germany-shooting#S5CV0401P0_19440623_HOC_9

20 "final tally of the 76 men": The Great Escape, Rob Davis, www.elsham.pwp.blueyonder.co.uk/gt_esc/

21 "It took 120 Klim cans": Colwell, p. 54

22 "On August 1, 1944": BBC: On This Day – August 1, 1944, http://news.bbc.co.uk/onthisday/hi/dates/stories/august/1/news-id_3932000/3932555.stm

23 "Keith Fleming": Allison and Hayward, p. 232

24 "the first V2 rocket": www.information-britain.co.uk/m/famdates.php?id=77

25 "The Battle of Arnhem": BBC: On This Day – September 17, 1944, http://news.bbc.co.uk/onthisday/hi/dates/stories/september/17/newsid_3662000/3662264.stm

26 "T. Eaton Company Limited": Historica Canada, The Canadian Encyclopedia, www.thecanadianencyclopedia.com/articles/t-eaton-company-limited

27 "Simpsons Limited": Historica Canada, The Canadian Encyclopedia, www.thecanadianencyclopedia.com/articles/simpsons-limited

28 "the St. Louis Cardinals": www.baseball-reference.com/postseason/1944_WS.shtml

29 "Caterpillar Club": The Caterpillar Club Story, Irvin Aerospace, Belleville, Ontario

30 "battleship Tirpitz": www.bombercommandmuseum.ca/tirpitz.html

31 "More than a million men": BBC: On This Day, Dec. 17, 1944, http://news.bbc.co.uk/onthisday/hi/dates/stories/december/17/newsid_3515000/3515538.stm

32 "only half a Red Cross Parcel": Report on the Forced Evacuation of Allied Officers and Other Rank Prisoners of War from Stalag Luft III, Sagan, Germany – January/February 1945, Gp/Capt D.E.L. Wilson, National Archives of the UK, AIR 40/269, Section B, Part 6

CHAPTER 6: PRISONER OF WAR - THE FIRST FORCED MARCH: JANUARY 27 to FEBRUARY 5, 1945

1 "Auschwitz liberation": BBC: On This Day, Jan. 27, 1945, http://news.bbc.co.uk/onthisday/hi/dates/stories/january/27/news-id_3520000/3520986.stm

2 "Geneva Convention lays down": Wilson, Section A, Part 4

3 "factors contributing to the harshness of the marches": Ibid., Section B, Parts 5 - 8

4   "Little information about route or destination": Ibid., Section L, Part 79

5   "The absence of any agreed system of halts": Ibid., Section E, Part 33

6   "German women refused to take anything": Ibid., Section E, Part 34

7   "At least 23,000 Red Cross Food Parcels:" Ibid., Section C, Parts 18 - 22

8   "this and other accommodations": Ibid., Section L, Part 79

9   "more than one Officer had frostbite": Ibid. Section E, Part 49

10 "One of them had a baby pram": Ibid., Section E, Part 49

11 "On the outskirts of Spremberg": Ibid., Section E, Part 52

12 "The hot meal provided at Spremberg": Ibid., Section L, Part 79

13 "The supply of German rations on the march": Ibid., Section L, Part 83

14 "thirst was serious": Ibid., Section F, Part 58

15 "lack of drinking water": Ibid., Section L, Part 79

16 "apart from the exhaustion": Ibid., Section G, Part 61

17 "Norwegian newspaper, Aftenposten": Ibid., Section K, Parts 75 and 77

18 "the three Allied leaders": BBC: On This Day, Feb. 7, 1945, http://news.bbc.co.uk/onthisday/hi/dates/stories/february/7/news-id_3517000/3517236.stm

19 "over 2,600 tons of bombs": BBC: On This Day – February 14, 1945, http://news.bbc.co.uk/onthisday/hi/dates/stories/february/14/newsid_3549000/3549905.stm

20 "He's made all kinds of things": Colwell, p. 113

21 "Heard that 1 of our boys got shot": Report on the Forced Evacuation of Allied Officers and Other Rank Prisoners of War from Stalag Luft III, Sagan, Germany – January/February 1945, Marlag Milag Nord – Lager Luft, Gp/Capt D.E.L. Wilson, National Archives of the UK, AIR 40/269, Section II, Part 19

22 "The Japanese army and naval troops": BBC: On This Day – February 23, 1945, http://news.bbc.co.uk/onthisday/hi/dates/stories/february/23/newsid_3564000/3564547.stm

23 "Foodacco cigarette prices": Buckham, p. 52

24 "the Grand Slam bomb": Royal Air Force, Bomber Command Famous Raids, Grand Slam Raids, www.raf.mod.uk/history/bombercommandgrandslamraids.cfm

25 "repeated attempts to advocate": Wilson, Marlag Und Milag – Lager Luft, Section I, Part 8

26 "Still no power in the camp": Buckham, p. 58

27 "Goon order says": Buckham, p. 58

28 "Used it to spell a huge message": Colwell, p. 114

CHAPTER 7: PRISONER OF WAR – THE SECOND FORCED MARCH: APRIL 10 to MAY 2, 1945

1 "G/C Wray was later made an Officer": Air Force Association of Canada, http://airforce.ca/awards.php?search=1&keyword=&page=809&mem=&type=rcaf

2 "Our news is that Mussolini": BBC: On This Day – April 28, 1945, http://news.bbc.co.uk/onthisday/hi/dates/stories/april/28/newsid_3564000/3564529.stm

3 "Hitler is dead": BBC: On This Day – May 1, 1945, http://news.bbc.co.uk/onthisday/hi/dates/stories/may/1/newsid_3571000/3571497.stm

EPILOGUE

1 "Bomber Command Memorial": Vintage Wings of Canada, www.vintagewings.ca/VintageNews/Stories/tabid/116/ArticleType/ArticleView/ArticleID/369/language/en-CA/Default.aspx

2 "Heroes on radx": produced by Crista Bazos, February 2011. radX is owned and operated by High Fidelity HDTV

APPENDIX 6: THE TWO FORCED MARCHES ESTIMATED MILEAGE, 1945

1 "G/C Wilson reported that travel on these days": Wilson, Section L, Part 79

Photo and Document Credits

CHAPTER 2: OVERSEAS

Forces Base, Cold Lake, Alberta, Book No. 5, Halifax Era, compiled by Vince Elmer, unofficial 419 archivist (Photo originally provided to the archive courtesy of Wm. McNicol). Reproduced with permission of Lieutenant-Colonel R.K. "Midas" Vogan

CHAPTER 3: SHOT DOWN

CHAPTER 4: PRISONER OF WAR – STALAG LUFT III, 1943

War. Hamilton Spectator collection

131 POW doing laundry with a dhobi stick and bucket. Albert Wallace Collection

133 Transcript of Kriegsgefangenenpost dated July 3, 1943. Albert Wallace Collection

135 Transcript of Kriegsgefangenenpost dated July 4, 1943. Albert Wallace Collection

136 Transcript of Kriegsgefangenenpost dated July 4, 1943. Albert Wallace Collection

140 Stalag Luft III camp orchestra. Albert Wallace Collection

142 Transcript of Kriegsgefangenenpost dated August 13, 1943. Albert Wallace Collection

143 Transcript of Postkarte dated August 19, 1943. Albert Wallace Collection

145 Transcript of Kriegsgefangenenpost dated August 27, 1943. Albert Wallace Collection

146 POWs checking out the class schedule. Albert Wallace Collection

147 Transcript of Kriegsgefangenenpost dated September 5, 1943. Albert Wallace Collection

150 Technical POW crew backstage in the Stalag Luft III camp theatre. Albert Wallace Collection

150 Transcript of Postkarte dated September 25, 1943. Albert Wallace Collection

151 Transcript of Kriegsgefangenenpost dated September 25, 1943. Albert Wallace Collection

152 Bob and Kate Wallace; Betty and Eleanor Wallace. Albert Wallace Collection

153 Aunt May and barn cat. Albert Wallace Collection

154 Transcript of Kriegsgefangenenpost postmarked October 16, 1943. Albert Wallace Collection

155 Cousin Dorothy. Albert Wallace Collection

157 Eleanor and Betty Wallace; Kate and Betty Wallace. Albert Wallace Collection

158 Transcript of Kriegsgefangenenpost dated November 4, 1943. Albert Wallace Collection

159 Scene from a camp theatre production. Albert Wallace Collection

160 Transcript of Kriegsgefangenenpost dated November 12, 1943. Albert Wallace Collection

CHAPTER 5: PRISONER OF WAR – STALAG LUFT III, 1944

Albert Wallace Collection

194 Transcript of Kriegsgefangenenpost dated May 28, 1944. Albert Wallace Collection

195 Transcript of Kriegsgefangenenpost dated June 3, 1944. Albert Wallace Collection

197 Transcript of Kriegsgefangenenpost dated June 21, 1944. Albert Wallace Collection

199 Transcript of Kriegsgefangenenpost dated July 9, 1944. Albert Wallace Collection

200 Transcript of Postkarte dated July 14, 1944. Albert Wallace Collection

201 G/C Wray and G/C Wilson judging at Sports Day. Albert Wallace Collection

201 Art Hawtin doing the broad jump at Sports Day. Albert Wallace Collection

202 Transcript of Kriegsgefangenenpost dated July 23, 1944. Albert Wallace Collection

203 Transcript of Postkarte dated August 2, 1944. Albert Wallace Collection

204 Transcript of Kriegsgefangenenpost dated August 21, 1944. Albert Wallace Collection

205 Transcript of Postkarte dated August 21, 1944. Albert Wallace Collection

205 Transcript of Kriegsgefangenenpost dated August 22, 1944. Albert Wallace Collection

206 Earl Clare's Cardinals – 1944 Major League softball champs. Albert Wallace Collection. Names courtesy of Art Hawtin

206 Albert's 1944 softball team. Albert Wallace Collection

209 Transcript of Kriegsgefangenenpost dated September 26, 1944. Albert Wallace Collection

210 Transcript of two Postkartes dated October 5, 1944. Albert
211 Wallace Collection

212 Transcript of Kriegsgefangenenpost dated October 13, 1944. Albert Wallace Collection

213 Transcript of Kriegsgefangenenpost dated October 1944. Albert Wallace Collection

214 Transcript of Kriegsgefangenenpost dated November 4, 1944. Albert Wallace Collection

215 Transcript of Postkarte dated November 16, 1944. Albert Wallace

Collection

CHAPTER 6: PRISONER OF WAR – THE FIRST FORCED MARCH: JANUARY 27 to FEBRUARY 5, 1945

CHAPTER 7: PRISONER OF WAR – THE SECOND FORCED MARCH: APRIL 10 to MAY 2, 1945

CHAPTER 8: FREE AT LAST

EPILOGUE

262 Bomber Command Memorial, Green Park, London. Albert Wallace Collection

APPENDICES

RECENT PHOTOGRAPHS

Recent Photographs

Albert at current-day 419 'Moose' Tactical Fighter (Training) squadron in Cold Lake, Alberta,   June 2011

Lieutenant-Colonel R.K. 'Midas' Vogan, then Commanding Officer 419 'Moose' squadron, Albert & Albert's daughter Barbara at Fulton Field, Kamloops, B.C. for the 70th Anniversary celebration of 419 squadron May 2011

Albert, and fellow mid upper gunner and prisoner of war Frank Boyd, at the Bomber Command Memorial dedication and unveiling ceremony in Green Park, London
June 28, 2012

Albert, and fellow RCAF navigator, 419 squadron ex-pat and Stalag Luft III ex prisoner of war Fred Stephens, at the Runnymede Memorial, England
June, 2012

293

Glossary, Slang and Abbreviations

88	88 millimeter cannon used by the Germans
Ablutions	Personal hygiene such as bathing, showering
Abort	Washroom/outhouse
A/C	Aircraft
AG	Aircrew position: Air Gunner
AFC	Air Force Cross. British military decoration
Appell	Counting (roll call) parade
Axis Powers	A group of nations that fought against the Allies: primarily Germany, Italy and Japan. Later included Hungary, Romania, Bulgaria, Croatia and Slovakia.
AYPA	Anglican Young People's Association
B-17 Flying Fortress/Fort	4-engine heavy bomber used by the US Army Air Forces
B&G	Bombing and Gunnery
Balloon Barrage	Huge balloons attached to anchored steel cables that floated at 2-3,000 ft. to protect key targets like cities, factories and ports
Bash (noun)	A special or extra large meal
Bash (verb)	As in "bash a few circuits", walk laps around the camp perimeter
Battledress	Combat uniform
Batwoman/Batman	A person assigned to a commissioned officer as a personal servant
Belt up	Tightening one's belt because food would be scarce, usually when Red Cross parcels were cut
Big X	Roger Bushell's code name as head of the X Organization, Stalag Luft III organizers of The Great Escape
Billet	Living quarters for soldiers
Billy tin	A light weight cooking pot
Bit it	Slang for killed
Block Captain	Most senior officer in a hut/barrack block
Bolingbroke ("Boly")	Bomber training aircraft made by Bristol
Bomber Command	Royal Air Force organization that controlled the strategic bombing offensive of World War II
Bought the farm	Slang for killed in a military action
Boulton Paul (BP) Turret	A type of gun turret used in Bomber Command aircraft
Brew	A drink of some kind (tea, coffee, cocoa or alcohol)

Bristol B1 Mid Upper Gun Turret	A type of gun turret used in Bomber Command aircraft
Browning	Machine gun
BCATP	British Commonwealth Air Training Plan
Bully Beef	Corned beef
Bumf	Slang for toilet paper
Buzz	To fly dangerously low to the ground
C.N.E.	Canadian National Exhibition. Permanent home to a fair that has taken place annually in Toronto since 1879
CO	Commanding Officer
Colditz Castle	German prisoner of war camp for Allied repeat escapers
Cooler	Slang for jail
Cone	To pinpoint an aircraft with searchlights to temporarily blind the crew. Once "coned", a master blue searchlight marked the aircraft as a target for the German fighters
Cookie	4,000 lb bomb
Corkscrew	Evasive maneuver taken by the pilot to avoid being caught in German searchlights
D Bar	US army chocolate bar ration. A thick rectangular 5 ounce bar contained in the American Red Cross food parcel
Deutsche	German
DFC	Distinguished Flying Cross. British military decoration
Dhobi stick	Tin cans on a stick used by the POWs as a hand washing machine
Dick	Code name for one of the three main escape tunnels at Stalag Luft III (Tom, Dick and Harry)
Ditch	Crash land an aircraft in water
D ring	Metal ring in the shape of a "D" used to deploy a parachute
DRO	Daily Routine Orders. Any relevant daily news posting such as training vacancies, transfers etc.
DSO	Distinguished Service Order. British military decoration
Drogue	A windsock type of nylon target towed behind a plane for air-to-air firing practice
Dummkopf	German for idiot
Dulag Luft	A transit camp in German-occupied Poland where Allied Air Force prisoners passed through for interrogation before they were assigned to a permanent POW camp
Eatons	Canadian department store

Evader	A person isolated in hostile territory who eludes capture
Fags	Cigarettes
Fairey Battle	A British single-engine light bomber
FE	Aircrew position: Flight Engineer
Feather the prop	To turn the propeller blades of a malfunctioning engine into the wind to minimize drag. Prevents further damage, conserves fuel and allows the remaining engines to better fly the plane
Ferret	A German who snoops in, around and under the huts in a POW camp looking and listening for signs of tunnels and escape activity
Flak	Anti-aircraft fire from the ground
Focke-Wulf 190	A German fighter; one of their best
Foodacco	A prisoner-run camp organization for POWs to market surplus food or other items based on bartering
Frazer Nash (FN)	A type of gun turret used in Bomber Command aircraft
Führer	German for leader
Gardening	An operation involving dropping mines by parachute from low altitude into the sea to target ships. Also known as mining.
GEE	Generalized Estimating Equation. British radio navigation
Gen	The news
Geneva Convention	International rules regarding the humanitarian treatment of victims of war, including prisoners of war
George	Code name for the fourth and lesser-known tunnel at Stalag Luft III. Built after The Great Escape and never used
Gestapo	The secret state police of Nazi Germany
Get the chop	Slang for being killed in active service
GIS	Ground Instruction School
Glop	A food concoction made out of whatever ingredients were available
Goering	Hermann Goering. Adolf Hitler's leader of aviation and head of the German Luftwaffe (Air Force)
Gone for a Burton	RAF slang for "dead". Coined from the name of a UK brewery "Burton Ale" (gone for a beer)
Goon	Any German
Goon box	A sentry lookout built on stilts in a POW camp
Griff	The news

Halifax	Four-engine heavy bomber aircraft
Hally or Hallies	Nickname for the Halifax bomber
Hang up	Slang for something gone wrong
Harry	Code name for one of the three main escape tunnels at Stalag Luft III (Tom, Dick and Harry). The tunnel used for The Great Escape
Harvard	A training aircraft
H.E.	High explosive
Hauptmann	German for Captain
Home run	Escaping and making it to safety
Horlicks tablets	An energy boosting treat used by the military for survival
IFF	Identification Friend or Foe. An electronic system for quickly identifying enemy aircraft
Incendiary	Small bomb
JU-88	Luftwaffe aircraft
Kein trinkwasser	Vessel for fetching water from the prison camp kitchen
Klim	Powdered milk (16 oz tin). "Milk" spelled backwards
Kommandant	German Commanding Officer
Kriegie	Short for kriegsgefangener (German for war prisoner)
Kriegsmarine	The German Navy
Lancaster or "Lanc"	Four-engine British heavy bomber aircraft made by Avro
Line shooting	Telling a lie or a tall tale
Luftwaffe	The German Air Force
Mae West	A life vest worn when flying over water
MC	Military Cross. British military decoration
ME	German *Messerschmitt* fighter aircraft
Met. Officer	The weatherman
Mossie	Slang for Mosquito, a British bomber that was made of wood. Fast
M.U.A.G.	Aircrew position: Mid Upper Air Gunner
NCO	Non-commissioned officer (Sergeant and Flight Sergeant)
Nissen hut	A half cylinder steel structure used to build air and army bases

Oberfeldwebel	German for Warrant Officer
Op	Operation
Palliasse	Rough mattress made from burlap stuffed with wood chips or straw
Pathfinder or Pathfinder Force (PFF)	Aircraft that flies ahead of the bomber stream at a lower altitude and drops target markers to assist the bombers
Penguin	A POW who helps disperse sand removed from a tunnel
Perspex	Aircraft window
Purge	A group of prisoners being moved in or out of the camp
Quartermaster	A military officer who is responsible for issuing quarters, rations, clothing and other supplies
RAF	Royal Air Force (British)
RAAF	Royal Australian Air Force
RCAF	Royal Canadian Air Force
Real McCoy	An expression meaning "the genuine article"
RG	Aircrew position: Rear Gunner
Remuster	To change military classification
RNZAF	Royal New Zealand Air Force
SBO	Senior British Officer
Schweinehund	Derogatory German word for "pig-dog"
Semaphore	Man-to-man communication with flags
Shizenpanzerwagen	Kriegie slang for the cart used to pump out the aborts (toilets)
Simpson's	Canadian department store
Sisman's Scampers	A brand of everyday shoes
Sprog	Slang for a rookie
SS	*Schutzstaffeln* (German for protection squads)
Stalag	Shortened version of *Stammlager* (a German prisoner of war camp)
Stand-down	A rest from operations
Stooge	The clean-up person or helper on a cooking team
Strafed	Shot at on the ground by low-flying aircraft machine guns
Tail End Charlie	Slang for the Rear Gunner aircrew position

TI	Target indicator. A flare dropped by a Pathfinder aircraft to mark a target for the bombers
Tin Basher	A prisoner skilled at making useful articles out of tin cans
Tom	Code name for one of the three main escape tunnels at Stalag Luft III (Tom, Dick and Harry)
U/s	Unserviceable (aircraft)
USAAF	United States Army Air Forces
V1	*Vergeltungswaffen*, an early German pilotless flying bomb with a range of up to 200km
VC	Victoria Cross. The highest military decoration
Very pistol	A flare gun. A different colour cartridge was used for each day
Verboten	German for not allowed
Vorlager	German compound outside the camp gate that housed the sick quarters, the cooler, Red Cross parcel storage, coal shed
WAAF	Women's Auxiliary Air Force
Waafery	Slang for the women's barracks that housed the WAAFs
WD	Women's Division of the Air Force
Wehrmacht	German armed forces
Wellington	Twin-engine medium bomber aircraft made by Vickers. The main British bomber in the early part of the war. Preceded the Halifax heavy bomber
York Roll	Processed meat (pork)

Acknowledgements

From the time I began collecting stories and materials about Dad's wartime experiences to the time I finished this book, my "Dad Project" took on a life of its own. I'm glad I didn't know going in what a long road it would be. I couldn't have done it without many helping hands along the way.

There was the Wartime Log that fellow Canadian prisoner of war Johnny Colwell meticulously kept throughout his time at Stalag Luft III, now carefully preserved in the Comox Air Force Museum at the Canadian Forces Base in Comox, B.C. Mr. Colwell's logbook provided a detailed account of prison camp life, along with a solid timeline of camp events that helped me time and again. Too, it gave me insight into some of the blunt, de-personalized things Dad had said in his letters. In his first letter home from Dulag Luft, he matter of factly wrote "5 of the crew are here. 2 were killed." Similarly, one of Johnny's logbook entries reads "1 American NCO shot dead in the kitchen door. Made a potato masher." Keep calm and carry on.

It was the U.K. Wartime Memories Project web site, devoted to collecting and preserving recollections, documents, photographs and artifacts from the two World Wars, which showed me the potentially rich but sometimes sad world of message boards and forums. There I came across a post from Gail Wasson, a Canadian woman looking for a particular photograph of her uncle Bruce Baker who had also been imprisoned in Stalag Luft III. A bell rang in my head as I recalled the name Bruce Baker from a few of Dad's letters written home from the camp. What were the odds? So I mentioned this to Dad and replied to Gail's post. After much to and fro, we determined that her late uncle and the Bruce Baker of Dad's letters were one and the same. They had known each other in Toronto before the war and then ended up in the same POW camp in Germany.

Gail's post also mentioned that her uncle Bruce had been shot down off the coast of Denmark in April 1943, which caught the attention of Finn Buch, a Dane whose family were Danish resistance members during the war. Through his father, who had witnessed many Allied air crashes during the war, Finn himself became personally interested in researching and writing about the stories and fate of airmen lost over Denmark. Gail put me in touch with Finn who generously shared his knowledge and sent me new information, including an official report on Dad's final air operation. Buoyed by this success, I put up a post of my own on another prisoner of war site, and 18 months later was contacted by Vicki Sorensen, whose late father Frank Sorensen too had been in Stalag Luft III and turned out to have many POW acquaintances in common with Dad. Dad and Frank may well have known each other, but as Dad put it, "it's lost in the memory banks."

Too, there was *They Shall Grow Not Old,* a book of remembrance published by the Commonwealth Air Training Plan Museum in Brandon, Manitoba. This sobering two-inch thick memorial book contains a brief biography of the over 18,000 men and women, Canadians and other nationals who died in the air war from 1939 to 1945 wearing the uniform of the RCAF. A huge undertaking, it was generously created to provide a central record of what had happened to the deceased and where they were buried. Sadly, it was through this book that I was able to track many of Dad's air gunner training classmates from the No. 1 Bombing and Gunnery School at Jarvis, Ontario. They were all so young.

I was touched by the goodness of volunteers who maintain the War Graves Photographic Project, a web site that operates in conjunction with the Commonwealth War Graves Commission, to make available a photographic database of war graves and memorials. It was there I found the photos of the graves of Dad's two lost crew mates, Warrant Officer First Class Glen McMillan and Sergeant Dave Alison. That they were perfectly maintained gave me some comfort.

In May 2011, Dad's squadron, which still exists as 419 Tactical Fighter Training squadron based in Cold Lake, Alberta, invited him to a 70th anniversary celebration held in Kamloops, B.C. I tagged along and was privileged to meet some of the current generation of Moosemen. And then the following month, at the invitation of the Commanding Officer, Dad and I made the trek to Cold Lake. While Dad took a spin in a fighter simulator, I spent time in the squadron archive poring over old photos and official records of war operations, thanks to the late Vince Elmer, a former 419 squadron electrician and unofficial archivist. For this unique and exceptional opportunity I must thank Lieutenant-Colonel R.K. "Midas" Vogan, then Commanding Officer, and Major Stig Lorentzen, then Deputy Commanding Officer, 419 squadron.

Then I stumbled upon Dan Logan, the son of veteran Danny Logan, also from 419 squadron. In honour of his father, Dan had created a web site to preserve the photos and memories of the 419 Moosemen. We quickly struck up a conversation. As it turned out, someone had previously sent him an old photo of a young airman in uniform labeled only "Wallace". Dan had saved it in hopes of someday being able to put a full name and more information to the face. I was happy to oblige. In the middle of our correspondence and, interestingly enough, the day after Remembrance Day 2012, Dan received an email out of the blue from Don Machan, a nephew of the late WO1 Glen Allan McMillan, the pilot killed in that last air operation to Germany. The coincidences were piling up and giving me the shivers. Dan told me it had happened more than a dozen times that aircrew family members, who had no knowledge of each other, had emailed him within hours of each other looking for information. In one of the many emails that Don and I exchanged, I learned that the Province of Saskatchewan, Department of Natural Resources named McMillan Island "in memory of a valiant one from Saskatchewan who gave his life in preservation of ideals of free men". Don and I also connected Dad with Don's mother (pilot McMillan's sister). Dad phoned her on her 98th birthday. I hope it brought them both some closure. Thank you Dan and Don.

Richard Koval, through his RCAF 6 Group Bomber Command web site, patiently helped me with numerous official 419 squadron reports and microfiche. Thank you Richard.

Special thanks also to Allyson Latta for all her support, and especially for introducing me to readers and encouraging me to find other readers who provided valuable feedback when I could no longer see the forest for the trees.

- Mary McIntyre, Cheryl Andrews and Ruth Zaryski Jackson of Life Writers Ink
- Greg Zweng, a member of the RCAF, a pilot, an overseas veteran (Afghanistan), and a military historian
- Stuart Hunt, a friend of Dad's going back to 1944 when they were roommates in Hut 107 at Stalag Luft III
- Lieutenant Colonel R.K. (Midas) Vogan, former commander of 419 squadron
- Ted Barris, author, journalist and broadcaster

Thanks also to Stalag Luft III ex-POWs and friends of Dad who took the time to talk to and correspond with me: Art Hawtin of Beaverton, Ontario, and George Sweanor of Colorado Springs, Colorado.

Most of all I thank my dad for his love and patience in enduring hours of interviews and the endless peppering of questions about personally challenging events that took place 70 years ago.

This book would not have been possible without the considerable books, archives, web sites and museums I consulted:

Allison, Les, and Hayward, Harry. They Shall Grow Not Old: A Book of Remembrance. Commonwealth Air Training Plan Museum Inc., Brandon, Manitoba

www.bombercommandmuseum.ca/, Bomber Command Museum of Canada

Barris, Ted. The Great Escape: A Canadian Story. Thomas Allen Publishers, 2013

Buckham, Robert. Forced March to Freedom. Canada's Wings, Inc., 1984

www.thecanadianencyclopedia.com/index.cfm?PgNm=T-CE&Params=A1ARTA0001002 British Commonwealth Air Training Plan, Historica Canada, The Canadian Encyclopedia

The Moose Squadron 1941-45: The War Years of 419 Squadron. Canadian Forces Training Material Production Centre (CFTMPC) Winnipeg, June 1977

www.canadianletters.ca/collections.php?warid=4, The Canadian Letters and Images Project, Vancouver Island University

Chorley, W.R. Royal Air Force Bomber Command Losses of the Second World War 1943. Ian Allan Publishing, 1992

Colwell, John. A Wartime Log. Original resides in the Comox Air Force Museum, Canadian Forces Base, Comox, B.C.

www.cwgc.org/default.asp, Commonwealth War Graves Commission

www.elsham.pwp.blueyonder.co.uk/raf_bc/, Rob Davis

419 Squadron Archive, compiled by Historian Vince Elmer, Canadian Forces Base, Cold Lake, Alberta

www.419squadronbewarethemoose.com/home.html, 419 Squadron, RCAF 1941 to 1945, Dan Logan

http://hansard.millbanksystems.com/people/mr-anthony-eden, Official Report of Debates in British Parliament, Anthony Eden remarks: May 19, 1944, May 23, 1944, June 7, 1944, June 21, 1944, June 23, 1944, July 26, 1944

Hehner, Barbara. The Tunnel King: The True Story of Wally Floody and The Great Escape. HarperTrophy Canada, HarperCollins Publishers Ltd., 2004

Hunt, Stuart Gardner. Twice Surreal: A Memoir of World War II and Korea. 2005

www.icrc.org/Web/Eng/siteeng0.nsf/htmlall/genevaconventions, Convention Relative to the Treatment of Prisoners of War. Geneva, 27 July 1929.

International Committee of the Red Cross, 2005

www.journal.forces.gc.ca/vo3/no1/doc/65-69-eng.pdf, The Great Canadian Air Battle: The British Commonwealth Air Training Plan and RCAF Fatalities During the Second World War, Dr. Jean Martin, Canadian Military Journal, Spring 2002

The King's Regulations and Air Council Instructions for the Royal Air Force 1943, Air Ministry, Air Publication 958

Library and Archives Canada, Ottawa. S.S. Queen Elizabeth Passenger Lists, Archival Microfilm HQS 63-302-551-2, Reel #C-5619

Library and Archives Canada, Ottawa. Canadian Prisoners of War – Official Reports on Camp Conditions, Europe: Reports on Prisoner of War Camps, Germany, 1942-1945, Archival Microfilm Reel #C-5339

Middlebrook, Martin and Everitt, Chris. The Bomber Command War Diaries: An Operational Reference Book 1939-1945. Viking, 1985

National Archives of the UK, Kew. Report on the Forced Evacuation of Allied Officers and Other Rank Prisoners of War from Stalag Luft III, Sagan, Germany – January/February 1945. Gp/Capt D.E.L. Wilson, AIR 40/269

http://news.bbc.co.uk/onthisday/default.stm, On This Day, BBC web site

Schweyer, Robert. Sights on Jarvis, No. 1 Bombing and Gunnery School, 1940 – 1945. Heronwood Enterprises, 2003

www.6grouprcaf.com/Operations.html, 6 Group Bomber Command, Richard Koval

Sweanor, George. It's All Pensionable Time: 25 Years in the Royal Canadian Air Force. Gesnor Publications, 1979

Tweddle, Paul. Into The Night Sky, RAF Middleton St. George: A Bomber Airfield at War. Sutton Publishing, an imprint of NPI Media Group Limited, Gloucestershire, England, 2007

www.twgpp.org, The War Graves Photographic Project

Vance, Jonathon F. A Gallant Company: The Men of the Great Escape. Pacifica Military History, California, 2000

www.warmuseum.ca/cwm/exhibitions/newspapers/intro_e.shtml, Democracy at War: Canadian Newspapers and the Second World War

Wolter, Tim. POW Baseball In World War II: The National Pastime Behind Barbed Wire, McFarland & Company, December, 2001